16th International Conference Mobile Learning 2020

Sofia, Bulgaria
2-4 April 2020

Editors:

Inmaculada Arnedillo Sanchez
Pedro Isaías
Boyan Bontchev
Luís Rodrigues

ISBN: 978-1-7138-1012-4

Printed from e-media with permission by:

Curran Associates, Inc.
57 Morehouse Lane
Red Hook, NY 12571

Some format issues inherent in the e-media version may also appear in this print version.

Printed with permission by Curran Associates, Inc. (2020)

For permission requests, please contact International Association for Development of the Information Society (IADIS) at the address below.

International Association for Development of the Information Society (IADIS)
Rua Sao Sebastiao Da Pedreira
No. 100, 30, 1050-209
Lisbon, Portugal

Phone: 351 21 3151373
Fax: 351 21 3151244

secretariat@iadis.org

Additional copies of this publication are available from:

Curran Associates, Inc.
57 Morehouse Lane
Red Hook, NY 12571 USA
Phone: 845-758-0400
Fax: 845-758-2633
Email: curran@proceedings.com
Web: www.proceedings.com

16th INTERNATIONAL CONFERENCE

MOBILE LEARNING 2020

PROCEEDINGS OF THE 16th INTERNATIONAL CONFERENCE

MOBILE LEARNING 2020

2 - 4 APRIL, 2020

Organised by

iadis

international association for development of the information society

Co-Organised by

SOFIA UNIVERSITY
ST. KLIMENT OHRIDSKI

As a member of Crossref (a non-profit membership organization for scholarly publishing working with the purpose to make content easy to find, link, cite and assess) each published paper in this book of proceedings will be allocated a DOI (Digital Object Identifier) number for its fast and easy citation and indexation.

Edited by Inmaculada Arnedillo Sánchez, Pedro Isaías and Boyan Bontchev

Associate Editor: Luís Rodrigues

TABLE OF CONTENTS

FOREWORD vii

PROGRAM COMMITTEE ix

KEYNOTE LECTURE xi

FULL PAPERS

USING MOBILE TECHNOLOGY TO CROWDSOURCE THE AUGMENTATION OF DEEP LEARNING DATASETS 3
Chantelle Saliba and Dylan Seychell

A META-ANALYSIS OF SERIOUS MOBILE GAMES TO SUPPORT MUSEUM'S INFORMAL EDUCATIONAL 11
Meng Wang and Miguel Baptista Nunes

MOBILE TECHNOLOGY AFFECTING TEACHING AND LEARNING IN RURAL SCHOOLS 23
Marlien Herselman, Adele Botha, Keneilwe Maremi, Sifiso Dlamini and Mario Marais

INVESTIGATING MOOC PLATFORMS AS A PROSPECTIVE TOOL FOR MOBILE LEARNING 31
Albena Antonova and Boyan Bontchev

MOBILE LEARNING ADOPTION AT THE SCIENCE MUSEUM GROUP 39
Ruel Welch, Temitope Alade and Lynn Nichol

MOBILE PERFORMANCE SUPPORT SYSTEM FOR TEACHERS AND PARENTS TEACHING FIRST GRADERS TO READ 47
Roberto Araya

CONCEPTUALIZING MOBILE DIGITAL LITERACY SKILLS FOR EDUCATORS 55
Farshida Jahoor, Adele Botha and Marlien Herselman

MOBILE LEARNING IN OUTDOOR SETTINGS: A SYSTEMATIC REVIEW 63
Johan Stymne

EXPLORATION OF VIDEO E-LEARNING CONTENT WITH SMARTPHONES 71
Stefan Räbiger, Tuğberk Dalkılıç, Alperen Doğan, Buket Karakaş, Berk Türetken and Yücel Saygın

VIRTUAL REALITY AND ITS IMPACT ON LEARNING SUCCESS 78
Thomas Keller, Elke Brucker-Kley and Christian Wyder

M-LEARNING FOR THE RECRUITMENT AND SELECTION OF HUMAN TALENT. CASE: INTERVIEW 87
Paula Asto Machaca and Luis Alfaro Casas

SHORT PAPERS

MOBILE LEARNING IN HIGHER EDUCATION 97
Petra Bauer, Christine Kolb and Jasmin Bastian

USING MOBILE LEARNING AND RESEARCH BASED LEARNING TO ATTRACT STUDENTS INTO QUANTUM INFORMATION RESEARCH 102
Francisco Javier Delgado-Cepeda and Marco Benjamín Enríquez-Flores

MODELING A SECURE EXAM MANAGEMENT SYSTEM (SEMS) FOR MOBILE ENVIRONMENT BASED ON FACE RECOGNITION AND GPS TECHNIQUES 107
Hervé B. Olou and Eugène C. Ezin

STUDENT ACCEPTANCE OF LEARNING WITH TABLETS IN A HISTORY MUSEUM 111
Alan J. Wecker, Merav Yosfan, Billie Eilam and Joel Lanir

SPOC, FUTURE OF MLEARNING AND LANGUAGE LEARNING? 115
Hamed Asgari and Georges Antoniadis

THE EFFECT OF TEACHING BY (MOBILE LEARNING) IN UNIVERSITY STUDENTS'S ACHIEVEMENT 121
Omar M. K. Mahasneh

REFLECTION PAPER

TEACHERS DIALOGUING ABOUT STATISTICAL LITERACY WITH SUPPORT OF MESSENGER APP FOR SMARTPHONES 129
Sérgia Oliveira, Liliane Carvalho, Carlos Monteiro and Carolina Carvalho

POSTER

ENABLING MLEARNING TECHNOLOGIES INTO INTEGRATING OFF-CAMPUS INTERNSHIP AND CAPSTONE COURSES FOR TECHNOLOGICAL UNIVERSITY IN TAIWAN 135
Su-Chang Chen, Hsi-Chi Hsiao, Jen-Chia Chang and Dyi-Cheng Chen

FOREWORD

These proceedings contain the papers and poster of the 16th International Conference on Mobile Learning 2020, which was organised by the International Association for Development of the Information Society and co-organised by the Sofia University "St. Kliment Ohridski", 2 - 4 April 2020. Due to an unprecedented situation caused by the COVID-19 pandemic, this year the conference was hosted virtually.

The Mobile Learning 2020 Conference seeks to provide a forum for the presentation and discussion of mobile learning research which illustrate developments in the field. In particular, but not exclusively, we aim to explore the theme of mobile learning under the following topics:

- Learning analytics and mobile learning
- Cloud computing and mobile learning
- Pedagogical approaches, models and theories for mLearning
- mLearning in and across formal and informal settings
- Strategies and challenges for integrating mLearning in broader educational scenarios
- User Studies in mLearning
- Learner mobility and transitions afforded by mLearning
- Socio-cultural context and implications of mLearning
- Mobile social media and user generated content
- Enabling mLearning technologies, applications and uses
- Evaluation and assessment of mLearning
- Research methods, ethics and implementation of mLearning
- Innovative mLearning approaches
- Tools, technologies and platforms for mLearning
- mLearning: where to next and how?

The Mobile Learning 2020 Conference received 58 submissions from more than 17 countries. Each submission has been anonymously reviewed by an average of 4 independent reviewers, to ensure that accepted submissions were of a high standard. Out of the papers submitted, 11 received blind referee ratings that signified acceptability for publication as full papers (acceptance rate of 19%). A few more papers were accepted as short papers, reflection papers and posters. An extended version of the best papers will be published in the Interactive Technology and Smart Education (ITSE) journal (ISSN: 1741-5659) and in the IADIS International Journal on WWW/Internet (ISSN: 1645-7641).

Besides the papers' presentations, the conference also features a keynote presentation from an internationally distinguished researcher. We would therefore like to express our gratitude to Professor Mike Sharples, Emeritus Professor of Educational Technology, Institute of Educational Technology, The Open University, UK, for accepting our invitation as keynote speaker.

A successful conference requires the effort of many individuals and this year we faced a new challenge that brought us more together. We would like to thank the members of the Program Committee for their hard work in reviewing and selecting the papers that appear in this book. We are especially grateful to the authors who submitted their papers to this conference and to the presenters who provided the substance of the meeting. We wish to thank all members of our organizing committee.

Last but not the least, we hope that everybody enjoyed the presentations and we invite you all to next edition of the International Mobile Learning Conference.

Inmaculada Arnedillo Sánchez, Trinity College Dublin, Ireland
Program Chair

Pedro Isaias, The University of New South Wales (UNSW – Sydney), Australia
Boyan Bontchev, Sofia University, Bulgaria
Conference Co-Chairs

April 2020

PROGRAM COMMITTEE

PROGRAM CHAIR

Inmaculada Arnedillo Sánchez, Trinity College Dublin, Ireland

CONFERENCE CO-CHAIRS

Pedro Isaias, The University of New South Wales (UNSW – Sydney), Australia
Boyan Bontchev, Sofia University, Bulgaria

COMMITTEE MEMBERS

Adamantios Koumpis, Berner Fachhochschule, Switzerland
Alessandro Pagano, University of Bari, Italy
Alex Voychenko, Irtc, Ukraine
Anastopoulou Stamatina, The Open University, UK
Angelos Michalas, TEI of Western Macedonia, Greece
Antoanela Naaji, Vasile Goldis Western University, Romania
Antonio Panaggio, Ministry of Education, Universities and Research, Italy
Ben Bachmair, London Mobile Learning Group, Germany
Bren Taylor, Service Birmingham, United Kingdom
Charalampos Karagiannidis, University of Thessaly, Greece
Chorng-Shiuh Koong, National Taichung University of Education, Taiwan
Christos Bouras, University of Patras, Greece
Claudia Steinberger, University of Klagenfurt, Austria
Dumitru Dan Burdescu, University of Craiova, Romania
Elisabetta Parodi, Lattanzio Learning Spa, Italy
Emad Bataineh, Zayed University, United Arab Emirates
Euripides Loukis, University of the Aegean, Greece
Fahriye Altinay, Near East University, Cyprus
Farshad Badie, Aalborg University, Denmark
Gabor Kiss, J. Selye University, Slovakia
George Magoulas, Birbeck College, United Kingdom
Giasemi Vavoula, University of Leicester, United Kingdom
Giuliana Dettori, ITD-CNR, Italy
Herman Van Der Merwe, North-West University, South Africa
Huseyin Bicen, Near East University, Cyprus
Ivana Marenzi, University of Hanover, Germany
Jozef Hvorecky, Vysoka Skola Manazmentu, Slovakia
Juan Manuel Santos-Gago, University of Vigo, Spain
Jun-Ming Su, National University of Tainan, Taiwan
Kateryna Synytsya, IRTC ITS, Ukraine
Kuo-Liang Ou, National Hsin-chu University of Education, Taiwan
Lam-for Kwok, City University of Hong Kong, Hong Kong
Li Yushun, Beijing Normal University, China
Maiga Chang, Athabasca University, Canada
Maria Uther, University of Wolverhampton, United Kingdom
Mario Vacca, Italian Ministry of Education, Italy

KEYNOTE LECTURE

20 YEARS OF MOBILE LEARNING – WHAT HAVE WE LEARNED

by Professor Mike Sharples,
Emeritus Professor of Educational Technology,
Institute of Educational Technology, The Open University, UK

Abstract

It is exactly 20 years since the publication in Computers and Education of my paper 'The Design of Personal Mobile Technologies for Lifelong Learning'. In my keynote I will reflect on what we have learned about mobile learning during the past two decades. The talk will cover four major mobile learning projects: HandLeR, MOBILearn, MyArtSpace, and nQuire. For each project, I will discuss its main contributions to mobile learning research and development, including: mobile technology for personal lifelong learning, the mobilised learner, importance of context, how to support learning between classrooms and informal settings, ways to evaluate mobile learning, pedagogy-led design and mobile learning at massive scale. I will end the talk by asking "What do we know now that we didn't know 20 years ago" and by offering four challenges for the future.

FULL PAPERS

USING MOBILE TECHNOLOGY TO CROWDSOURCE THE AUGMENTATION OF DEEP LEARNING DATASETS

Chantelle Saliba and Dylan Seychell
Department of Artificial Intelligence, University of Malta
Msida MSD2080, Malta

ABSTRACT

In the past decade, mobile communications have seen drastic changes and improvements with an estimate of over 3.5 billion mobile phone users worldwide. In addition, the average mobile phone has gone from being a simple communication device to a smartphone device capable of web browsing, video conferencing, gaming, photography, and videography and intelligent applications. For this reason, companies and industries have been exploring this technology to create opportunities to enhance their communications with clients and to create further business opportunities. In this research, we analyze the approach of using mobile technologies as a technique to crowdsource data that would be used to enhance research by creating digital resources. In today's modern and technological world there are areas and fields which are still unexplored by technology due to their lack of digital resources. Modern machine learning techniques such as deep learning methods, require a large volume of data that is not always available. Such a case is the example of classifying Maltese flora. Malta is a small island in the middle of the Mediterranean with an area of 316 km^2. Being such a small island with unique and indigenous flora makes it a challenging feat to find already available digital data to be able to conduct technological research. For this reason, we turn to mobile technology and how this can aid in the collection of such data to augment existing datasets that enhance academic research and render classification more effective and feasible.

KEYWORDS

Mobile Technology, Research, Data, Crowdsourcing, Machine Learning

1. INTRODUCTION

Mobile technology has seen great advancements in the past years and mobile technology has become more and more advanced, encouraging the population of mobile users to drastically infatuate worldwide. Smartphones nowadays are equipped with higher memory storages and higher performance ratings. In addition, the simple mobile phone is now capable of web browsing, photography, videography and gaming. Organizations and business have taken this opportunity to create mobile applications to feel closer to their customers and audience and to understand better the customer needs and wants. In this research, we would be analyzing the prospects of using mobile communications for academic research. Academic research has been strengthened by technological advancement, helping in the collection of data and the analysis of data by performing complex computations that apply machine learning techniques to analyze it accurately and efficiently. In this research, we will be analyzing the concept of implementing a mobile communication medium to crowdsource data to create digital resources that will be used to enhance deep learning datasets that enable better analysis of artefacts. For technology to aid academic research, digital resources are required and even though we live in an advanced and technological era, there are unexplored fields by technology due to their lack of digital resources. In this research, we would be analyzing Maltese flora [Lanfranco and Lanfranco, 2003] and the idea of introducing an image classification system using deep learning algorithms from the digital data crowdsourced by a mobile technology system.

1.1 Motivation

The motivation behind this system has two different perspectives. Firstly, the system revolves around the idea of collecting data that is sparse and needed to enhance datasets for deep learning algorithms. Gathering this digital data will enable further research as well as introduce other technological techniques such as machine learning to unexplored fields.

In addition, by conducting this experiment on an island's botany, we would be shifting the mobile user's attention to areas that are usually taken for granted. Moreover, through this study we will be raising awareness about Malta's flora and natural surroundings and its conservation. This is further enhanced by other data, such as location, available on mobile phones that adds context and features to the visual data being collected.

2. BACKGROUND RESEARCH

2.1 Mobile Technology

Mobile phones and smartphones have seen drastic changes and improvement in both performance, and features. The simple mobile phone that used to enable communication between two distant individuals, has now been transformed into a technological device capable of web browsing, video conferencing, videography, phone photography and gaming. Smartphones nowadays are also equipped with high-performance processors and higher memory storage. This encouraged the creation of applications from various fields and areas with personal or global interest to communicate with mobile users. By the year 2013, there were roughly 13000 applications that provided medical and health advice [Trueland, 2013]. Business and retailers have also taken this opportunity to expand their horizons and use this medium as an excellent business and marketing tool. Businesses have been making use of applications to enhance customer experience [Mclean et al, 2018] and as a branded marketing strategy [Li, 2018] where the traditional membership card is being traded to a more attractive and gamified mobile application. A substantial number of applications are also for educational purposes both for formal learning and also for informal learning [Churchill et al, 2016]. Demographically the largest number of mobile users is between the ages of 18 and 29, which makes it a perfect opportunity for educational institutions to provide learning mechanisms beyond the traditional classroom [Crompton and Burke, 2018]. Incorporating mobile learning to the classrooms has proven to improve the student's motivation and engagement towards their education [Camilleri et al, 2019].

2.1.1 Mobile Communication for Data Collection

With the population of mobile phone users increasing globally, mobile communication could be considered as an excellent source of data collection. Data collection can be performed for various institutions from businesses to understand their customer's preferences and trends to academics that gather data for further research. The expansion of mobile phones has enabled data collection to be made more efficient and representative by reaching a more geographically spread number of people. Conducting survey research by making use of mobile technology will also enable the researchers to make use of the location of the individuals participating in the survey by making use of GPS features. This will enable the researchers to have more in-depth information in understanding the participant. Furthermore, nowadays smartphones are equipped with cameras and audio recording features that can enhance data value as well as provide new opportunities for data collection. Moreover, gathering information through technological means gives the advantage of real-time data transfer and the information gathered can be manipulated and analyzed in real-time, therefore, saving costs while also being environmentally friendly. Data collection via a mobile communication system can be conducted through online surveys, questionnaires and mobile applications [Barzilay, 2019]. When conducting data collection via mobile communication, the privacy of the participants should be safeguarded and all the necessary precautions should be taken. The researchers should ensure that all the information is protected. GPS tracking and sharing of personal information and visual imagery should be done only upon informing the participant and getting the necessary permissions [Link et al, 2014].

2.1.2 User Engagement through Mobile Communication

The population of mobile users is increasing because mobile features are becoming more advanced and applications are becoming more engaging and addictive especially amongst college students [Kumar and Gera, 2016]. The methods and techniques that stimulate motivation depend on the area to which the application is being used. A learning application can be made motivating by taking into consideration the user's background as well as information about the environment before generating content. [Dingli and Seychell, 2012] generated a more engaging learning application by creating a system that makes use of

3 layers where the innermost layer represents the information generated from the user's environment and the outer layer represents the information that is most related to the user's profile. A technique that is widely used in learning applications as well as in business applications is gamification. Gamification is the process of adopting game design mechanics to mobile applications [Cechetti et al, 2017]. This engages the user through a number of game elements such as rewards, points, characters and personalized feedback [Tóth and Tóvölgyi, 2016].

2.2 Machine Learning

Machine Learning (ML) is one of the fundamental concepts of Artificial Intelligence and it is playing a key role in the advancement of technology. One can find ML in various fields such as in robotics, computer games, data mining, medical diagnosis, social media services, pattern recognition, natural language processing, product recommendation, online fraud detection to name a few [Ray, 2019]. Conventional machine learning techniques made use of extensive domain expertise that was transformed to data that the machine learning classifier was able to interpret and classify. Deep Learning algorithms are the new generation of machine learning techniques which are composed of multiple processing layers that will learn the raw data through a number of steps to which in each step the algorithm would be discovering more and more about the data. Deep learning has proven to outperform traditional machine learning algorithms in various fields such image recognition and classification. This research addresses the challenge that such techniques face when handling smaller sets of data and we propose a method that uses mobile technology to enhance the datasets that are needed for such techniques.

2.2.1 Convolutional Neural Networks

A Convolutional Neural Network (CNN) is a deep learning algorithm that is said to be biologically inspired [Ray, 2019]. The Convolutional Neural Network's architecture is composed of a number of stages. It first starts by receiving the data and passes it through a series of convolutional layers and pooling layers. The convolutional layer is used to learn the features by computing convolutions between the input and a set of kernels or filters. A kernel or filter can perform operations such as edge detection and sharpening. A non-linear activation function such as the rectified linear unit (ReLU) function is then performed on the convolutions. This introduces non-linearity in the convolutional network. The pooling layer tries to reduce the number of parameters by merging similar features while retaining important information [Lecun et al., 2015]. After feature extraction, the classification component receives the data as a matrix and after performing flatting, passes it through one or more fully connected layers. The results will then be passed through an activation function such as softmax or sigmoid to classify the outputs. CNNs can be seen at work in various areas such as music [Vishnupriya and Meenakshi, 2018] and hand gesture recognition [Han et al., 2016].

2.2.2 Convolutional Neural Networks for Flower Classification

Given their success rate in image classification, [Liu et al., 2016] suggested an eight layer CNN to classify flower images. The first five layers were convolutional layers while the remaining three were fully connected layers. This system was able to distinguish between 79 different flower classes and achieved an accuracy rate of 76.54%. Techniques that were introduced in the neural network to generate a higher accuracy rate included local response normalization, overlapping pooling and dropout to prevent saturation and overfitting in both the pooling layers and fully-connected layers.

2.3 Maltese Flora

Malta is composed of a group of small islands with the main islands being Malta, Gozo and Comino with Malta being the mainland. All the islands compose an average of 316km^2. In Malta, due to our central position in the Mediterranean Sea, one finds flora that is located in southern Europe and northern Africa as well as flora that is indigenous to the Maltese islands [Lanfranco, 2007].

3. METHODOLOGY

The introduction of a mobile communication system that will crowdsource data is human-centric and therefore it requires human input and collaboration. Hence, the methodology of this system was divided into two phases. A feasibility study was firstly conducted by performing an online survey about the people's opinion about crowdsourcing data. In this study we analyzed the participant's profiles and their relation with the Maltese nature and if they frequently go for hikes or picnics in the Maltese countryside. Moreover, in this survey, it was asked about their willingness to collaborate in this study by submitting their photos of flowers and their opinion about a mobile application about the Maltese flora. The second phase of the methodology included the designing of a proposed solution while keeping the data and the conclusions that were derived from the research in mind.

3.1 Conducted Research

In this research, a survey was conducted about the people's opinion of crowdsourcing data. In this survey, we also analyzed people's mobile behavioral patterns. In this research, a total of 243 participants took place where all the participants are of either Maltese descendent or British descendent between the ages of 12 and 80. All the participants that took place resided in one of the Maltese islands.

3.1.1 User's Profile

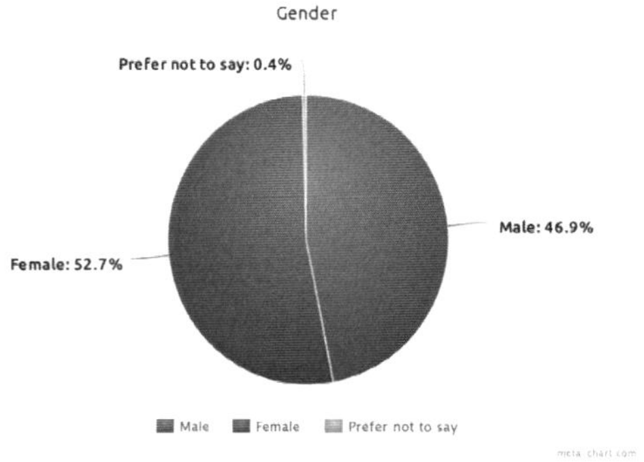

Figure 1. Gender of Participants

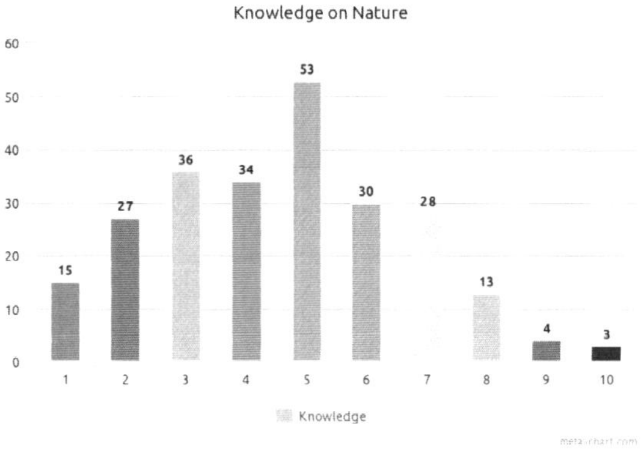

Figure 2. Knowledge on Nature

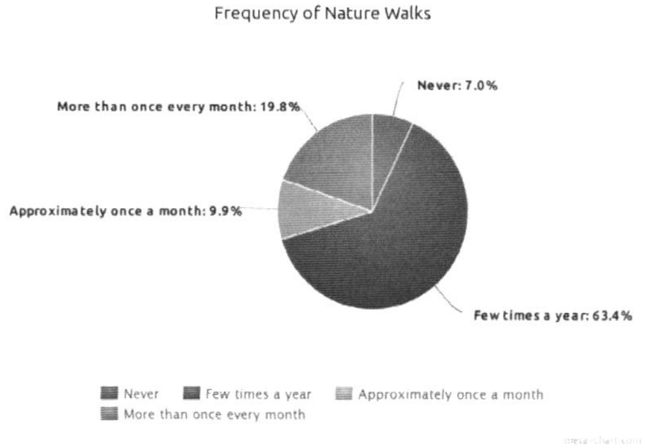

Figure 3. Frequency of Nature Walks

In this research, the male and female ratio was almost balanced with a 52.7% female representation and a 46.9% male representation as shown in Figure 1. 0.4% of the population preferred not to affiliate with any gender.

The research being conducted is human dependent and therefore understanding the participant needs and their willingness to contribute is important. Their contribution is also dependable on the area to which the academic research is being conducted. Therefore, a part of the conducted research involved around the user's opinion about Maltese nature and how knowledgeable the residents feel about the Maltese flora. It was concluded that the Maltese do not feel as knowledgeable as can be shown in Figure 2 were 21.8% of the participants ranked their knowledge as a 5 which is the middle of the scale. 32.1% of all the participants gave a scoring rate of higher than 5; while 46.1% gave a scoring of lower than 5. This show that overall the participants gave a scoring of 5 or lower. When asked about how frequent the participants go for walks or hikes in nature, the results showed that the Maltese with a percentage of 63.4% go for a walk a few times a year. In addition, there were 19.8% that stated that they go for hikes more than once every month, as shown in Figure 3. This research also considered the main reasons why the participants go into nature and some of the most popular opinions included admiring nature (74.9%), relaxing (74.1%), and taking photos (53.1%). Other activities included hanging out with family and friends and performing physical activities such as running and jogging.

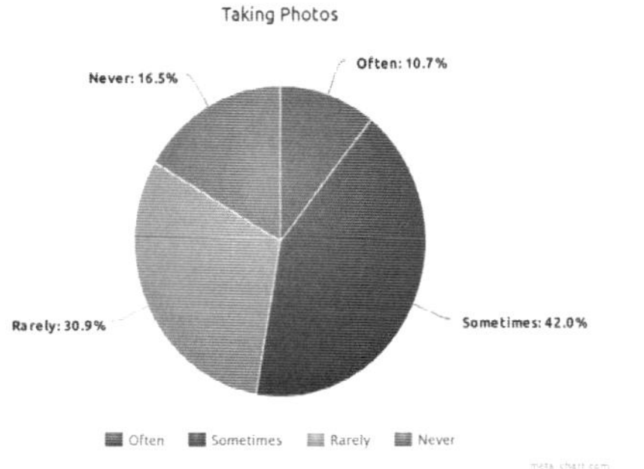

Figure 4. Photographing Photos

To gather digital resources about Maltese flora, the participants will need to photograph flowers. This research asked the participants how often they take photos of flowers. It results that the majority sometimes take flowers with a percentage of 42% as shown in Figure 4.

3.1.2 Mobile Behavior Patterns

An important element when it comes to data crowdsourcing is to understand the participants' mobile behaviour patterns and engagement. Gathering data using such methods involves that the audience is familiar with the technological medium and makes use of smartphone features such as the mobiles cameras and application. The participants in this study made use of two of the most famous operating systems: android and iOS with 83.5% of the participants making use of an android operating system and 16.5% of the participants making use of iOS as can be shown in Figure 5.

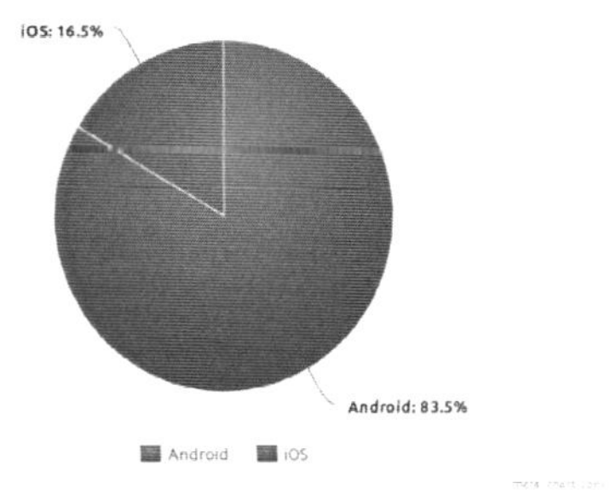

Figure 5. Operating Systems

It was found that the majority make use of Internet browsing (92.2%), Social Media (90.5%) and the camera (89.3%) when it comes to smartphone features. Another widely used feature is text messaging.

In addition, it was concluded that 91.8% have applications installed on their smartphone. Only 2.5% stated that they do not have applications on their phone while 5.8% stated that they are not sure if they have applications or not, as shown in Figure 6. This result shows that an application for crowdsourcing might be a possible solution since the number of application users is high.

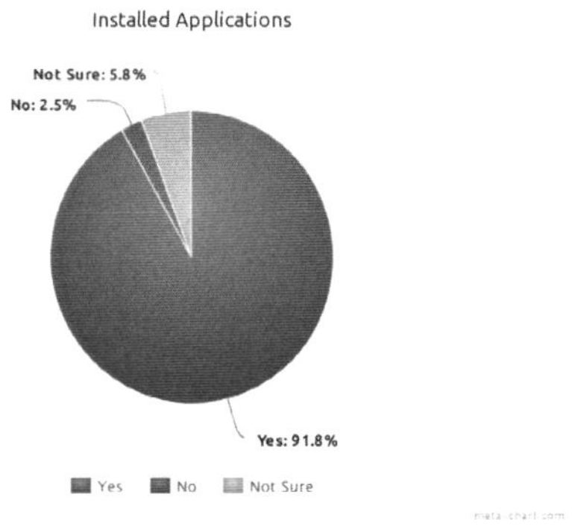

Figure 6. Installed Applications

3.1.3 Data Crowdsourcing

In its core principle crowdsourcing has the willingness of the participants to form part of the research and include themselves in the data gathering process. This can be achieved if the participants are willing to participate in the research and provide the data they collected. The study shows that 51.4% of the people that participated would be willing to share their photos of flowers. On the other hand, 15.2% would not be willing to share their photos even for research purposes. The other 33.3% said that it depends on the situation and the case study.

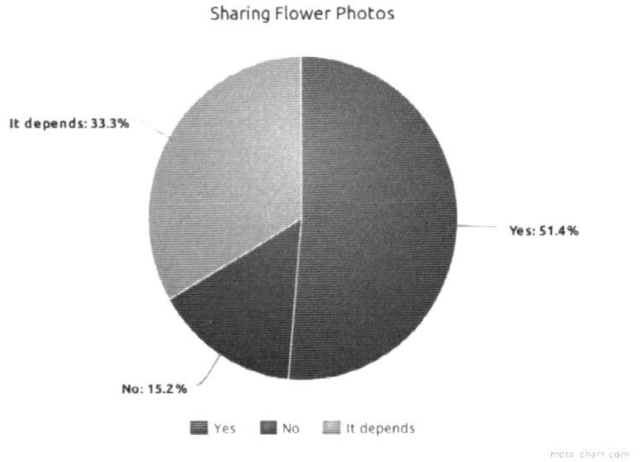

Figure 7. Willingness to share Flower Photos

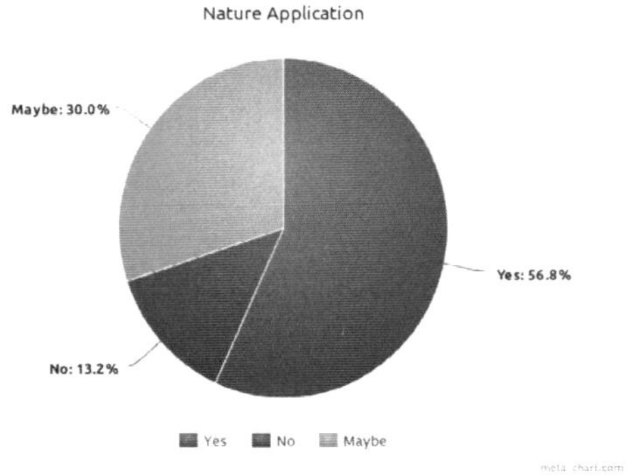

Figure 8. Use of a Nature related Application

A mobile application will be a good technique to enable crowdsourcing of data. As shown in Figure 8, the majority of the participants said that they would be interested in an application that is related to nature and that would provide related information. 30% answered that they are not sure if they would make use of such an application while 13.2% said that would not make use of such an application.

3.2 Proposed Solution

From the research conducted, it could be concluded that an application would be an ideal medium to crowdsource data. The application could provide the users with information about the species of the photographed image by making use of machine learning techniques such as a convolutional neural network (CNN) while storing the image photographed.

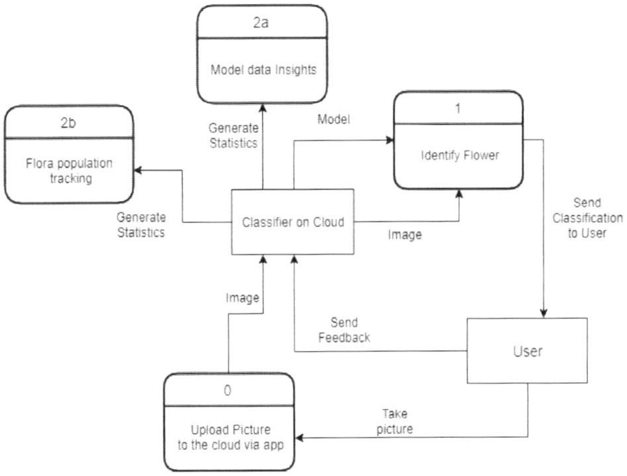

Figure 9. Block Diagram of Proposed Solution

The block diagram of the proposed solution can be seen in Figure 9. The participant will be interacting with the system through the use of an application and upon taking a photo through the application; the system will send this image to the cloud. This image will be stored in the cloud and will be used to add to the current digital resources related to Maltese Flora. A machine learning model would also be located in the cloud and this model will return the label along with some images of the same determined label. In addition, the app user will be requested to provide feedback on the label and the related images returned. This feedback would be used to generate insights on the machine learning model.

A prototype application has been set up for this purpose as shown in Figure 10. The first image in this figure shows the first part of the application where the user will be able to upload a photo of a flower to the flower either by choosing an image from the gallery or by taking a photo from the camera. This photo will be sent to the cloud and apart from storing this image to store as digital resources, the system will make use of a model to classify that photo with a level of confidence. The second image of the Figure shows the second part of the application where the user will be shown similar images and the user will be able to give feedback to the model by submitting the rating stars. The application is making use of Google services such as Firebase[1] and the ML Kit[2]. The application is currently locally based and can classify between five different types of flowers: roses, sunflowers, dandelions, tulips and daisies. This will, however, be extended and fine-tuned to Maltese flora to enable further testing and implementation.

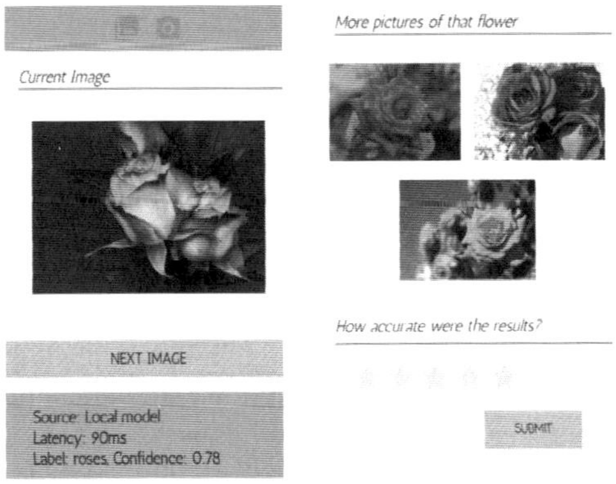

Figure 10. Prototype Application

[1] Google's cloud mobile back-end platform, available at https://firebase.google.com/

[2] Machine Learning for mobile development by Google, available at https://firebase.google.com/products/ml-kit

4. CONCLUSION

In this research study, presented the concept of creating a mobile application that uses crowdsourcing data to improve a dataset for machine learning models. The digital data collected will then be used for academic research and for the implementation of image classification through the use of machine learning techniques to classify Maltese flora that as of currently there is limited digital data available. This system would enable digital data to be collected from the citizens residing or visiting Malta through the use of an application with the mobile's photography features while providing them with information about the photographed flower. A survey was conducted to analyze the opinion of the citizens, about data crowdsourcing and it was concluded that only 13.2% stated that they will not make use of such an application, while 15.2% stated that they will not be willing to share their photos of flowers for academic research. This system can be applied to other areas and fields that have limited digital resources that would enable the collection of data for further academic research.

REFERENCES

Barzilay, M., 2019. *Data Collection and Mobile Technologies.* 10.13140/RG.2.2.31541.93929.

Camilleri, A., et al, 2019. Mobile learning via educational apps: an interpretative study.

Cechetti, N. P. et al., 2017. Gamification strategies for mobile device applications: A systematic review. *12th Iberian Conference on Information Systems and Technologies (CISTI).* Lisbon, Portugal, pp. 1-7.

Churchill et al., 2016. Mobile Learning Design Theories and Application 1st ed. 2016.

Crompton, H. & Burke, D., 2018. The use of mobile learning in higher education: A systematic review. Computers & Education, 123, pp.53–64.

Dingli, A. and Seychell, D., 2012. Motivating learning through mobile interaction. *Proceedings of IADIS International Conference on Mobile Learning.* Berlin, Germany, pp. 271-274.

Fox, B.I. & Felkey, B.G., 2014. Quick Survey of Smartphone Features and Functions. Hospital Pharmacy, 49(6), pp.585-586.

Han, M., et al., 2016. Visual hand gesture recognition with convolution neural network. *2016 17th IEEE/ACIS International Conference on Software Engineering, Artificial Intelligence, Networking and Parallel/Distributed Computing (SNPD).* Shanghai, pp. 287-291.

Kumar, A. & Gera, N., 2016. Mobile Addiction and Mental Health of College Students. Educational Quest, 7(2), pp. 87–90.

Lanfranco, E. and Lanfranco, G., 2003. *Il-Flora Maltija.* Pubblikazzjonijiet Indipendenza, Malta.

Lanfranco, G., 2007. *Fjuri Slavaġ.* Wise Old Publications, Malta.

Lecun, Y., et al., 2015. Deep learning. Nature, 521(7553), pp.436–444.

Li, C.-Y., 2018. Consumer behavior in switching between membership cards and mobile applications: The case of Starbucks. Computers in Human Behavior, 84, pp.171–184.

Link, M.W. et al., 2014. Mobile Technologies for Conducting, Augmenting and Potentially Replacing Surveys. Public Opinion Quarterly, 78(4), pp.779–787.

Liu, Y., et al., 2016. Flower classification via convolutional neural network. *2016 IEEE International Conference on Functional-Structural Plant Growth Modeling, Simulation, Visualization and Applications (FSPMA)*, Qingdao, pp. 110-116.

Mclean, G. et al, 2018. Developing a Mobile Applications Customer Experience Model (MACE)- Implications for Retailers. Journal of Business Research, 85, pp.325–336.

Ray. S., 2019. A Quick Review of Machine Learning Algorithms. *2019 International Conference on Machine Learning, Big Data, Cloud and Parallel Computing (COMITCon).* Faridabad, India, pp. 35-39.

Tóth, Á. & Tóvölgyi, S., 2016. The introduction of gamification: A review paper about the applied gamification in the smartphone applications. 000213-000218. 10.1109/CogInfoCom.2016.7804551.

Trueland, J., 2013. A smart use for mobiles. Nursing Standard (through 2013), 27(36), pp.16–8.

Vishnupriya, S., and Meenakshi, K., 2018. Automatic Music Genre Classification using Convolution Neural Network. *2018 International Conference on Computer Communication and Informatics (ICCCI).* Coimbatore, pp. 1-4.

A META-ANALYSIS OF SERIOUS MOBILE GAMES TO SUPPORT MUSEUM'S INFORMAL EDUCATIONAL

Meng Wang and Miguel Baptista Nunes[1]
School of Information Management, Sun Yat-Sen University, China

ABSTRACT

This paper uses a meta-analysis approach to explore the state-of-the-art of the use of mobile devices to support gamification for informal learning in museum contexts. This study addresses a complex interdisciplinary type of research where information technology is the catalyzer for a complex intersection of museology, information science and educational studies, and aims at helping game designers, museum educators and educational practitioners on their decision making concerning the selection of IoT components of serious mobile games. Specifically, the paper focuses on investigating IoT technological architectures and IoT technological affordances to serve the diversity of functions and features that can be used by different types of games. As a result, this paper presents 5 main categories of IoT technologies used for serious mobile games in museums and illustrates how each type of well-known types of games implements their functions and features through IoT. The paper recommends that for mobile technologies location aware architectures are crucial and the foundation for design and development of exploratory and geolocation serious mobile games for museums.

KEYWORDS

Museum, Informal Learning, Gamification, Serious Games, IoT Technologies, Serious Mobile Devices, Mobile Games

1. INTRODUCTION

> "Museums are, first and foremost, free-choice learning environments, that is, public institutions for personal learning" (Falk and Dierking, 2008).

Museums have long been seen as places that not only display their collections, but also contribute to cultural dissemination, informal education and social memory. As stated by Washburn (1975), "a museum collection is not its only excuse for being". Museums are regarded as informal learning places that can: complement school education; enhance knowledge of history; enable understandings of cultural backgrounds and environments; enrich awareness of natural and artificial surroundings (Efird, 2014, Akamca et al., 2017). Different types of museums display different exhibitions with different learning atmospheres. Researchers have proposed that the visualization, closeness and even manipulation of emulated items displayed in museums are fundamental to visitors' learning processes and have more impact on understanding and knowledge acquisition (Wang and Nunes, 2018; de Rijcke and Beaulieu, 2011). Visiting experiences and close interaction with artefacts, often in a more inclusive environment, are deemed to have a deeper and longer-lasting effect on learning than classrooms and textbooks (Akamca et al., 2017; Kang et al., 2009; Terreni, 2015; Williams, 1996).

According to Wang and Nunes (2018), the educational roles of museums fall into three categories: formal, informal and complementary. This paper focuses on informal learning roles of museums and how these can be supported by mobile serious games (also known in the literature as educational games). Informal learning is a learner-centered and learner-directed process, where the learner has agency over what is being learned, and how it is learned (Eshach, 2006). The process requires reflection and evaluation of the learning, and increases the likelihood that the learning will be used in future (Wang and Nunes, 2018). Gamification of museum visits aiming at reinforcing informal learning has become a hot topic for the development of museums' educational capabilities. Attempts to generate experiential learning based on

[1] Corresponding Author

visitor experiences through using mobile serious games has gained momentum both in academic circles and in practitioner environments. Therefore, in recent years, researchers have concentrated on developing museum mobile applications that go beyond the traditional visit guides or pure entertainment, and focus instead on meeting informal learning objectives though serious games. These edutainment applications aim to engage visitors in knowledge acquisition through playful experiences (Rubino et al, 2015). Advances in mobile technology and the Internet of Things (IoT) have also contributed to make serious games technology better suited to facilitate informal learning in the museum space (Jonhson et al, 2015). The study reported in this paper intended to review the state-of-the-art of the use of IoT technologies in the design, application and use of serious mobile games in museums. This paper first investigates the overall use of IoT technologies by serious mobile games aiming at support informal learning through gamification and then matches known types of games against previously identified IoT technologies.

2. RESEARCH METHODOLOGY AND DESIGN

2.1 Research Aim

This paper aimed at investigating the existing research on gamification supported mobile technology for museum learning and corresponding gamification activities. Moreover, study aimed at identifying the key factors and characteristics of game designs for this type of learning. Finally, based on identified literature review, the study aimed at establishing a framework for gamification design for mobile technologies and museum learning. Therefore, the underlying methodological approach adopted for this study is a combination of systematic literature with a critical meta-analysis review.

2.2 Research Question and Objectives

The following research question guided the research design and research process:

1. What types of serious mobile games and IoT technologies provide support for informal learning and enjoyable experiences in museum visits?

According to these research questions the following research objectives were set to:

1. Establish the state-of-the-art of gamification with mobile technology for museum learning.
2. Classify types of games or gamification activities that are supported by mobile technologies for museum learning. Highlight the highest frequency shown type of mobile game for museum learning.
3. Classify modes of mobile technology use in gamification for mobile learning.

2.3 Research Methodology

The research design created for this research is based on two-step a meta-analysis in the sense proposed by Wang and Nunes (2019), which consists of a systematic literature review, followed by a critical analysis based on a multi-matrix representation of findings and a conceptual visualization of this complex multidisciplinary area of use of mobile technology to support serious games in museums.

The first step of the research was conducted by following the systematic literature review general strategy proposed by Nunes et.al (2009) and specific protocol suggested by Jesson et al. (2001). The approach adopted consists of the following steps, which were proposed by Nunes et al. (2017):

1. Identification of keywords;
2. Production of search queries;
3. Definition of inclusion and exclusion criteria;
4. Identification of relevant database;
5. Query of databases and selection of relevant documents;
6. Analysis of the dataset selected.
7. Manual Backward and Forward Citation Search.

The second component of the research followed a critical analysis of the papers selected. This critical analysis aims at more than a mere description and synthesis of the existing literature on this research topic (Saunders et al. 2016). Such an approach requires a researcher to extensively search the literature as well as evaluate and criticize the quality and content of that body of knowledge (Booth et. al, 2009). It consists of a constructive critical analysis of theoretical propositions, models and frameworks, and includes rejections and acceptance of these different theoretical constructs (Nunes et al. 2017). The final product should be a clear, well-informed and well-argued critical narrative (Wallace and Wray, 2011; Saunders et al, 2016), which should identify seminal works related to the topic of the research, summarize current debate and theoretical propositions, critically analyze these propositions and present a conceptual model based on a synthesis of all of these debates.

2.3.1 Search Query Construction

In this research, the term "mobile technology" was operationalized in terms of three agreed synonyms "mobile device", "mobile phone" and "smart phone", which in other more specific researches may have specific and differentiated meaning, but for the purposes of this research were deemed to represent the same conceptualization.

Furthermore, the term "gamification" was interpreted based on its definition and search queries expanded though the use of three of its variants, namely "game", "serious game", "gamified".

Finally, due to the fast developments in the field, many of the papers retrieved addressed areas of augmented reality and virtual reality. These were deliberately excluded from the search.

As a result three generic search queries were created as follows:

1. "smart phone" AND "museum" AND (gamif* {gamification, gamified} OR "game" OR "serious game") NOT ("Augmented reality" OR AR OR "Virtual Reality" OR VR);
2. "mobile phone" AND "museum" AND (gamif* {gamification, gamified} OR "game" OR "serious game") NOT ("Augmented reality" OR AR OR "Virtual Reality" OR VR);
3. "mobile device" AND "museum" AND (gamif* {gamification, gamified} OR "game" OR "serious game") NOT ("Augmented reality" OR AR OR "Virtual Reality" OR VR).

Since a pilot search performed on the Web of Science (WoS) yielded very low numbers of publications in this area, it was decided to use the Google Scholar Hong Kong (https://www.google.com.hk) as the source for this research. The statistics and basic findings for each of the queries are presented in Table 1 in section 3.1.

2.3.2 Inclusion and Exclusion Criteria

There were no date limitations imposed on the findings of the search queries listed above. Although the study is primarily limited to the museum sector, many of the papers retrieved focus on historical places of interest, cultural attractions and cultural heritage institutions, etc. These were also included in the study.

Google Scholar is an inclusive search engine, retrieving papers even if only two of the AND components of the search query were found on the paper. Therefore, during the first reading of titles and abstracts papers were excluded from the study if they were solely technical, the games implemented did not make exclusive use of mobile devices, or the focus of the paper was not on gamification, but on orientation, visit guidance or mobile advertisement of the museum.

3. SYNTHESIS AND PRESENTATION OF FINDINGS

3.1 Descriptive synthesis of findings

This descriptive synthesis provides a very brief statistical overview of the systematic literature review. Table 1 shows the results of the different searches that composed the systematic review and were submitted to Google Scholar. The three searches had three distinct primary focuses of inquiry on the same context: smart phone, mobile phone and mobile device. All three search queries shared the same exclusion criteria and core keywords. All three searches returned similar numbers of articles in a total of 868 papers. However, as expected from the start there as significant amount of duplication in the final document set (circa 2/3).

After eliminating duplication and then screening the title, keywords, abstracts, which is a selection procedure for doing systematic literature review proposed by Nunes et al., (2017), this study has identified 61 full texts that were eligible for further reading a potential selection for the study. These 61 full papers were read in their entirety and filtered according to further exclusion criteria: (i) mention of mobile devices but no serious game application implemented; (ii) mention of gamification but only as future work; (iii) mention to mobile devices application as future work; (iv) mention of gamification and mobile devices in the same paper but not integrated into one application; and (v) mention of mobile devices and museums (including references to cultural information resources), but not gamification. Thus, finally there were 30 full texts identified for full inclusion in the critical review. This is a relatively small number of papers that reflects a small subfield of a complex interdisciplinary research are in the intersection of museology, information science and educational studies.

Table 1. Results distribution for each of the search queries and database

Query Order	Search query	Number of documents from Google Scholar	Relevant document from Google Scholar (title+ abstract)	Relevant document from Google Scholar (full paper)
1	"smart phone" AND "museum" AND (gamif* {gamification, gamified} OR "game" OR "serious game") NOT ("Augmented reality" OR AR OR "Virtual Reality" OR VR)	362	52	15
2	"mobile phone" AND "museum" AND (gamif* {gamification, gamified} OR "game" OR "serious game") NOT ("Augmented reality" OR AR OR "Virtual Reality" OR VR)	235	46	28
3	"mobile device" AND "museum" AND (gamif* {gamification, gamified} OR "game" OR "serious game") NOT ("Augmented reality" OR AR OR "Virtual Reality" OR VR)	271	57	18
Total documents returned		868		
Total documents after removal of duplicates and not-found articles		259		
Total number of relevant documents after title, abstract analysis and key words			155	
Total documents of relevant documents after full content analysis				61
Total documents after full content analysis and applying additional exclusion criteria				30
Total documents after manual backward and forward citation search				9
Final total of documents selected for the meta-analysis				39

Finally, in order to guarantee that no seminal paper was missed, a manual search was conducted using backward and forward citation analysis as proposed by Nunes et al (2017). This resulted in the addition of 9 (3 from backward and 6 from forward citation) extra full papers that were inspected by screening the title, keywords, abstracts and exclusion criteria as explained above. Therefore, the final article data set was composed by 39 full texts, which were subsequently subject to a critical analysis that resulted in the discussion in the next sections.

3.2 Critical Synthesis of Findings

3.2.1 IoT Technological Centered Discussion

Since this study addresses a complex interdisciplinary type of research where information technology is the catalyzer of a complex intersection of museology, information science and educational studies, the first instinct was to concentrate on technological architectures and technological affordances. In the case of this study the catalyzer is in itself complex formed by a combination of mobile devices and IoT.

Table 2. IoT Technologies for Mobile Serious Games in Museums

Individual IoT Technologies	Typical Technological Architectures for Mobile Games		Source
	Location-aware technology	Context-aware technology	
User Profiling			
Authentication		√	Kim et al. (2015)
Content Personalization		√	Stylianidis (2015)
Recommender Systems		√	Rosmansyah and Rosyid (2017), Sweetser and Wyeth (2005),
Interaction			
Sharing with others via Social Media (e.g. Facebook)	√	√	Rosmansyah and Rosyid (2017), Hughes and Moscardo (2017), Russo et al. (2009). Nilsson et al., (2016).
Communicating with others via VOIP (e.g. from inside the game itself such as points rankings, points mechanic)	√	√	Jones et al. (2017)

Reading others posts and comments		√	Jones et al. (2017).
Real-time competition based on a navigation system (e.g. Interactive guide)	√		Kuflik et al. (2011), Jones et al. (2017). Swacha (2019), Massaty et al (2017), Chiou (2010).
Manipulation of Virtual Artefacts			
3D Models (e.g. Senses of touching)		√	Jones et al. (2017), Rowe et al. (2014).
Virtual Reality Models (e.g. Senses of touching)		√	Laine et al. (2007), Jones et al. (2017),
Augmented Reality Models (e.g. Senses of touching)		√	Froschauer et al (2012), Jones et al. (2017)
Mixed Reality Models (e.g. Senses of touching)		√	Jones et al. (2017)
Geo-location Information			
Near Field Connection (NFC)	√	√	Sánchez et al. (2011)
Radio frequency identification (RFID)	√	√	Sánchez et al. (2011)
Quick Reponses (QR) code	√	√	Kristianto, Dela and Santoso (2018), Fitz-Walter and Tjondronegoro (2011), Su and Cheng (2013), Meishar-Tal and Ronen (2016), Rhee & Choi, (2015).
Bar code	√	√	Fitz-Walter and Tjondronegoro (2011)
Global positioning system (GPS)	√	√	Amato et al, (2013), Greenspan and Whitson (2013), Chiou (2010), Tal (2019).
GPS maps and sensors	√	√	Fitz-Walter and Tjondronegoro (2011).
Automatic location detection	√	√	Stylianidis (2015), Kim et al. (2015)
Location detection via QR or RIFD codes	√	√	Tal (2019), Kristianto, Dela and Santoso (2018), Greenspan and Whitson (2013).
Automatic target detection		√	Su and Cheng (2013), Wang et al. (2017)
Target detection via QR or RIFD codes (e.g. Icon/ sticker, presence of marine animals in detail)		√	Su and Cheng (2013), Cesário et al. (2017), Ballagas and Walz(2007).
Target detection using video camera to read bar code.		√	Fitz-Walter and Tjondronegoro (2011)
Content Management and Adaptation			
Cloud storage and access (e.g. data base of introduction information for each historical place)		√	Kim et al. (2015)
Learning analytics (e.g. actively and free choice for learning, self-monitoring and reflection, progressive challenges, immediate feedback)		√	Rowe et al. (2014), Kim et al. (2015).
Image capture, manipulation and description (e.g. photographic, video or 3D model)		√	Kim et al. (2015); Stylianidis (2015); Bujari et al.(2017),

The analysis of the 39 papers selected revealed that there seems to be a developing dichotomy in the design of this type of serious game for museums around the concepts of location aware and context aware technology (Hwang et al., 2011). Most of the papers in the dataset explicitly use one or both of these types of technological architectures. However, the definition and discussion of these could only be found in depth on papers outside the scope of the systematic literature review.

Location aware technologies were initially developed in the 1980s. Early versions of this type of applications relied on location-sensing technologies to determine positions and corresponding surroundings nearby that location (Want and Schilit, 2001; Hazas et al., 2004). However, the services using these early location aware technologies were limited by low accuracy, weak coverage, low frequency of location updates. Moreover, as stated by Kaasinen (2003) location aware services differ considerably from other more traditional mobile services, since they are not just being carried by the user and operated when convenient, but they are actually used on the move and therefore not be the user's primary task that may be the movement itself. This may cause loss of information that is not caused by a weaknesses in the service but because the demands of the physical environment (e.g. background noise, illumination, weather, cross contact with other movers, etc.) may distract user's attention and disturb usage. Finally, one of the early problems with location based systems were the costs of installation and maintenance that at the time were very high (Hazas et al., 2004).

Hwang et al. (2011) use this same argument to justify that before 2010 due to these costs of developing context aware device/ technology and due to the lack of instant support for collaborative discussions, mobile learning applications were mainly based on location factors rather than the context. In fact, concept of context aware technology was firstly proposed in 1994, but the only put into practice in the early 2010s.

Context aware systems are predicated on the principle that geographical information by itself does not meet the increased locality information needs of users, but should take the broader contextual information of that location to support users' activities, searches and objectives (Want and Schilit, 2001). Context aware mobile systems respond to this criticism by using context to provide relevant information and services to the user, where relevance depends on the user's task not just geographical location (Dix et al., 2000; Dey, 2001). Hong et al., (2009) pointed out that this very nature of the context aware technologies can provide better services by meeting the user's personal needs based on a combination of physical and personal contexts. However, this is a rather difficult task since as proposed by Kaasinen (2003) in mobile environments all elements of the context of use may vary according to the needs of the different users who are engaged in many different tasks that cannot all be anticipated in the application design. Therefore, context aware technologies extract data from surroundings of a device and present it by analyzing user behaviors or responding explicitly stated requirements (e.g. find me a restaurant) (Gellersen et al., 2002; Byun and Cheverst, 2004).

Having identified the two main types of architectures that can be used in serious mobile games to provide support for informal learning and enjoyable experiences in museum visits, the next step in our critical analysis was to compare and contrast the IoT technologies that support these two architectures (Table 2) and how these IoT technologies are used in different the different types of serious mobile games (Table 3). The typology of games used in Table 2 was presented by Wang and Nunes (2019). The IoT technologies referred to in Table 2 are directly related with the features and implementation of the two types of architectures. In-door location aware architectures for instance commonly use radio frequency identification (RFID) tags, whilst out-door (open-air museums) ones use global positioning system (GPS) (Amato et al, 2013; Greenspan and Whitson 2013; Chiou, 2010; Tal, 2019). On the other hand, context aware architectures use quick response codes (QR), recommender systems and semantic web applications (Miyata and Kozuki, 2008; Hwang et al., 2011).

Table 2 focuses on the IoT technologies that have been used in support of gamification applications for museums with an educational purpose. In addition, table 2 provides a mapping and comparison of the use of these IoT technologies for location and context aware architectures.

As shown on table 2, these IoT technologies could be classified into the following 5 main categories: user profiling; interaction; manipulation of virtual artefacts; geo-location information; content management and adaptation.

The first category of user profiling includes the following types of technologies: authentication, content personalization and recommender systems. The major advantage of setting up a user profiling component is customization that is based on the record of users' information seeking and searching behavior. This record is collected as the user engages with the museum collection and employs other user profiles and similarity algorithms to provide personalized information and specific recommendations that may maximize satisfaction of the visiting experience (Kim et al. 2015, Stylianidis 2015, Rosmansyah and Rosyid, 2017, Sweetser and Wyeth, 2005).

The second category of IoT technologies focuses on enhancing visitor's museum experiences by offering an interactive approach. For instance, interaction may happen when the players share their gaming experiences or a specific interest in an artefact in the collection with peer players or even widely on their social media applications (Rosmansyah and Rosyid, 2017, Hughes and Moscardo, 2017, Russo et al., 2009). In addition, interaction may occur if the serious game application includes chat facilities or VOIP function that enable the player to communicate, discuss and comment experiences with the others during the playing activity. These interaction features make full use of common facilitates afforded by the mobile devices (Jones et al., 2017). Moreover, interaction may be achieved through asynchronous facilities that allow the reading previous players' posts and comments (Jones et al., 2017). Finally, interaction may take place through competition and become part of the game design by using external motivation triggers such as points, badges, and leaderboard membership to motivate players and prove their sense of worth and winning and complete the serious game (Jones et al., 2017, Kuflik et al., 2011).

Thirdly, the capacity of manipulation of virtual artefacts is increasingly becoming more realistic and therefore more interesting in terms of artefact visualization, understanding and even providing a sense of touching. This type manipulation requires the support of a particular type of technologies such as 3D visualization, Virtual Reality, Augmented Reality and Mixed Reality (Jones et al., 2017).

One of the most important and significant categories of IoT are geo-location information technologies which also one of the most important affordances of mobile technologies. This type of IoT uses sensors or recognition technologies to capture and identify local positioning information that can be used to navigate, guide, control, re-direct and complete the serious games. These types of IoT ranges from Global positioning system (GPS which is usually only used in outdoors museums, heritage sites and exhibitions) to more common Quick Reponses (QR) code reading devices; automatic location detection; automatic target detection; target detection via QR, Radio Frequency Identification (RFID) codes or bar code; target detection using video camera; location detection via QR or RIFD codes. (Kristianto, Dela and Santoso, 2018; Fitz-Walter and Tjondronegoro, 2011; Su and Cheng, 2013; Meishar-Tal and Ronen, 2016). The developments of mobile phones have contributed to the seamless incorporation of these technologies on the devices, such as readers for Near Field Connection (NFC), RFID. These can automatically be used for location and target identification and offer easier operation and access (e.g. no need to open phone camera to scan or read codes) as well as resulting in significant savings in development and extra HW resources when compared with early technologies such as QR and barcode (Sánchez et al., 2011). One successful example of NFC technology used for museum objects detection was described by Cesário et al. (2017) that used stickers for reading with mobile phones to offer information on marine animal's specimens and complemented the existing information on the text tags.

Finally, content management technologies are probably the earliest to have been adopted in this type of application but have been enhanced with the emergence of recent technological developments such as cloud storage and access that has been implemented for storage data and sharing data in a wide variety of aspects, ranging from descriptive information about the artefacts (text, images, video, metadata) to actual user profile and behavioral information (Kim et al., 2015). In addition, Kim et al (2015) stressed that learning analytics plays a role in profiling, customization, content management and recommendation. Moreover, these researchers stated that these content management technologies can be extremely useful for photographic image capture, video, and 3D model manipulation and description (Kim et al., 2015).

3.2.2 Game Type Centered Discussion

As part of an earlier research effort, Wang and Nunes (2019) proposed a classification of serious games for informal learning in museums. This classification was a general one, not specifically aiming at IoT mobile gamification, and divided games according to their purpose and features. The study reported in this paper identified a variety of mobile game types used specifically in IoT mobile games that are consistent with the Wang and Nunes (2019) proposition as shown in Table 3. This table illustrates the features and functions of IoT technologies as identified in Table 2 against its use in each of the mobile games types.

As Table 3 shown that out of 13 types of games that compose Wang and Nunes (2009) classification, only 8 types were identified in the current data set. From the 5 types not found, *documentary games* are the most traditional type. This type of game was very prevalent in non-interactive technologies of the 20th Century, such as video and audio presentations and documentaries. Mobile devices are part of a new generation of ICT devices and provide much more rich interactivity features and it is quite reasonable to expect that this classic type of documentary game is not part of modern IoT mobile game designs. *Stimulation and strategy games* are also classic types of educational games, but they require long periods of engagement that are not compatible with nowadays relative short visits to museums. This type of game was widely developed for informal learning in the museum in complement to classroom education and are still very successfully used in this type of setting, where the engagement with the museum may imply day visits and even multiple visits. One the other hand, there is not clear reason to justify the absence of role play games or pervasive games. One possible explanation for the absence of role play games is the complexity of the game script necessary to implement multiple roles and corresponding game plots. The design and development of IoT mobile games is still in its infancy and the lack of this type of game may just be due to an early stage of evolution of gamification using this type of technological setting. Similarly, pervasive games are usually associated with Virtual Reality (VR) applications that are still rather inefficiently used by mobile devices.

The meta-analysis of the literature selected shows quite clearly that in relation to the IoT technologies 5 categories identified in Table 3, *geo-location* IoT technologies are the most used, in fact used by all of the 8 identified types of games. This reflects the optimal use of IoT applications, that is, the use of sensors or tags to identify spaces and artefacts and help in navigating through the museum physical environment while obtaining rich information and detailed explanations. This use of geo-location can therefore stimulate informal learning through discovery, exploration and challenges set around artefacts in disparate locations in the museum. Moreover, apart from the exploration games and adventure games, all other types of games that are supported by geo-location information technologies also used other technologies (i.e. *content management and adaptation* and *interaction*) complementarily in order to achieve their purpose and implement game plots. For instance, treasure hunt games set challenges for learners aiming to locate, understand and relate artefacts in disparate locations in the museum. The ocean game designed by Cesário et al (2017) is a point treasure hunt game and challenges players to collect 13 marine species and answer a quiz to gain points and acquire digital badges. In addition, once the player used the mobile device to identify the sensor (*sticker*) that corresponds to a certain marine species, he receives both a written text explanation of that species as well as 3 related curiosity scientific facts. After collecting all 13 marine species, the visitor is presented with a quiz that evaluates players' newly acquired understandings from reading the textual information and curiosity scientific facts for the different species (Radeta et al, 2017; Cesário et al, 2017).

Location based game is the type that uses the highest number (4 out of 5) of the IoT technologies identified in Table 3. In addition, it is also the game type that implements the larger diversity types of functions under these main technologies. Wang and Nunes (2019) proposed that the features of location games are navigation systems combined with informative descriptions and explanations of items in the museum. Navigation features of location games require location detection or target detection through the use of GPS in open air museums (Sedano et al., 2012; Greenspan and Whitson, 2013); of sensors in conventional museums (Heumer et al., 2007); or by scanning the QR code (Hwang et al., 2011; Ceipidor et al., 2009). Modern versions of this type of game draw narratives, explanations, multimedia objects and quizzes related to museum artefacts and/or locations by accessing cloud storage (Kim et al., 2015) and implementing learning analytics for customization and recommendation purposes (Hsu et al., 2018). The combination of these two technologies allows players to make active choices for learning, self-monitor their progress and reflect on the progressive game challenges through immediate feedback. In addition, modern games actively encourage social interaction with other learners and visitors by sharing experiences, scores and even frustations with others via social media, such as Facebook (Machado, 2016; Nilsson et al., 2016; Rosmansyah and Rosyid, 2017).

Table 3. Implemented Mobile Features and Functions by Serious Mobile Games
matched against Wang and Nunes (2019) classification

Types of Games	**Features and Functions Supported by Mobile Technology**	**Sources**
Documentary games	➢ No mobile phone application found in the selected data set.	
Treasure hunt/Scavenger hunt motif (Discovering game)	➢ Geo-location information • GPS maps and sensors • Location detection via QR and RIF codes, • Quick response (QR) code, • Target detection using video camera to read bar code, • Target detection via QR and RIF codes, • Bar code • Location detection via QR and RIF codes. ➢ Content management and adaptation • Cloud storage and access, • Learning analytics.	Kim et al. (2015), Jones et al. (2017), Tal (2019), Meishar-Tal and Ronen (2016), Fitz-Walter and Tjondronegoro (2011), Cesário et al. (2017)
Puzzle (Gamified learning activities, Tasks Games)	➢ Geo-location information • GPS maps and sensors ➢ Content management and adaptation • Learning analytics	Su and Cheng (2013), Cabrera (2005)
Trivia (quiz)	➢ User profile • Content personalization ➢ Geo-location information • GPS maps and sensors ➢ Interaction • Share with others via social media • Communicating with others via VOIP	Rosmansyah and Rosyid (2017), Ieiri et al. (2017)
Mini games	➢ Geo-location information • GPS maps and sensors ➢ Content management and adaptation • Learning analytics	Stylianidis (2015),
Individual or group task games (Quest Game)	➢ Interaction • Real-time competition based on a navigation system	Cabrera (2005), Wang et al. (2017)
Stimulation games	➢ No mobile phone application found in the selected data set.	
Exploration games (Tangible User Interface (TUI) game/ Discovering game)	➢ Geo-location information • Global positioning system (GPS) • GPS maps and sensors • Location detection via QR and RIF codes, • Quick response (QR) code, • Target detection using video camera to read bar code, • Target detection via QR and RIF codes, • Bar code • Location detection via QR and RIF codes.	Xhembulla (2014), Kim et al. (2015), Wang et al. (2017), Sánchez et al. (2011)
Role play games	➢ No mobile phone application found in the selected data set.	
Adventure games	➢ Geo-location information • Global positioning system (GPS)	Amato et al, (2013), Greenspan and Whitson (2013), Chiou (2010), Tal (2019).
Strategy games	➢ No mobile phone application found in the selected data set.	
Location based games	➢ Geo-location information • Global positioning system (GPS), • GPS maps and sensors,	Wang et al. (2017), Kristianto et al., (2018), Greenspan and Whitson (2013), Kim et al. (2015), Xhembulla (2014), Kim et al. (2015),

	• Quick response (QR) code, • Location detection via QR and RIF codes, • Target detection using video camera to read bar code, • Target detection via QR and RIF codes, • Bar code, • Location detection via QR and RIF codes. • Near Field Communication (NFC) ➢ Interaction • Share with others via social media • Communicating with others via VOIP • Real-time competition based on a navigation system	Wang et al. (2017), Sánchez et al. (2011), Jones et al. (2017), Tal (2019), Meishar-Tal and Ronen (2016), Cesário et al. (2017), Rosmansyah and Rosyid (2017), Ieiri, Nakajima, Ayaki and Hishiyama (2017),Amato et al, (2013), Chiou (2010), Tal (2019).
	➢ Content management and adaptation • Learning analytics, • Cloud storage and access. ➢ User profile • Content personalization • Recommendation system	
Pervasive games/ Live action role-playing game	➢ No mobile phone application found in the selected data set.	

Ghosts is an exploratory and geolocation experimental mobile game designed by Nilsson et al. (2016) that aims to draw attentions to museum artefacts with the help of all knowing "ghosts" that pop-up according to the location in the museum. When playing the game, players are supposed to encounter series of designed ghosts randomly based on their positions and to these ghosts help to find out artefacts in the museum. Therefore, by receiving the feedback about player's real time position, the ghosts help to make sure the players are on the right path to visit the museum, as well as get information on how far they are from the artefacts. In addition, after completion of the game with the support of the ghosts, user are encouraged to share their visiting experiences and achievements through Facebook (Nilsson et al., 2016). This is the type of game that is expected to appear more and more in modern museums. An exploratory and geolocation game that makes use of multiple IoT technologies embedded trough a diverse number of game features and functions.

4. CONCLUSIONS

This paper first investigates and identifies the overall use of IoT technologies by serious mobile games aiming at supporting informal learning and improving museum visiting experiences through gamification. Moreover, the paper then studies known types of games, following categorization by Wang and Nunes (2019) and pinpoints which of the identified IoT technologies are used by each of the types of games according to their features and functions. IoT technologies categorization is presented in Table 2 and the study of technologies, features and functions used by each game types is presented in Table 3.

From a theoretical perspective, this meta-analysis study proposes 5 main categories of IoT technologies used by mobile games in the museum context. The study also illustrates features and functions and corresponding use of IoT technologies against its use in each of the mobile games types previously proposed by Wang and Nunes (2019). From the analysis performed, this study proposes the geo-location information function as the crucial facet of mobile serious games to support informal learning in museums. Consequently, this study also concludes that the combination exploratory location games are at the optimal choice of game architecture and design.

From a practical perspective, this study can be used to guide serious game designers on which IoT technologies to select and features to design, according to the types of games they selected and the informal learning they want to support in the museum context in which the games are to be implemented in. The paper also suggests that designers engaging with this type of game should preferentially use location aware architectures supported by geo-information functions.

ACKNOWLEDGEMENT

The study reported in this paper was partially funded by the Guangdong Social Science Foundation Project No. 2019A1515011260. The paper is part of the contractual agreed output of this project.

REFERENCES

Akamca, G. O., Yildirim, R. G., & Ellez, A. M. (2017). An alternative educational method in early childhood: Museum education. Educational Research and Reviews, 12(14), pp.688-694. doi:10.5897/err2017.3145

Amato, F., Chianese, A., Mazzeo, A., Moscato, V., Picariello, A., & Picciali, F. (2013). The talking museum project. Procedia Computer Science, 21, pp. 114-121.

Booth, A., Carroll, C., Papaioannou, D., Sutton, A. and Wong, R., (2009), "Applying findings from a systematic review of workplace based e learning: implications for health information professionals", Health Information & Libraries Journal, 26(1), pp.4-21.

Byun, H. E., & Cheverst, K. (2004). Utilizing context history to provide dynamic adaptations. Applied Artificial Intelligence, 18(6), pp.533–548.

Cabrera, J.S., Frutos, H.M., Stoica, A.G., Avouris, N., Dimitriadis, Y., Fiotakis, G. and Liveri, K.D., 2005, September. Mystery in the museum: collaborative learning activities using handheld devices. In Proceedings of the 7th international conference on Human computer interaction with mobile devices & services. pp. 315-318. ACM.

Ceipidor, U. B., Medaglia, C. M., Perrone, A., De Marsico, M., & Di Romano, G. (2009, June). A museum mobile game for children using QR-codes. In *Proceedings of the 8th international conference on interaction design and children* (pp. 282-283). ACM.

Cesário, V., Radeta, M., Matos, S., & Nisi, V. (2017, October). The Ocean Game: Assessing Children's Engagement and Learning in a Museum Setting Using a Treasure-Hunt Game. In Extended Abstracts Publication of the Annual Symposium on Computer-Human Interaction in Play. pp. 99-109. ACM.

Chiou, C. K., Tseng, J. C., Hwang, G. J., & Heller, S. (2010). An adaptive navigation support system for conducting context-aware ubiquitous learning in museums. Computers & Education, 55(2), pp.834-845.

De Rijcke, S. and Beaulieu, A., 2011. Image as interface: consequences for users of museum knowledge. library trends, 59(4), pp.663-685.

Dey, A. K. (2001). Understanding and using context. Personal and Ubiquitous Computing, 5(1), pp. 4–7.

Dix, A., Rodden, T., Davies, N., Trevor, J., Friday, A., & Palfreyman, K. (2000). Exploiting space and location as a design framework for interactive mobile systems. ACM Transactions on Computer–Human Interaction (TOCHI), 7(3),
pp.285–321.

Efird, R. (2014). Learning places and 'little volunteers': an assessment of place- and community-based education in China. Environmental education research, 21(8), pp.1143-1154. doi:10.1080/13504622.2014.976607

Eshach, H. (2006). Bridging In-school and Out-of-school Learning: Formal, Non-Formal, and Informal Education. Journal of Science Education and Technology, 16(2), pp. 171-190.

Falk, J.H., & Dierking, L.D. (2008). Enhancing visitor interaction. In L. Tallon & K. Walker (Eds.), *Digital technologies and the museum experience: handheld guides and other media* (pp. 19-33). Lanham: Altamira Press.

Fitz-Walter, Z., & Tjondronegoro, D. W. (2011, September). Exploring the opportunities and challenges of using mobile sensing for gamification and achievements. In UbiComp 11: Proceedings of the 2011 ACM Conference on Ubiquitous Computing. pp. 1-5. ACM Press.

Gellersen, H. W., Schmidt, A., & Beigl, M. (2002). Multi-sensor context-awareness in mobile devices and smart artefacts. Mobile Networks and Applications, 7(3), pp.341–351.

Greenspan, B., & Whitson, J. R. (2013, May). Whether to play or preserve the past?: Creating The Forgotten Worker Quest. In FDG pp. 298-305.

Hazas, M., Scott, J., & Krumm, J. (2004). Location-aware computing comes of age. Computer, 37(2), pp.95-97.

Heumer[1], G., Gommlich[1], F., Jung[1], B., & Müller, A. (2007). Via Mineralia–a pervasive museum exploration game.

Hong, J. Y., Suh, E. H., & Kim, S. J. (2009). Context-aware systems: A literature review and classification. Expert Systems with applications, 36(4), pp. 8509-8522.

Hsu, T. Y., Liang, H., Chiou, C. K., & Tseng, J. C. (2018). CoboChild: a blended mobile game-based learning service for children in museum contexts. *Data Technologies and Applications*, *52*(3), 294-312.

Hughes, K., & Moscardo, G. (2017). Connecting with new audiences: Exploring the impact of mobile communication devices on the experiences of young adults in museums. Visitor Studies, 20(1), pp.33-55.

Hwang, G. J., Wu, C. H., Tseng, J. C., & Huang, I. (2011). Development of a ubiquitous learning platform based on a real-time help-seeking mechanism. British Journal of Educational Technology, 42(6), pp.992-1002.

Ieiri, Y., Nakajima, Y., Ayaki, R., & Hishiyama, R. (2017, July). A Walk Rally Application to Motivate Users to Visit Potential Sightseeing Resources. In 2017 IEEE 41st Annual Computer Software and Applications Conference (COMPSAC) 2, pp. 637-642). IEEE.

Jesson, J., Mstheson, L., & Lacey, F. M. (2011). Doing Your Literature Review: SAGE.

Jones, C. E., Liapis, A., Lykourentzou, I., & Guido, D. (2017, May). Board game prototyping to co-design a better location-based digital game. In Proceedings of the 2017 CHI Conference Extended Abstracts on Human Factors in Computing Systems.pp. 1055-1064. ACM.

Kang, C., Anderson, D., & Wu, X. (2009). Chinese perceptions of the interface between school and museum education. Cultural Studies of Science Education, 5(3), pp.665-684. doi:10.1007/s11422-009-9197-2

Kim, S. Y., So, H. J., Kwon, S., Oh, S., Park, K., Ko, M., & Oh, G. (2015, July). Towards designing a mobile social learning application with meaningful gamification strategies. In 2015 IEEE 15th International Conference on Advanced Learning Technologies. pp. 170-174. IEEE.

Kirci, P., & Kahraman, M. O. (2015, May). Game based education with android mobile devices. In 2015 6th international conference on modeling, simulation, and applied optimization (ICMSAO). pp. 1-4. IEEE.

Krassmann, A. L., Falcade, A., Bernardi, G., & Medina, R. D. (2017). Exploring Student's Motivational Aspects by Developing and Applying a Ubiquitous Digital Serious Game Approach. *Journal of Creative Education*, 8(3), pp.405.

Kristianto, K., Dela, K., & Santoso, H. (2018). Implementation of Gamification to Improve Learning in Museum.

Kuflik, T., Stock, O., Zancanaro, M., Gorfinkel, A., Jbara, S., Kats, S., ... & Kashtan, N. (2011). A visitor's guide in an active museum: Presentations, communications, and reflection. Journal on Computing and Cultural Heritage (JOCCH), 3(3), pp.11.

Laine, T. H., Sedano, C. I., Vinni, M., & Sutinen, E. (2007, October). Engagement, motivation and inspiration: the SciMyst framework in museums. In *Proc. of the Fourth Conference on New Exploratory Technologies*.

Machado, M. (2016, July). Participatory Culture and Digital Concept at the Favela Museum, Rio de Janeiro, Brazil. In *3rd European Conference on Social M di R h Media Research EM Normandie, Caen, France* (p. 180).

Marcus, A. (2015). The Story Machine: Combining Information Design/Visualization with Persuasion Design to Change Family-Story Sharing Behavior. In Mobile Persuasion Design. pp. 163-260. Springer, London.

Meishar-Tal, H., & Ronen, M. (2016). Experiencing a Mobile Game and Its Impact on Teachers' Attitudes towards Mobile Learning. International Association for Development of the Information Society.

Miyata, H., & Kozuki, N. (2008, July). Mobile & Collaborative Learning Development by a Concept of "Mobile-As-Participation-Platform". In ITC-CSCC: International Technical Conference on Circuits Systems, Computers and Communications. pp. 829-832.

Nilsson, T., Blackwell, A. F., Hogsden, C., & Scruton, D. (2016). Ghosts! A location-based bluetooth LE mobile game for museum exploration. In *Mapping the Digital: Cultures and Territories of Play*. pp. 129-138. Brill.

Nunes, J. M., Kainwal, S., & Arif, M. (2017). Knowledge Management practices in Higher Education Institutions: a Systematic literature Review. Creative Commons Attribution, 4, pp.1-16.

Nunes, M., McPherson, M., Annansingh, F., Bashir, I., & Patterson, D. (2009). The use of elearning in the workplace: a systematic literature review. Impact: Journal of Applied Research in Workplace E-learning, 1(1), pp.97-112.

Radeta, M., Cesario, V., Matos, S., & Nisi, V. (2017, November). Gaming versus storytelling: understanding children's interactive experiences in a museum setting. In *International Conference on Interactive Digital Storytelling* (pp. 163-178). Springer, Cham.

Rosmansyah, Y., & Rosyid, M. R. (2017, October). Mobile learning with gamification for Alquran memorization. In 2017 International Conference on Information Technology Systems and Innovation (ICITSI) pp. 378-383. IEEE.

Rowe, J. P., Lobene, E. V., Mott, B. W., & Lester, J. C. (2014). Play in the museum: Designing game-based learning environments for informal education settings. In *FDG*.

Rubino, I., Barberis, C., Xhembulla, J., & Malnati, G. (2015). Integrating a location-based mobile game in the museum visit: Evaluating visitors' behaviour and learning. Journal on Computing and Cultural Heritage (JOCCH), 8(3), pp.15.

Russo, A., Watkins, J., & Groundwater-Smith, S. (2009). The impact of social media on informal learning in museums. Educational Media International, 46(2), pp.153 166.

Sánchez, M., García, O., Alonso, R. S., Guevara, F., Sancho, D., & Bajo, J. (2011). ARTIZT: applying ambient intelligence to a museum guide scenario. In Ambient Intelligence-Software and Applications (pp. 173-180). Springer, Berlin, Heidelberg.

Saunders, M., Lewis, P. and Thornhill, A., (2016), Research methods for business students, 7/eî, Pearson Education limited, Italy.

Sedano, C. I., Sutinen, E., Vinni, M., & Laine, T. H. (2012). Designing hypercontextualized games: a case study with LieksaMyst. *Journal of Educational Technology & Society*, *15*(2), 257-270.

Stylianidis, P. (2015, November). Mobile learning: open topics, concept and design of a learning framework. In 2015 International Conference on Interactive Mobile Communication Technologies and Learning (IMCL) pp. 421-424. IEEE.

Su, C. H., & Cheng, C. H. (2013). A mobile game-based insect learning system for improving the learning achievements. Procedia-Social and Behavioral Sciences, 103, pp. 42-50.

Sweetser, P., & Wyeth, P. (2005). GameFlow: a model for evaluating player enjoyment in games. Computers in Entertainment (CIE), 3(3), pp.3-3.

Tal, H. M. (2019). Strategies for Developing Mobile Location-Based Learning Activities by Teachers. In Mobile Technologies in Educational Organizations. pp. 85-95. IGI Global.

Terreni, L. (2015). Young children's learning in art museums: a review of New Zealand and international literature. European Early Childhood Education Research Journal, 23(5), pp.720-742. doi:10.1080/1350293x.2015.1104049

Wallace, M. and Wray, A. (2011), ìCritical reading and writing for postgraduates (2nd ed.)î, Sage.

Wang, L., Gunasti, K., Gopal, R., Shankar, R., & Pancras, J. (2017, January). The Impact of Gamification on Word-of-Mouth Effectiveness: Evidence from Foursquare. In Proceedings of the 50th Hawaii International Conference on System Sciences.

Wang, M. and Nunes, M.B., (2018). Identification of Serious Games for Museum's Educational Roles: A Critical Literature Review. In M. Macedo & P.Kommers(Eds.). *Proceedings of international conference on ICT society and Human Beings,* Madrid, Spain, pp. 131-140.

Wang, M., & Nunes, M. B. (2019). Matching serious games with museum's educational roles: smart education in practice. Journal of Interactive Technology and Smart Education. 6(4), pp. 319-342.

Want, R., & Schilit, B. (2001). Expanding the horizons of location-aware computing. Computer, 34(8), pp.31-34.

Washburn, W. E. (1975). Do museums educate? Curator: The Museum Journal, 18(3), pp.211-218.

Williams, B. L. (1996). An Examination of Art Museum Education Practices Since 1984. Journal of National Art Education Association, 38(1), pp.34-49.

MOBILE TECHNOLOGY AFFECTING TEACHING AND LEARNING IN RURAL SCHOOLS

Marlien Herselman[1,2], Adele Botha[1,2], Keneilwe Maremi[1,2] ,Sifiso Dlamini[1] and Mario Marais[1]
[1]*CSIR, P.O. Box 395, Pretoria, South Africa*
[2]*University of South Africa, School of Computing, Florida Campus, South Africa*

ABSTRACT

The purpose of this paper is to provide monitoring and evaluation results of how teaching and learning were affected in 24 rural schools in 7 provinces of South Africa after a three-year mobile technology implementation project. Teachers face many challenges in rural schools as access to the Internet, electricity, basic amenities and training to use technology in the classroom are often not attained. Large classes and unsupportive principals can also influence the sustainable use of mobile technology in these schools. Two theories of change (implementation success and improved quality of teaching and learning) were applied through an End-line survey to determine how the Information Communication Technology for Education (ICT4E) project, affected teaching and learning in the selected rural schools. Funded by the Department of Agriculture and Rural Development (DARD) in South Africa, the Council for Scientific and Industrial Research (CSIR), Pretoria campus was mandated to implement the project. The implementation involved providing mobile tablets to all teachers, and schools, training the teachers through a university accredited Teaching Professional Development (TPD) course, training 48 ICT Technicians to support teachers and doing a baseline and end-line survey. At the end of the project, 184 teachers successfully completed the TPD training and 6895 learners were affected. The methodology that was applied is a sequential explanatory mixed-method approach where data was collected using firstly a survey, followed by one-to-one interviews. Data were analyzed using descriptive statistics (quantitative data) as well as coding through Nvivo (qualitative data). The main results indicated that 97% of the teachers will continue to use mobile technology for teaching rather than traditional teaching. The teachers also indicated that for them the most outstanding benefit of the TPD was to learn new teaching strategies. Teachers reported an 80% improvement in school attendance and that learners were much more involved and eager to learn when using mobile tablets in the schools. Teachers continued to develop their own communities of practice to share lesson plans and ideas in specific subjects (Mathematics and Science). The project, therefore, had a very positive affect on teaching and learning and was statistically proven to be a success.

KEYWORDS

Monitoring and Evaluation, Teaching and Learning, Mobile Tablets, Teacher Professional Development, Rural Schools

1. INTRODUCTION

The Council for Scientific and Industrial Research (CSIR) in Pretoria, South Africa, was mandated by the Department of Agriculture and Rural Development (DARD) to implement the ICT for Education Project (ICT4E) over a period of three years (2017-2019). The overarching objective of the mobile technology project was to improve the quality of teaching and learning in a rural context through the introduction of proven technologies, frameworks and approaches that have been tested, creating an enhanced teaching and learning process.

The purpose of the project's monitoring and evaluation function was to contribute evidence (through surveys) that informed the responsive evolution of ICT4E's implementation; and also to compile evidence that would inform the design and implementation of similar projects in future (Herselman, Botha & Maremi, 2019). The DARD selected 24 schools in 7 provinces of South Africa (Gauteng, Eastern Cape, Free State, Northwest, Northern Cape, Kwa-Zulu Natal and Limpopo) and the principals of the selected schools had to identify 10 suitable teachers who received Teacher Professional Development through accredited training materials. The IDEAS Lab at the University of the Free State won the open tender process to facilitate all training of teachers and two selected youths from the respective community where the school is situated who should provide technical support to the teachers (Dlamini & van der Vyver, 2019).

For the purpose of this paper, the focus will be on sharing the monitoring and evaluation results of the End-line survey results that were applied after the training over a period of two years. These results will reflect the difference this project has made on the teaching and learning in these schools.

Rural schools in South Africa are struggling to implement the White Paper on e-education (Department of Basic Education, 2004), especially at the organizational level (Kotzé, Van der Westhuizen & Barnard, 2017; Vandeyar, 2010). The reason for this relates to contextual issues, lack of resources and infrastructure as well as the ability to translate the country's national policies to provincial policies.

The research question of this paper is: *What evidence was found to indicate implementation success and improved quality of teaching and learning when mobile technology was used in training teachers in selected rural schools in South Africa?* This will be addressed in the results section.

The focus is specifically on rural schools in resource-constrained environments where low-income communities reside and power as well as bandwidth are challenges (Botha & Herselman, 2018). Other constraints in this type of context can include cultural issues and people are usually not familiar with or have the anxiety to use technology (Adukaite, van Zyl, Er & Cantoni, 2017).

2. CHALLENGES FACED BY TEACHERS WHEN USING TECHNOLOGY TO TEACH

There is an expectation that all teachers should have 21st-century skills to teach with technology to enhance their teaching practice (Botha, Herselman, Musgrave & Jaeschke, 2017). Vosloo (2011) however indicates that investments in technology should rather be channeled towards training teachers to use these technologies effectively. Investing time and money to improve teachers, and teaching, is viewed by members of School Governing Bodies (SGBs) as pivotal (Botha *et al.*, 2017). For this to happen teachers have to be trained to apply and develop the content of a digital nature and to use technology in their specific subject areas (Ekanayake & Wishart, 2014).

Apart from TPD training, the teacher has to be seen as part of a system and their attitudes, beliefs and anxiety levels, when integrating mobile technology into their classrooms, are essential to respect (Dagdilelis, 2018). Anxiety can be overcome if teachers can learn new skills to use the technology to support their teachning to enhance classroom practices and learn from their fellow colleagues (Scherer, Siddiq & Tondeur, 2019; Chiu & Churchill, 2016; Jantjies & Joy, 2016; Teo, Lee & Chai, 2008).

Thoughtfulness, creativity, and commitment to sustain specific action plans are required to successfully integrate technology to support teaching (Naiman, 2016). Successful integration of mobile technology to support collaborative learning has also been indicated by Fu and Hwang (2018) and explained by Hwang, Chu and Lai (2017) when a mobile learning project was conducted in Taiwan. Training teachers to use applications during their teaching can enhance their own skills and also influence the learning of their learners (Adukaite *et al.*, 2017). Teachers should also consider creating learning communities of practice amongst themselves to support their own development and to enhance their 21st-century skills development (Karam, Straus, Byers, Kase & Cefalu, 2018). Even if there are concerns about the integration of technology into educational settings (Bates, Swennen & Jones, 2014), it is believed that with the support of adequate leadership and the potential of digital content to support teaching, these challenges can be counteracted (Terhoven & Fataar, 2018; Rikkerink, Verbeeten, Simons & Ritzen, 2016).

In order to eliminate poverty, reduce inequality and spur economic development, South Africa's National Development Plan (NDP) identifies education, training, life-long learning and innovation as key priorities (National Planning Commission, 2012). As is indicated by Mabila, Van Biljon and Herselman (2017) there are four major features supported by the E-education policy framework for the use of ICT in teaching and learning in South Africa which is: equity, access to ICT infrastructure, capacity building and norms and standards. Education systems must change to facilitate mobile access to education and one of the most important changes is training teachers to prepare them for the mobile world (Ally, 2009). The infrastructure of a school also affects the sustainable use of mobile technology, as some schools, especially in rural areas of South Africa lack basic equipment like desks and many computer facilities at these schools are under-serviced and dysfunctional (Terhoven & Fataar, 2018). Better qualified teachers move to better-equipped schools where there is adequate infrastructure, buildings, electricity, lavatories, learning materials, and resources, as these factors directly affect teachers' and learners' performances (Ramorola, 2018).

The challenges of the educational school system in South Africa should not be underestimated as conditions in which teachers work are complex due to the pervasive legacies of South Africa's history (Ramorola, 2018). The subsequent changes in policies and implementation that have occurred since the dawn of democracy in 1994, did result in different education departments (Mabila *et al.*, 2017). However, teachers have had to cope with the changes amid other challenges, as new curricula have been introduced (Terhoven & Fataar, 2018). Teachers, therefore, face many challenges in schools in South Africa (Ramorola, 2018).

Therefore in order to counteract these challenges, the DARD with the CSIR decided to invest in these communities throughout South Africa by providing infrastructure and training to teachers to use the infrastructure (mobile tablets, servers, and learner tablets) more effectively.

3. THE SCOPE OF THE ICT4E PROJECT IS TO SUPPORT TEACHING AND LEARNING IN RURAL SCHOOLS

The scope of the ICT4E Project was to deploy ICT infrastructure to 24 beneficiary schools, to design, develop and accredited training material for use during the project, to provide teacher professional development (TPD) training and accreditation, and to training School ICT technicians (two for each school to support teachers with technical issues.

The implementation model, therefore, involved the deployment of tablets to learners, teachers and ICT Technicians. Each school received 40 mobile Android tablets (30 learners and 10 teacher tablets), another 48 tablets were provided to the ICT Technicians (2 per school). Another technology infrastructure that was provided to each school was connectivity (Mi-fi hotspot device with a SIM card with 3G access), content servers (one for each school) and other electronic resources (e-textbooks on the servers, lesson plans for specific subjects when using mobile tablets, quizzes, tests and curriculum-related support material).

The TPD training commenced in the afternoons, for four (4) hours after school hours. TPD training was divided into six separate sessions of two consecutive days each. The TPD had two objectives: 1) To position the rural participating teacher for further lifelong learning, and 2) To change the classroom practice of the rural participating teachers to reflect an enhanced teaching and learning engagement through pedagogy for the information age.

The requirement for successful completion of TPD was that teachers needed to be selected by their school principal to attend the training; they had to be registered as a student for this training at the University of the Free State (UFS); they had to attend at least 90% of the classes (one class can be excused due to illness or a funeral); and they had to hand in and complete three reflective entry journals and two assignments. If they comply with these requirements teachers then received the credit-bearing Certificate in Teacher Professional Development for Digital Mobile Learning (CTPDDML) that is part of the introduction to the ICT module as part of the Advanced Certificates in Teaching at UFS. More detail on the teacher training is provded in another paper: Botha *et al.* (2017).

UFS trained two ICT Technicians per school (48 in total) in two sessions (one week each) at the DARD training facility (Free State Province). They each received certificates for each of the 6 modules they completed. The ICT Technicians were deployed to the school after the first training session and they were given specific roles and responsibilities to support the teachers (who already completed their training).

4. METHODOLOGY

Monitoring and evaluation were done through the application of developmental evaluation, which repositions evaluation as an internal, collaborative function and aligned best with the projects' Research and & Development character. The purpose and objectives of the project, as well as its program components and activities, were conceptualized in two theories of change (implementation success and improved quality of teaching and learning) that frame the rationale for the project and its evaluation. The Funnell and Rogers (2011) definition of theory of change was applied which indicates that a program theory should contribute to a chain of intermediate results and finally to the intended or observed outcome.

In addition, the evaluation employed an array of mixed methods to address the two theories of change. A sequential, explanatory mixed methods approach was followed during the End-line survey where the use of both the qualitative and quantitative research methods in a singular study is applied (Creswell & Clark, 2017). Quantitative data were analyzed using statistical and mathematical techniques (Principal Component

Analysis/PCA and stepwise multiple regression analysis) in order to observe specific variables in a data set (Mouton, 2006). The thematic analysis of qualitative data (from one-to-one interviews was carried out using the Nvivo software version 11 (NVIVO, 2017). The data analysis for the quantitative phase of the survey was conducted using the SPSS version 24. The data analysis consisted of both descriptive and inferential statistics (associational and comparative).

5. RESULTS

The results will be provided by addressing the two theories of change: Implementation success and improved quality of teaching and learning (End-line survey). The results also address the research question posed in this paper under section 1: *What evidence was found to indicate implementation success and improved quality of teaching and learning when mobile technology was used in training teachers in selected rural schools in South Africa?*

- **Implementation success**

This was measured by tracking a) the consistent participation of the teachers in their TPD; b) tracking the technical training of the ICT Technicians to support teachers; c) identify how the project positively influenced the learners and finally d) how consistent the functionality of the technology was to support training and use of the mobile tablets.

a) Out of the 240 selected teachers, **56 dropped** out (**meaning 184 completed**) mainly because they could not cope with doing this course on top of their teaching load. Upon completion of TPD, **67.7% of the final group of teachers complied with the accredited training criteria of the UFS**. Five teachers have also enrolled for the Online Advanced Certificate in Teaching at UFS starting 2019 based on the successful completion of the TPD training. This is evidence of how this project definitely influenced the **lifelong learning** of the teachers at the 24 schools and influenced the **rural education system of South Africa positively.** Many teachers, principals, and learners expressed their gratitude to have been part of the project, and this is particularly the case in the deep rural areas where such opportunities are scarce. Their confidence levels using the technology grew, this encouraged the UFS team to continue, and to make sure that the program remains relevant. The human factor, where one pays attention to their joys and concerns, is an important factor to take note of. The statistical (both descriptive and inferential) evidence indicated that after the training of the teachers, 97% of the teachers indicated that they will continue to use ICT for teaching rather than traditional teaching and also 98% of the teachers indicated that they are willing to use ICT to teach. The teachers also indicated that for them the most outstanding benefit the training was to learn new teaching strategies.

b) The ICT Technician's technical training was successful as t**he average pass rate was 82%**. Their training and deployment were noted by most schools to be an advantage and huge support to assist them to integrate the technology into the teacher's teaching and learning practices. **Twenty schools** indicated that the trained ICT Technicians are **consistently diligent** and organized and support the schools by searching for Apps to support specific subjects and to organize a timetable to ensure each teacher can use the tablets for their classes during the week. They also support teachers in resolving technical problems. The existence of the Communities of Practice or Professional Learning Communities (**79.5% of the teachers indicated that they have established Communities of Practice with teachers during the end-li**ne) that were formed amongst the teachers in each province and even across provinces is further evidence that the intervention was a success and has a possibility for sustainable use in future. Teachers use **WhatsApp** groups to share lesson ideas, especially in subjects like **Mathematics** and **Biology**. An important observation from UFS was that when young and motivated youth, who take an interest in building ICT skills of teachers at the school; teachers get motivated to make use of the technology in the classroom. Subsequently, integration occurs, which means that ICT integration becomes sustainable beyond formal training. This has an impact on educators and learners at the schools.

c) Learners positively affected by the project were **6895 (Boys = 3346 Girls = 3549).** The feedback of the teachers about the learners indicates that overall the discipline has improved, there are less absent learners, they find working with the technology very exciting and are more attentive in class. Teachers also indicated that for them **80% of the learners are more participative** in Grade 11 and the lowest mark in one of the Mathematic classes was only **40% which was a huge improvement** since the use of the tablets in the classroom. The coding of the feedback of the teachers revealed the following themes: ICT acceptance and use through collaborations with peers and teachers, positive change in **classroom practice** and **positive attitude** changes in learners. This is therefore evident that the ICT4E project has had a **very positive influence on the behaviour, attendance, effort, and attention of the learners and has also supported the attainment of 21st-century skills in the learners.**

d) Results on the functionality of the technology were that theft of tablets and tablets that freeze or do not want to operate were regarded as the biggest challenges that influenced the teachers' motivation to use the technology. However, most of the teachers did complete the course successfully and were satisfied and grateful for the provided technology and training. Another major findings was that if principals support the project then everyone is eager to use the technologies. Three schools also reported that they will get their own Internet and buy more tablets from their own funds to ensure the sustainability of the project.

- **The measurement of the improved quality of teaching and learning**

This was done by doing a baseline and End-line assessment (survey questionnaire). This paper will only provide some significant End-line results (descriptive and inferential statistical analysis).

Demographics: A quarter (26.1%) of the participants was male and 73.9% female; the ages ranged from 27 to 59 years and the average age of the group of teachers was 45.5 years; more than three-quarters of the teachers (77.3%) had a Bachelor's or higher degree. The home language of 23% of the teachers was Afrikaans, 20% Sepedi, 18% isiZulu, 14% isiXhosa and 13% Setswana.

After the TPD training inferential statistics (Pearson correlation coefficient that measures the strength of a linear association between two variables and is denoted by *r*), indicated that the three highest statistically significant correlated items with **'Extent of training'** were:

- 'Basic usage of ICTs in education', $r = .823$, $p < .01$;
- 'Integrating ICT in the curriculum using the World Wide Web', $r = .652$, $p < .01$;
- 'Integrating ICT in classroom projects', $r = .617$, $p < .01$; and

The three highest statistically significant correlated items with the teachers' **'Attitudes towards technology'** were:

- 'The use of the tablet computer as a learning tool excites me', $r = .721$, $p < .01$;
- 'The tablet computer helps students understand concepts in more effective ways', $r = .711$, $p < .01$;
- 'The tablet computer helps educators to teach in more effective ways', $r = .709$, $p < .01$; and

Regarding the teachers **digital literacy and acceptance levels of ICT** the teachers indicated that they feel they have good ICT skills ($r = .759$, $p < .01$) and that they are confident to obtain information from the Web to support their teaching and learning activities in the classroom ($r = .735$, $p < .01$).

Three multiple regression analyses were conducted. The first analysis used **'Self-confidence in integrating ICT'**, the second analysis used the '**Level of digital literacy'** of teachers and the third analysis used '**Attitudes towards technology**' as dependent variables. Each of these scales was separately used as a dependent variable in a stepwise multiple regression analysis with the remaining scales as independent variables. Before the Stepwise regression analyses were performed, a bivariate correlation analysis was conducted to establish the strength of the bivariate associations.

Table 1. Bivariate correlation matrix of developed scales for the survey population

Standardized scales	Extent of training	Attitudes towards technology	Self-confidence in integrating ICT	Digital literacy and ICT acceptance	I think my level of digital literacy is:	Attributes of ICT acceptance in
Extent of training	-					
Attitudes towards technology	0.171	-				
Self-confidence in integrating ICT	0.152	.675 **	-			
Digital literacy and ICT acceptance	0.280 **	.407 **	.564 **	-		
I think my level of digital literacy is	0.066	.405 **	.395 **	.562 **	-	
Attributes of ICT acceptance in teaching	0.185	.554 **	.715 **	.600 **	.336 **	-

***. Correlation is significant at the 0.01 level (2-tailed).*

The following statistically significant correlations were highly correlated:

- 'Self-confidence in integrating ICT' and 'Attributes of ICT acceptance in teaching', $r = .715$, $p < .01$.
- 'Self-confidence in integrating ICT' and 'Attitudes towards technology', $r = .675$, $p < .01$.
- 'Digital literacy and ICT acceptance' and 'Attributes of ICT acceptance in teaching', $r = .600$, $p < .01$.
- 'Self-confidence in integrating ICT' and 'Digital literacy and ICT acceptance', $r = .564$, $p < .01$.

At the end of the training, 67% of teachers indicated that they have developed digital content and using Apps in class to teach (72%). In the end-line, 100% of the teachers indicated that 'The tablet computer helps the teacher to teach in more effective ways'.

The three highest statistically significant correlated items with 'Attributes of ICT acceptance in teaching' after the teacher's training was completed, were as follows:

- **'Using ICT will enable me to exercise my teaching work easier'**, $r = .818$, $p < .01$;
- **'Using ICT will enable me to positively teach more learners**', $r = .811$, $p <.01$;
- **'My intentions are to continue using ICT for teaching rather than traditional teaching**, $r = .726$, $p < .01$; and

The $r= .818$ is a significant indication that after the training the teachers feel that using ICT will enable them to exercise their teaching easier and they feel ICT will enable them to teach more learners positively and that they want to continue to use ICT for teaching rather than traditional teaching. This is also the first known project (that CSIR researchers are aware of) in South Africa that has statistical evidence to prove its success.

6. CONCLUSIONS AND RECOMMENDATIONS

ICT in Education initiatives notoriously falter in their implementation when unique obstacles to uptake are not addressed. One of this project's highest level outcomes was to avoid implementation failure precisely by providing for these obstacles in its design, and in so doing modelling implementation success. To assess implementation success, the evaluation posed 3 questions: 1) Were the program components, and the project overall, feasible to implement? 2) Which factors support, inhibit or prevent implementation (theft, demotivated teachers and teachers not coping seem to be the biggest contributors)? And 3) What are the lessons learned about the implementation of this project that should be transferred to others (below these are provided)?

The implementation experience of ICT4E is instructive in distinguishing between factors inhibiting successful implementation that are within the control of the project, and those inhibiting factors external to it. A crucial inhibiting factor is the state of technology infrastructure in rural areas. Even with a project design that assumes full responsibility for installing a complete technology ecosystem, some functionality, especially electricity, remains independent of project efforts.

Despite a comprehensive design that accounted for the common obstacles within its control, ICT4E's implementation was nevertheless tested, with mixed results. Particularly challenging was the availability of the ICT Technicians, technical problems with the tablets and theft. The level of committed collaboration also varied from school to school. While there is evidence of the use of technology by teachers in the classroom the quality and relevance of teaching materials employed for this (which the content servers were expected to facilitate) is unclear.

The thorough and inspiring teacher and ICT Technicians training and deployment were enabling factors, which was evident in the fact that many teachers kept using technology and teaching practices. A system-wide approach – parents, administration and District officials (especially subject advisors) - is required to create a conducive environment for the use of technology as a conventional teaching practice to be adopted widely.

A success story is the teacher training and the apparent changes in teaching practice as well as the teacher's feedback on the effect the project has had on the attitudes, discipline, and attendance of learners. Their marks improved in some subjects where they are using mobile tablets, especially at the secondary school level (Grade 8-12).

The long term sustainability will only become apparent over time. A key issue is what are the components of an enabling environment? Ongoing evaluation is therefore required to develop recommendations for supporting teachers and schools. To sustain technology in future the identified barriers in the whole system (a project at District/Circuit level and the supporting systems of the department) need to be addressed. The lack of sufficient e-content to support all subjects at all levels and in the various South African languages was identified as a significant need.

The lessons learned in ICT4E should be used by all provincial Departments of Education to guide the design and implementation of "teaching with technology" strategies.

The main lessons learned were:

- If there is a lack of commitment from the principal then teachers are not eager to participate or to integrate mobile technology in their classrooms;
- To import international e-content sources does not work as it has to be contextualized;
- The lack of reliable and fast Internet in South Africa, especially in resource constraint/rural areas, hinders the use of technology – this is coupled with high data prices;
- Sustainability is a challenge as once a project is done usage of mobile technology fades. This has to be part of the exit strategy from the beginning and involvement from the district side is crucial;
- Security of devices is a concern in most projects as devices are stolen and not replaced (when outdated);
- Technical support during and after implementation is important;
- Change management should be a priority since the inception of any mobile technology project;
- Teachers need to be empowered through ICT integration courses and refreshment courses at least once a year;
- Establishing collaborations and networks amongst teachers to share content can influence sustainability.

ACKNOWLEDGMENT

This paper acknowledges the funding support of the National Research Foundation (NRF) in South Africa with grant number: 112252. It also acknowledges the DRDLR ICT4E Project which is funded by the DARD and where the UFS provides the training of the teachers in every school.

REFERENCES

Adukaite, A., Van Zyl, I., Er, Ş. & Cantoni, L. 2017. Teacher perceptions on the use of digital gamified learning in tourism education: The case of South African secondary schools. *Computers & Education,* 111:172-190.

Ally, M. 2009. *Mobile learning: Transforming the delivery of education and training.* Edmonton: AU Press.

Bates, T., Swennen, A. & Jones, K. 2014. *The professional development of teacher educators.* Routledge.

Botha, A. & Herselman, M. 2018. Teachers become cocreators through participation in a teacher professional development (TPD) course in a resource constraint environment in South Africa. *The Electronic Journal of Information Systems in Developing Countries,* 84(1):e12007.

Botha, A., Herselman, M., Musgrave, S. & Jaeschke, G. 2017. Dimensional evaluation of a rural mobile learning teacher professional development curriculum. The Institute for Science and Technology Education (ISTE). Kruger Park. https://researchspace.csir.co.za/dspace/handle/10204/10048.

Chiu, T.K. & Churchill, D. 2016. Adoption of mobile devices in teaching: Changes in teacher beliefs, attitudes and anxiety. *Interactive Learning Environments,* 24(2):317-327.

Creswell, J.W. & Clark, V.L.P. 2017. *Designing and conducting mixed methods research.* Sage publications.

Dagdilelis, V. 2018. Preparing teachers for the use of digital technologies in their teaching practice. *Research in Social Sciences and Technology,* 3(1):109-121.

Department of Basic Education. 2004. *White paper on E-Education: Transforming learning and teaching through information and communication technologies.* [Online]. Available: http://www.education.gpg.gov.za/Legislation/White%20paper%207%20on%20e-Education.pdf [Accessed.

Dlamini, S. & Van Der Vyver, A. 2019. A Qualitative Analysis of an E-education Initiative in Deep Rural Schools in South Africa: A Need to Build Resilience. Cham: Springer International Publishing.

Ekanayake, S.Y. & Wishart, J. 2014. Integrating mobile phones into teaching and learning: A case study of teacher training through professional development workshops. *British Journal of Educational Technology*:n/a-n/a.

Fu, Q.-K. & Hwang, G.-J. 2018. Trends in mobile technology-supported collaborative learning: A systematic review of journal publications from 2007 to 2016. *Computers & Education.*

Funnell, S.C. & Rogers, P.J. 2011. *Purposeful program theory: Effective use of theories of change and logic models.* John Wiley & Sons.

Herselman, M., Botha, A. & Maremi, K. 2019. Evaluating a mobile tablet project in rural South Africa against criteria to comply with being an innovative educational ecosystem. 3rd International Conference on Education and Multimedia Technology. . Nagoya, Japan

Hwang, G.-J., Chu, H.-C. & Lai, C.-L. 2017. Prepare your own device and determination (PYOD): a successfully promoted mobile learning mode in Taiwan. *International Journal of Mobile Learning and Organisation,* 11(2):87-107.

Jantjies, M. & Joy, M. 2016. Lessons learnt from teachers' perspectives on mobile learning in South Africa with cultural and linguistic constraints. *South African Journal of Education,* 36(3):1-10.

Karam, R., Straus, S.G., Byers, A., Kase, C.A. & Cefalu, M. 2018. The role of online communities of practice in promoting sociotechnical capital among science teachers. *Educational Technology Research and Development,* 66(2):215-245.

Kotzé, T., Van Der Westhuizen, M. & Barnard, E. 2017. Teaching strategies to support isiXhosa learners who receive education in a second/third language. *South African Journal of Education,* 37(3):1-12.

Mabila, J., Van Biljon, J. & Herselman, M. 2017. A sustainability framework for mobile technology integration in schools: The case of resource-constrained environments in South Africa.

Mouton, J. 2006. *How to Succeed in Your Master's and Doctoral Studies: A South African Guide and Resource Book.* Pretoria: Van Schaik.

Naiman, L. 2016. *Design thinking as a strategy for innovation.: Creativity at work.* [Online]. Available: http://www.creativityatwork.com/design-thinking-strategy-for-innovation/ [Accessed.

National Planning Commission. 2012. National Development Plan 2030: Our future–make it work. *Presidency of South Africa, Pretoria,* 1.

Nvivo. 2017. *Homepage.* [Online]. Available: https://www.qsrinternational.com/ [Accessed 31 January].

Ramorola, M.Z. 2018. Transforming teaching and learning through technology integration.

Rikkerink, M., Verbeeten, H., Simons, R.-J. & Ritzen, H. 2016. A new model of educational innovation: Exploring the nexus of organizational learning, distributed leadership, and digital technologies. *Journal of Educational Change,* 17(2):223-249.

Scherer, R., Siddiq, F. & Tondeur, J. 2019. The technology acceptance model (TAM): a meta-analytic structural equation modeling approach to explaining teachers' adoption of digital technology in education. *Computers & Education,* 128:13-35.

Teo, T., Lee, C.B. & Chai, C.S. 2008. Understanding pre-service teachers' computer attitudes: applying and extending the technology acceptance model. *Journal of Computer Assisted Learning,* 24:128-143.

Terhoven, R. & Fataar, A. 2018. The role of leadership practices in establishing a curriculum policy platform at working-class schools. *South African Journal of Education,* 38(2):1-10.

Vandeyar, T. 2010. *The appropriation of education policy on information and communication technology in South African schools.* Pretoria, South Africa: University of Pretoria.

Vosloo, S. 2011. *The teacher crises, UNESCO Mobile learning week.* UNESCO, Paris.

INVESTIGATING MOOC PLATFORMS AS A PROSPECTIVE TOOL FOR MOBILE LEARNING

Albena Antonova and Boyan Bontchev
Faculty of Mathematics and Informatics, Sofia University
5, James Baucher Blvd., 1164 Sofia, Bulgaria

ABSTRACT

The Massive Open Online Courses (MOOCs) provides new m-learning solutions for "learning-on-the-go", packing in one educational content, pedagogical framework and community support. Reaching millions of users world-wide, the MOOCs have the potential to fully transform educational landscape. However, the spread of the MOOCs is still limited, the retention rate and the degree of completion is small and the MOOCs efficiency remain doubtful. Thus, the present research aims to make an overview of the recent developments in MOOCs and m-learning solutions to recommend strategies for prospective learning providers. Considering the opportunities, it investigates suitable approaches for learning institutions to design and deliver m-learning MOOCs that will empower learners' experience. The paper is structured as follows. On first place, it makes an introduction to the MOOCs main concepts and identifies common features and classifications. Then, a short overview is made on the most popular MOOCs platforms. After that, the paper analyzes the MOOCs providers' approaches, including learners, technologies, instructional design, factors of success and lessons' learned of the MOOCs implementation. Finally, the discussion makes an overview of the steps and recommendations for implementing a successful MOOC.

KEYWORDS

MOOC, User-Centered Learning, M-Learning, MOOC Learning Provider

1. INTRODUCTION

The Massive Open Online Courses (MOOCs) build on the long history of the distance education, boosting knowledge democratization and access to learning. In addition to the wide spread of mobile technologies, the MOOCs promise to improve the access to learning for anyone, anytime and anyplace. Facilitated by m-learning technologies, it can combine a large set of solutions for learning-on-the-go, promoting personalized and situated mobile learning (Kukulska-Hulme, 2009), bridging formal and informal learning experiences, virtual collaboration and communication (Duncan-Howell and Lee, 2007). Aiming to be both open and massive, today MOOCs involve millions of learners across the world and include hundreds of MOOCs technology platforms. Even more, thousands of MOOCs courses are produced by the most renown universities, learning providers, technology institutions and not-for-profit organizations. Combined, m-learning and MOOCs are two developments with the potential to fundamentally reshape the landscape of education. However, there are still many technical, educational and social challenges for learning providers in order to guarantee equal access to education for all (Sharples et al. 2015). More importantly, the efficiency of the MOOCs courses is small, the drop-out rate of the learners is high, and many employers are still skeptic about the effectiveness of the MOOCs, finding them superficial, too general, and incomparable with traditional learning. Therefore, learning providers have to be better prepared to design appropriate MOOCs solutions, considering MOOCs platforms, pedagogical methods and learners' experiences.

The present research aims to make an overview of the MOOCs recent developments for prospective learning provider, in order to derive to structured recommendations for design and delivery of learner-oriented course offerings. Considering portable m-learning solutions, it will investigate strategies for developing m-learning MOOCs, reflecting on the MOOCs functions, application fields, and learners' experiences, focusing on features, tools and functionality to support knowledge transfer.

The paper is structured as follows. On first place, it makes an introduction to the MOOCs main concepts, common features and classifications, and characteristics of the MOOCs platforms. Then, the paper investigates the main specifics of the MOOCs implementation, taking into account the learners, the learning process and MOOCs technologies and institutions. Finally, the discussion presents practical recommendations for MOOCs users. The conclusion outlines the next directions for implementing successful m-learning and portable MOOCs.

2. BACKGROUND – MOOC DEFINITION AND CHARACTERISTICS

Hollands and Tirthali (2014) define MOOCs as online courses that: "allow hundreds of thousands of students to participate simultaneously in a course and are free and open to any interested participant ...". The main characteristics of MOOCs remain the open access (anyone can participate) and scalability (supporting indefinite number of learners). The term MOOC was first used in 2008 to describe the online course "CCK08: Connectivism and Connective Knowledge" (Downes, 2008). This is the first example of a course, where twenty-five students taking the course for fee and for credit are accompanied by another 2,300 'open' participants. This first MOOC was delivered as an "open" and "massive" course, providing both course materials and a certificate of completion free of charge. Few years later, in 2011, the lecture "Introduction to Artificial Intelligence" of Thrun from Stanford University reached over 160 000 enrolled students (Kopp and Lackner, 2014). The both courses are online courses, massively attended and open to everybody. Since then, the number of MOOCs increased tremendously worldwide, stimulated largely by the emergence of the popular MOOC platforms (Yuan & Powell, 2013).

2.1 Classification and Categories of MOOCs

The majority of the MOOC categorisations were created from the viewpoint of a MOOC providers and cover issues such as the number of participants, the degree of openness and pedagogy (Liyanagunawardena et al., 2019). During the years, the main categories of MOOCs are defined as: cMOOCs (based on connectivism) and xMOOCs (based on behaviorism). The main difference between these two MOOCs types lies in their didactic approach (Kopp and Lackner, 2014). First, the cMOOCs are built on the connectivist learning theory, valuing interaction within the community, social media interaction and peers' discussions. It facilitates learning in the network and encourages participants to create, share, and reflects upon each other's artifacts (such as videos, blog posts and others). Second, the xMOOCs are delivered as an "extension" of the traditional learning environment, providing education at scale. Thus, xMOOCs reproduce online the traditional lecture: video lectures, computer-based assignments and tests, and peer assessment. It is media- or teacher-centered, focusing on instruction and delivery of content usually from professors by prestigious institutions, such as Harvard and Stanford (Daniel, 2012). Today, the vast majority of existing MOOCs classifies as xMOOCs. The MOOC classification of Pilli and Admiraal (2016) focuses on the level of which a MOOCs is Massive and Open. They define four cases: (1) Small scale/less open courses (limited enrolments and a fee); (2) Small scale/ more open, (free courses with limited enrolment); (3) Large scale/less open (courses with some course material freely available, but restricted access to other material and assessments); (4) Large scale/more open (content is freely available to all).

Working on a MOOCs taxonomy, Clark (2013) suggested a taxonomy from a pedagogical perspective oriented to MOOC delivery methods. Liyanagunawardena et al. (2019) made a review of different MOOCs classifications and made the following proposal. They defined 13 common categories for every MOOC: (a) brief description; (b) syllabus; (c) subject area; (d) educators; (e) institution; (f) supporter; (g) provider; (h) timings; (i) pre-requisites; (j) certification; (k) cost; (l) reviews; and (m) language. As well, the authors analyzed how each of the MOOC providers and aggregators match each of these 13 categories.

2.2 MOOCs Platforms

The raising MOOCs' popularity is due to the large number of MOOCs platforms, divided on MOOCs aggregators and MOOCs content providers. The MOOCs platforms collect and provide information about the MOOCs courses in a learner-oriented form. In general, MOOCs platform can classify on MOOCs aggregators and MOOCs providers. For instance, the MOOCs aggregator services focus on course ratings and reviews; while in contrast, the MOOCs providers address specific course details such as openness of the MOOCs, course pre-requisites and available certificates. The mobile app market places, such as Google Play and iTunes host numerous educational apps for m-learning MOOCs solutions. However, the massiveness of the MOOCs, including statistics and popularity, is not reflected neither by the MOOCs providers nor by the aggregators.

2.2.1 MOOCs Aggregators

The aggregator services aim to collect in one place courses from several MOOCs providers. This facilitates prospective participants to navigate through the courses of different MOOCs providers, exploring extensive search options and specific categories, generated by the aggregator services (Table 1). For example, on the MOOC aggregator listed last – MOOC List, there are currently available courses on 32 languages, provided by universities and learning institutions from 61 countries.

Table 1. The most popular MOOCs aggregators (data from aggregators' websites, March 2020)

Name	Website	Features
Classcentral	https://www.classcentral.com/providers	45 MOOCs providers
Coursebuffet	https://www.coursebuffet.com/providers	16 MOOCs providers
Coursetalks	https://www.coursetalk.com/providers	46 MOOCs providers
MOOC List	https://www.mooc-list.com/	77 MOOCs providers

2.2.2 MOOCs Content Providers

The majority of the MOOCs are delivered via MOOC content providers, even developed by leading academic institutions. Coursera, edX, and Udacity were the first major MOOC platforms, based in North America. Today, many MOOC providers come from Europe such as EMMA (European Multiple MOOC Aggregator), FutureLearn (UK), iversity (DE), MOOIN (DE) and iMooX (Austria). While initially the MOOC platforms supported only English, now many MOOC platforms are multilingual. Other language MOOCs are Edraak (Arabic), MiriadaX (Spanish and Portuguese) and XuetangX (Chinese).

Furthermore, some governments promoted national-wide MOOCs platforms, such as the platform France Université Numérique (FUN) and platform MéxicoX. Even more, Finland, recognizing the role of Artificial Intelligence, organized a specialized MOOC platform for AI training (https://course.elementsofai.com/) first, providing it on Finnish and English, and lately, translating it on all other EU languages.

Table 2. The numbers of learners, courses and degrees of MOOCs providers (data from Classcentral, 2019)

Name	Learners	Courses	Degrees	Mobile app
Coursera	45 million	3800	16	X
edX	24 million	2640	10	X
Udacity	11.5 million	200	1	Not available
FutureLearn	10 million	880	23	Not available
Swayam	10 million	1000	0	X

In Table 2, there are presented some of the main figures for the top 5 MOOC content providers, as identified by the aggregator Class central for 2019 and including the number of learners and number of courses. Based on its statistics, for 2019 the course topics by subject are distributed as follows: Technology (19,8%), Business (19,7%), Social Sciences (11%), Science (9%), Humanities (8,9%), Education and teaching (8%), Engineering (7,8%), Health and medicine (7,4%), Arts and Design (5,2%), and Mathematics (2,9%).

2.2.3 MOOCs m-Learning Platforms

The m-learning solutions for MOOCs increasingly gain popularity, exceeding tens of millions of downloads. The most popular m-learning MOOCs providers are still Coursera and edX, but Udemy and LinkedIn Learning emerge as increasingly popular mobile learning platforms (Table 3). All these platforms support Android, iPhone, and iOS mobile devices.

Table 3. The most popular MOOCs mobile platforms (data from Google Play and iTunes, March 2020)

Name	Courses	Installs Google Play	Reviews/ Google Play	Reviews/ iTunes
Udemy	>2000 topics >130 000 videos	10 Mio +	194,6 K 4,5/5	17 K 4,6/5
Coursera	>2000	5 Mio +	99,45 K 4,3/5	54,8 K 4,8/5
edX	2000	1 Mio +	56,31 K 4,7/5	2,8 K 4,7/5
LinkedIn learning	>4000	1 Mio+	18,7 K 4,6/5	47K 4,8/5
Khan Academy	Students/ Teachers	10 Mio+	114,4 K 4,5/5	4,9K 4/5

For example, Udemy attracts learners with access to more than 2000 courses on wide number of topics, provided by more than 50 000 instructors, teaching on more than 60 different languages. The Udemy platform supports course downloads, audio-only mode, video streaming, learning personalization and speed control. The mobile application of Coursera allows learners to browse courses in a variety of subject areas. It supports both online streaming of video lectures and downloads for offline viewing. The edX mobile platform promotes the access to wide range of online classes, quizzes and exams, supporting extended search functions. LinkedIn Learning offer another m-learning approach, allowing learners to download courses for offline viewing, to share courses with the network and to add certificates of completion into LinkedIn profile. Finally, Khan Academy is an application, designed mainly for secondary school students, however gaining attention of adult learners by providing free courses and thousands of interactive exercises, videos, and articles.

3. INVESTIGATING MOOC SPECIFICS

3.1 Defining MOOCs Learners' Profile

The MOOCs learners' profiles largely vary across courses, countries and subjects. In general, the MOOCs audience is widely heterogeneous, and can include multiple learning profiles, such as students, academics, employees, unemployed and retirees, all having different motivation, learning approaches and expectations. However, the studies reveal that 70% to 80% of the MOOC participants are already well-educated with at least a B.A. degree (Hollands & Tirthali 2014; Kopp and Lackner 2014). Even the participants from emerging countries belong to the educated and wealthy part of society. As Fyle (2013) concludes, besides technical infrastructure, the learners in MOOCs should have specific soft skills, including strong academic self-concept, good interpersonal and communication skills, basic understanding of collaborative learning, self-directed learning skills and cognitive learning strategies. In informal learning settings, for achieving one's own learning goal, the willingness to learn is supported by discipline to cope with autonomous, self-directed, self-organized and self-paced learning processes and good time management (Lackner et al., 2015). All this reduces the chances for people of limited educational background and experience to join MOOCs.

3.1.1 Learners' Drop Out

The numerous drop-outs and the small success rate (below 10%, most often 7,5%) of successful MOOCs learners are largely discussed in the literature. Lackner et al. (2015) classify the reasons for dropping out of a MOOC within two categories: personal (internal), and imposed (external). First, in adult learning a difference should be made between learning for personal and for professional purposes. Whereas professional purposes are often externally motivated, linked to enterprises and to the labor market, it is more difficult to identify and validate the personal purposes and internal motivations. The employers position on MOOCs, how they recognize the MOOCs certificates and their attitude can impact on the learners' motivation. Sometimes MOOC participants just "shop around" and pick up different elements of a course but do not want to finish the course itself; sometimes it is not the whole course that seems to be interesting but only parts of it. Thus, learning goal can differ from the objectives or learning outcomes, set up by the institution or the lecturers (Lackner et al., 2015). The success rate depends as well on the main antecedents of learning, including the students' prior experiences with education, their motivations, previous performance and perceived effectiveness in learning (Vigentini et al., 2016).

3.1.2 Learning Engagement

The individual's motivation to participate in a MOOC can largely vary from achieving an academic certification, to acquire specific skills, for personal enrichment and self-satisfaction. More recently, Deng et al. (2020) identifies four type of learners' engagement: behavioral, cognitive, emotional, and social engagement. Considering that most learners are university graduates, they can participate in MOOCs for variety of reasons, expecting different benefits, based on the MOOCs recognition and accreditation. The learners can be classified in three main groups (Alario-Hoyos et al., 2014b): (1) lurkers, who register in a course but never log in or enter without completing the tasks, (2) participants that do not complete the course, but take part in some activities and (3) participants that complete the course. In the empirical study of Alario-Hoyos et al. (2014b), the group of lurkers is the biggest one (26,5% are no-shows and 42% are just observers). The participants, who completed successfully the course are about 8%, among which engaged participants, who take all the assignments are only 6% from all enrolled. The most engaged participants used to act as mentors, assisting their peers and enriching the MOOC with additional content and discussion.

3.2 The MOOC Learning Process

The MOOCs learning process depends on the chosen form. Most of the xMOOCs are designed as weekly sequences of instruction, combining short video lectures punctuated with quizzes, supplemental readings and assignments. Thus, the learning process in the xMOOCs is structured in a linear way, building on the passive transmission-based learning strategy of the traditional classroom. Some courses allow learners to submit open assignment, but often the interaction between learners are limited to forum discussions. The learning process in cMOOCs aims to encourage participants to learn in the networks of people, tools, artefacts and organizations, reaching their individual and collective objectives (Tirthalli, 2016). The learning dynamic in cMOOCs is not one to many, but many to many, exploring learning as social and interactional, encouraging reflection, dialogue and collaboration, applying theory learnt to practice, creating community of peers, enabling creativity and motivating learners (Conole, 2013).

3.2.1 Instructional design for MOOCs

Building a MOOC is not an easy task, even for courses, based on an already existing and mature course. The inappropriate course design or the lack of a clear course structure can lead multiple learners to drop out. Kopp and Lackner (2014) find out that although the similarities, the design of the MOOCs courses actually differ from the other blended-, online- or m-learning methods. The main difficulty is that learners can come from different backgrounds, countries and social strata, making planning and designing increasingly challenging. Furthermore, Kopp and Lackner (2014) propose a checklist for the design and development phase of a MOOC, based on the ADDIE approach. Thus, instructional design process includes seven categories: core requirements, structure, participant requirements, assignments, media design, communication and resources. Conole (2013) discusses the 7C Learning Design framework for MOOCs, covering course Conceptualization (the vision for the course), Capture (a resource audit), Communicate (mechanisms to foster communication), Collaborate (mechanisms to foster collaboration), Consider (assessment strategies), Combine (overarching views of the design), and Consolidate (implementing and evaluating the design in a real learning context). Alario-Hoyos et al. (2014a) propose a MOOC Canvas as a simple and visual framework, facilitating educators to design a MOOC from scratch.

3.2.2 Technologies

Technologies offer many ways in which MOOCs can facilitate learning, such as interacting with multimedia or communicating and collaborating with peers. However, the MOOCs (and especially xMOOCs) do not need many features to be successful (Kopp and Lackner, 2014). It is the innovative combination of already known components like video lectures, forums and quizzes that make MOOCs special. This way, the MOOCs platform should contain the possibility to provide and to access videos, text transcripts, quizzes and further readings, a forum to communicate with other participants and a billboard, where news are announced.

A. Videos

Videos play a central role for students' learning experience in the current generation of MOOCs. Guo et al. (2014) find out that videos have a big influence on the student engagement in MOOCs. Based on that, they formulate several practical recommendations for MOOCs creators: (1) to use short videos (up to 6 min); (2) to make post-production editing and to display slides together with the instructor's head; (3) to film in more informal setting, encouraging instructors to speak fairly fast and with high enthusiasm; (4) to produce Khan-style tablet drawing tutorials, that are more engaging than PowerPoint slides or code screencasts; (5) to introduce motion and continuous visual flow into tutorials, along with extemporaneous speaking; (6) to consider that students engage differently with lecture and tutorial videos and thus for tutorials, to add options for re-watching and skimming (Guo et al. 2014).

B. Social tools

The main social tools, used to connect the MOOCs' participants are the forums and social networks, either built-in tools, available on the platform, or external tools, provided by third-parties (such as social networks, forums, microblogging and others). In all cases, using appropriate social tools play an important role to effectively build connections among MOOC participants, facilitating mentors and peers to create a vibrant MOOC community. Thus all MOOCs need to ensure appropriate level of interactivity and collaboration (Gamage et al, 2020). Open-ended, guided, or directed peer-to-peer assessments of course tasks and projects appear the most important social tool for providing individual feedback, and for engaging and motivating course participants, without any need of instructor intervention (Staubitz et al., 2016).

3.3 Motivation for Learning Institutions to Create MOOCs

The main factors, motivating learning institutions to create MOOCs can largely vary (Tirthali, 2016). Usually, learning institutions reflect on MOOCs as tools to extend the reach and the access to education, to build and maintain the brand, to lower costs or increase revenues, to improve educational outcomes for MOOC participants and on-campus students, to innovate in teaching, learning and research (Hollands and Tirthali, 2014). There exist different strategies how learning institutions can adopt MOOCs courses in their learning offerings (Ebner et al., 2020). This way, many institutions can implement MOOCs to improve the quality of campus education, to increase the visibility of its brand and to open education to reach the global masses (Stöhr et al., 2015). However, MOOCs are expensive to produce (Tirthali, 2016), as it is a team effort, involving considerable amount of time and investments from faculty, teaching staff, instructional designers and videographers, graphic designers and programmers. Many institutions find out that MOOCs can bring additional revenue streams and not-direct benefits, such as savings for ongoing courses and increasing in the in-campus enrollments. Most often, the revenue from MOOCs come from delivering certificates and on-line degrees. However, it depends from the level that the learning institution can offer learning credits for MOOCs, making them equivalent to face-to-face or formal online courses.

4. DISCUSSIONS

The raising popularity of the MOOCs mobile platforms is expected to encourage more learning institutions to investigate strategies to successfully design and develop mobile MOOCs offerings. They need to take into account the following considerations, including both methodological and technological issues:

- First, taking into account that most of the MOOCs learners are University graduates, learning providers (LP) can design user-centered learning paths, recognizing learners' personal and professional motivations to engage in life-long-learning. As m-learning MOOCs require specific prior skills and motivation to enroll and to successfully complete, LPs can introduce personalization approaches, including course contextualization and adaptation in larger scale, reducing some common learners' barriers such as language, time constraints and cognitive overload.
- On second place, many statistics prove that teachers and lecturers are among the main group of the MOOCs learners, motivated to gain personal reward and a sense of intrigue and altruism (Hew and Cheung, 2014). Therefore, LPs can design specific learning paths for teachers and lecturers, allowing them not only to

upgrade their professional knowledge and skills, but explicitly introducing pedagogical practices and teaching approaches that can be used later in face-to-face class interactions.

- Third, younger generations are increasingly expecting to interact with mobile learning, videos, and MOOCs in their formal and informal studies. Thereby, LPs should increasingly prepare for the raising demands and expectations for m-learning by the new generation of learners (Gómez-Ramirez et al, 2019).
- Fourth, the experience of xMOOCs and cMOOCs suggests that LPs should increasingly encourage passive learners to engage and interact with their peers (e.g., by forum discussions or peer assessments), to produce individually or in-group artefacts, and to reflect on their learning. Designing interactive exercises, building trust and sense of community and engaging in social discussions will increase the success of MOOCs learning and knowledge building. Especially for m-learning MOOCs, the mobile MOOC design should offer clear navigation, simple layout, liner display, and full interaction (Jia and Zhang, 2018).
- Fifth, due to the ever-growing popularity of mobile applications and m-learning, all MOOCs platforms should provide client applications at least for Android, iPhone, and iOS mobile devices. By applying appropriate adaptation to the smaller screen sizes of both the user interface and learning content, MOOCs mobile clients should support the same functionality as the Web clients. For example, they should provide learner dashboard, multi-screen support, discussion forums, peer-to-peer assessment, offline learning, and multi-language support.
- Finally, LP have to define appropriate strategies and criteria for selecting and implementing a MOOC platform. Thus, LP should consider the overall costs for installation, maintenance and management of the MOOC platform, including its mobile learning component. Furthermore, LP should define the platform functionality, including on-line/off-line video-and audio lectures, peer assessment, automatic quiz assessment, and supporting enough options for interactivity and collaboration (Gamage et al., 2020).

5. CONCLUSION

Increasingly, the MOOCs become accessed as mobile learning solution, improving the access and portability of learning. Supporting learners in all phases of learning, it facilitates pre-learning experience (browsing courses, enrolling), learning-on-the go (watching online video, making quizzes, downloading content), and post-learning experience (commenting, socializing, consulting content and recommendations, sharing learning artefacts). Therefore, building adaptable and contextualized mobile learning strategies is especially important for MOOCs learning providers. Furthermore, the MOOCs' experience can help a large group of learning providers to build better strategies for adopting e-learning, m-learning and blended learning approaches.

Nowadays, MOOCs are offered for both Web and mobile client applications, where upon difference between their functionalities become ever less essential. While the technological issues are steadily resolved by the modern mobile devices offering high resolution of display, higher performance, and faster mobile throughput, there are still some pedagogical and methodological concerns that will continue attracting the attention of MOOC designers in the next years. Future MOOCs should address the great percentage (up to 90%) of learners dropping out due to lack of incentive, failure to understand the course content and having no help (Hew and Cheung, 2014), by offering a better personalization, contextualization, and adaptation to the knowledge and needs of each individual learner.

ACKNOWLEDGEMENT

The research in this paper is partially supported by The National Science Program "Information and Communication Technologies for Unified Digital Market in Science, Education and Security" financed by the Ministry of Education and Science, Bulgaria.

REFERENCES

Alario-Hoyos, C., Pérez Sanagustín, M., Cormier, D. and Delgado Kloos, C., 2014. Proposal for a conceptual framework for educators to describe and design MOOCs. *In J. of Universal Computer Science*, vol. 20, no. 1 (2014), pp.6-23.

Alario-Hoyos, C., Pérez-Sanagustín, M., Delgado-Kloos, C. and Munoz-Organero, M., 2014. Delving into participants' profiles and use of social tools in MOOCs. *In IEEE Transactions on Learning Technologies*, 7(3), pp.260-266.

Clark, D. 2013. MOOCs: taxonomy of 8 types of MOOC. Donald Clark Plan B, Blog post. Retrieved from http://donaldclarkplanb.blogspot.co.uk/2013/04/moocs-taxonomy-of-8-types-of-mooc.html

Conole, G.G., 2013. MOOCs as disruptive technologies: strategies for enhancing the learner experience and quality of MOOCs. *In Revista de Educación a Distancia*, (39).

Daniel, J., 2012. Making sense of MOOCs: Musings in a maze of myth, paradox and possibility. *In Journal of interactive Media in education*, 2012(3).

Deng, R., Benckendorff, P. and Gannaway, D., 2020. Learner engagement in MOOCs: Scale development and validation. *British Journal of Educational Technology*, *51*(1), pp.245-262.

Downes, S., 2008. Places to go: Connectivism & connective knowledge. Innovate. *In J. of Online Education*, 5(1), p.6.

Duncan-Howell, J.A. and Lee, K.T., 2007. *M-Learning–Innovations and Initiatives: Finding a place for mobile technologies within tertiary educational settings*. Ascilite.

Ebner, M., Schön, S. and Braun, C., 2020. More Than a MOOC—Seven Learning and Teaching Scenarios to Use MOOCs in Higher Education and Beyond. In *Emerging Technologies and Pedagogies in the Curriculum* (pp. 75-87). Springer, Singapore.

Gamage, D., Perera, I. and Fernando, S., 2020. MOOCs lack interactivity and collaborativeness: Evaluating MOOC platforms. International Journal of Engineering Pedagogy (iJEP), 10(2), pp.94-111.

Gómez-Ramirez, I., Valencia-Arias, A. and Duque, L., 2019. Approach to M-learning Acceptance Among University Students: An Integrated Model of TPB and TAM. *International Review of Research in Open and Distributed Learning*, *20*(3).

Guo, P.J., Kim, J. and Rubin, R., 2014, March. How video production affects student engagement: An empirical study of MOOC videos. *Proceedings of the first ACM conference on Learning@ scale conference*, pp. 41-50.

Fyle, C.O., 2013, June. Teacher education MOOCs for developing world contexts: Issues and design considerations. *Proc. of Sixth International Conference of MIT's Learning International Networks Consortium (LINC)*.

Jia, J., and Zhang, B. (2018, July). Design Guidelines for Mobile MOOC Learning—An Empirical Study. *Proc. of Int. Conference on Blended Learning*, Springer, Cham., pp.347-356.

Hew, K. F., and Cheung, W. S. (2014). Students' and instructors' use of massive open online courses (MOOCs): Motivations and challenges. *In Educational research review*, 12, pp.45-58.

Hollands, F.M. and Tirthali, D., 2014. *MOOCs: Expectations and reality*. Center for Benefit-Cost Studies of Education, Teachers College, Columbia University, 138.

Hollands, F.M. and Tirthali, D., 2014. Why Do Institutions Offer MOOCs?. *In Online Learning*, 18(3), p.n3.

Kopp, M. and Lackner, E., 2014. Do MOOCs need a special instructional design. *Proc. of EDULEARN14,* 71387147.

Kukulska-Hulme, A., 2009. Will mobile learning change language learning?. *In ReCALL*, 21(2), pp.157-165.

Lackner, E., Ebner, M. and Khalil, M., 2015. MOOCs as granular systems: design patterns to foster participant activity. *In eLearning papers*, (42), pp.28-37.

Littlejohn, A. and Milligan, C., 2015. Designing MOOCs for professional learners: Tools and patterns to encourage self-regulated learning. *In eLearning Papers*, 42.

Liyanagunawardena, T.R., Lundqvist, K., Mitchell, R., Warburton, S. and Williams, S.A., 2019. A MOOC taxonomy based on classification schemes of MOOCs. *European Journal of Open, Distance and E-learning*, *22*(1).

Pilli, O. and Admiraal, W., 2016. A taxonomy of massive open online courses. *In Contemporary Educational Technology*, 7(3), pp.223-240.

Sharples, M., Delgado Kloos, C., Dimitriadis, Y., Garlatti, S. and Specht, M., 2015. Mobile and accessible learning for MOOCs. *In Journal of interactive media in education*, 1(4), pp.1-8.

Staubitz, T., Petrick, D., Bauer, M., Renz, J., and Meinel, C. (2016, April). Improving the peer assessment experience on MOOC platforms. *Proc. of the third (2016) ACM conference on Learning@ Scale*, pp.389-398.

Stöhr, C., Eriksson, T. and Adawi, T., 2015, June. Reasons for engaging in MOOC development: Management, faculty and support perspectives. *In MOOCs in Scandinavia Conference. Stockholm, Sweden*.

Tirthali, D., 2016. Are MOOCs Sustainable?. Corte & U. Teichler (Eds.), *From Books to MOOCs*, pp.115-123.

Yuan, L. and Powell, S.J., 2013. MOOCs and open education: Implications for higher education. *CETIS white paper*.

Vigentini, L. and Zhao, C., 2016, April. Evaluating the'Student'Experience in MOOCs, pp.161-164.

MOBILE LEARNING ADOPTION AT THE SCIENCE MUSEUM GROUP

Ruel Welch, Temitope Alade and Lynn Nichol
University of Worcester
Worcester, United Kingdom

ABSTRACT

Mobile learning (mLearning) at the Science Museum Group (SMG) in the United Kingdom (UK) could reduce ICT support calls, increase productivity and develop technical knowledge SMG staff. However, challenges are pervasive in any technological adoption. This paper uses the unified theory of acceptance and use of technology (UTAUT) model to explain the determinants of mLearning adoption at the Science Museum Group (SMG).
Results indicate that the UTAUT constructs, performance expectancy, effort expectancy, social influence and facilitating conditions are all significant determinants of behavioral intention to use mLearning. A newly proposed construct, self-directed learning was not a significant determinant of behaviour intentions. Further examination found age and gender moderate the relationship between the UTAUT constructs. These findings present several useful implications for mLearning research and practice for ICT service desk at SMG. The research contributes to mLearning technology adoption and strategy.

KEYWORDS

Mobile Learning, Workplace Learning, Technological Adoption

1. INTRODUCTION

The Science Museum Group (SMG) service desk team in the United Kingdom (UK) faces Service Level Agreement (SLA) breaches due to an overstretched Service Desk team. Furthermore, this team suffers a recruitment freeze due to significant reductions in funding made by the Department for Culture, Media and Sport (DCMS) in the UK. Thus, service desk staff are required to manage incidents and other demands with minimal resources.

The aim of this paper is to derive models for adoption of mobile learning (mLearning) as a form of just-in-time knowledge acquisition. This will be achieved by addressing two objectives

1. Analyze questionnaire data establishing factors contributing to mLearning adoption at SMG
2. Provide recommendations to the SMG's service desk management on improving the implementation and adoption of mLearning in the SMG in order to achieve operational objectives.

1.1 mLearning in the Workplace

While mLearning research has grown in popularity in the milieu of educational institutes i.e. schools, colleges and universities, its use as a knowledge acquisition method remains a relatively new concept in the field of organizational learning, more specifically, communities of practice (Lave and Wenger, 1991). It is widely accepted that staff training and staff propensity to be trained is a contributing factor in facilitating new technological adoption. Rossett and Marshall's (2010) research found the use of mobile devices for learning was uncommon practice. As a result, this presents a missed opportunity as mLearning provides useful just-in-time knowledge acquisition. The focus of most researchers over the last few years has been on evaluating the effects of mLearning (Chee et al., 2016).

1.2 Main Contributions

The extent to which mLearning can be used as a tool for knowledge acquisition and its impacts on productivity and specifically, the effective management of ICT support calls in the museum sector remain largely unknown. Due to lack of research in this area, this study on mLearning adoption in SMG is important to senior SMG ICT management as it will provide insight and help to illuminate important drivers for technological adoption. These contributions are useful within and outside the museum sector as it provides insights for technological adoption strategies.

2. RESEARCH MODEL AND HYPOTHESES

Venkatesh et al. (2003) research found that the constructs appear to be significant determinants of user acceptance and usage behaviour. The remainder of this section presents a definition of each of the determinants and their relationship across eight technology acceptance models. Additionally, stating the role of the key moderators (gender and age), and proposing the theoretical rational for the hypotheses that will be advanced in this study. Finally, this section will present the adaptation of the UTAUT model that will be used in this research.

Performance expectancy: Venkatesh et al. (2003) defines performance expectancy as the extent an individual considers the utility of an information system and the performance gains attained in their job from using it. There are five constructs pertaining to performance expectancy, namely perceived usefulness (TAM/TAM2 and C-TAM-TPB), extrinsic motivation (MM), job-fit (MPCU), relative advantage (IDT), and outcome expectations (SCT).

Modification to the performance expectancy construct to incorporate the mLearning context suggests SMG staff will find it useful to apply mLearning as a knowledge acquisition solution.

Numerous authors ((Morris and Venkatesh 2000; Venkatesh and Morris 2000) theorised that gender and age have been shown to play moderating roles in the context of technological adoption. Research conducted by Minton and Schneider (1980) on gender differences suggests that adult males tend to be more task-oriented than adult females. Whilst, research on job-related attitudes (Hall and Mansfield 1975; Porter 1963) suggests that younger workers place more emphasis on extrinsic rewards. Therefore, the influence of performance expectancy on behavioural intention will be moderated by gender and age, such that the effect of gender will be stronger for men, in particular, younger men Venkatesh et al. (2003). Therefore, this study will advance the following hypotheses:

Hypothesis 1: Performance expectancy has a positive effect on behavioural intentions to use mLearning

Hypothesis 2: Performance expectancy influences behavioural intention to use mLearning more strongly for male staff than for female staff

Hypothesis 3: Performance expectancy influences behavioural intention to use mLearning more strongly for younger staff than for older staff

Effort expectancy: Venkatesh et al. (2003) defines effort expectancy as the extent to which the use of the information system is achieved with ease. Three constructs from three models denote the concept of effort expectancy: perceived ease of use (TAM/TAM2), complexity (MPCU), and ease of use (IDT).

The notion of effort expectancy being a stronger determinant of an individuals' intention for women than men is supported by prior research (Venkatesh and Morris 2000; Venkatesh et al. 2000). Additionally, based on similar claims in the context of performance expectancy, it is anticipated that gender and age will have comparable moderating effects on effort expectancy. Accordingly, based on the same arguments presented in UTAUT, it is anticipated that individual acceptance of mLearning will depend on the extent to which the use of it will be achieved with ease. Additionally, Rossett and Marshall's (2010)'s research found the use of mobile devices for learning was uncommon in current practice and was hardly considered for staff training albeit formal, non-formal or informal work-based learning. Moreover, it is anticipated that gender and age will have comparable moderating effects on effort expectancy. Thus, the following hypotheses will be tested:

Hypothesis 4: Effort expectancy has a positive effect on behavioural intention to use mLearning

Hypothesis 5: Effort expectancy influences behavioural intention to use mLearning more strongly for female staff than for male staff

Hypothesis 6: Effort expectancy influences behaviour intention to use mLearning more strongly for older staff than for younger staff

Social influence: Venkatesh et al. (2003) defines social influence as the extent to which an individual perceives that either senior staff members or someone that can influence behaviour thinks they should use the information system. The construct social influence is represented as subjective norm in TRA, TAM2, TPB/DTPB and C-TAM-TPB, social factors in MPCU, and image in IDT.

Some authors (Venkatesh et al. (2003); Wu et al., 2008; Indrawati et al., 2010) suggest that social influence affects the intention to use new technology. It has been theorised that women tend to be more sensitive to the opinions of others and therefore find social influence to be more prominent when forming an intention to use new technology (Miller 1976; Venkatesh et al. 2000). Additionally, Rhodes' (1983) research suggests that older staff members are more likely to place emphasis on social influences. Transposing these arguments to the context of mLearning is the rationale for anticipating that social influence is a significant determinant of behaviour intentions to use mLearning, likewise, will be moderated by gender and age in the same way. Thus, the following hypotheses will be advanced.

Hypothesis 7: Social influence has a positive effect on behavioural intention to use mLearning

Hypothesis 8: Social influence influences behavioural intention to use mLearning more strongly for female staff than for male staff

Hypothesis 9: Social influence influences behavioural intention to use mLearning more strongly for older staff than for younger staff

Self-directed learning: Livingstone (2006) defines self-directed or informal learning as any activity involving the pursuit of understanding, knowledge, or skill that occurs without the presence of externally imposed curricular criteria' (p206) or instructor (Chee et al., 2016), research on mobile learning trends between 2010 and 2015 found, that informal learning was the most popular approach within mLearning research, compared to other learning approaches such as formal learning and non-formal.

From both a techno-centric and andragogical viewpoint, aspects of mLearning can be considered as a kind of self-directed eLearning via mobile devices. For example, both eLearning and mLearning are learner centred thus, self- learning (Behera, 2013). It is expected that a person's level of self-directedness of learning will have a positive influence on his or her behavioural intention to use mLearning as a knowledge acquisition intervention. Beck's (1983) research on cognitive therapy suggests evidence to support the notion that men are more likely to possess autonomous personality traits than women. As a result, it is anticipated that the effect of self-directed learning on mLearning acceptance will be moderated by gender and age, such that the effect will be stronger for men, particularly older men. Thus, the following hypotheses will be tested:

Hypothesis 10: Self-directed learning has a positive effect on behavioural intentions

Hypothesis 11: Self-directed learning influences behavioural intentions to use mLearning more strongly for Male staff than for Female staff

Hypothesis 12: Self-directed learning influences behavioural intention to use mLearning more strongly for older staff members than for younger staff members

Facilitating conditions: Venkatesh et al. (2003) defines facilitating conditions as the extent to which an individual perceives the organisational and technical infrastructure's ability to provide support for the information system. The construct facilitating conditions is typified by three different constructs from five models; perceived behavioural control (TPB/DTPB, C-TAM-TPB), facilitating conditions (MPCU), and compatibility (IDT).

Based on arguments presented by Venkatesh et al. (2003) it is anticipated that the effect of facilitating conditions on mLearning adoption will not be moderated by gender and age. Therefore, this study will advance the following hypothesis:

Hypothesis 13: Facilitating conditions does not impact behavioural intentions

Behaviour intentions to use mLearning: Based on arguments presented by Venkatesh et al. (2003) regarding behavioural intentions. This research expects that behavioural intention would have a significant positive effect on use behaviour. Thus, the following hypothesis will be tested:

Hypothesis 14: Behaviour intentions has a positive effect on Use behavior Learning, Workplace Learning, Technological Adoption.

3. METHODOLOGY

3.1 Data Collection

A structured questionnaire was created using an electronic form (google form) and disseminated to both SMG staff via emails to gatekeepers. Thus, convenience sampling, a non-random sampling technique was used. The questionnaire consisted of SMG specific questions, demographic questions, internet connected mobile device usage questions and reviewed UTAUT questions. Each item on the UTAUT survey is scored on a 5-point Likert scale. The wording of the items on the survey were reviewed by a selection of SMG staff for the purpose of clarity and completeness.

Data Screening: The data was screened for missing data, unengaged responses, outliers and data normality. There were no missing data in the dataset. Five cases were removed due to unengaged responses. Mahalanobis distance was calculated to locate and remove outliers. No cases were removed as the maximum value calculated for this dataset was 67.089 and the critical value is 69.3.

Data normality is examined by conducting a Skewness and Kurtosis test. The results of the analysis showed fairly normal distributions for the indicators of latent factors and all other variables were observed. However, mild Kurtosis was found in seven items. The Kurtosis observed ranged from benign to 3.17. This does fall below more lenient rules suggested by Sposito et al. (1983) who recommend 3.3 as the upper limit.

3.2 Data Analysis

Data was analysed using the Structural Equation Modelling (SEM) approach. SEM is a comprehensive statistical modelling technique used to specify confirmatory factor analysis models, regression models and complex path models. Thus, this approach was used in this study. Anderson and Gerbing (1988) recommend a two-step approach which this study adopted. First, an examination of the measurement model for reliability and validity was conducted. Secondly, the assessment of the structural model to test the suitability of the model and research hypotheses was carried out.

4. RESULTS AND DISCUSSIONS

4.1 Participants

This section describes the descriptive statistics for the 118 staff whose responses from the mLearning adoption survey was usable.

Sixty-eight (58%) of the staff were female, and fifty (42%) were male. Participants' age group were reported as follows: 3 (2%) <21; 41 (35%) 21 - 30; 36 (30%) 31 - 40; 23 (20%) 41 - 50; 15 (13%) >50;

The highest educational attainment of staff members was reported as 3 (3%) having attained a Secondary school education; 5 (4%) Further Education (FE) College; 11 (9%) Higher Education (HE) college 53 (43%) Bachelor; 46 (39%) Postgraduate.

All of the main departments of SMG were represented; 8 (7%) Collections Services; 6 (5%) Commercial Experience; 1 (1%) Curatorial / Library / Archives; 6 (5%) Development; 5 (4%) Directorate; 10 (9%) Exhibitions; 14 (12%) Finance / Procurement; 21 (18%) ICT; 9 (8%) Learning; 5 (4%) Marketing and Comms; 5 (4%) Masterplan, Estates & Design; 12 (10%) Operations (including Visitor Fundraising); 4 (3%) People & Culture; 6 (5%) Retail; 6 (5%) Other.

43 (36%) staff had management responsibilities, leaving 75 (64%) that did not.

A large majority (114; 97%) of the participants reported they had used a mobile device at home with Internet access. Seventy-seven (65%) said they had used a mobile device at work, seventy (59%) of staff members reported that they used their mobile device to acquire knowledge or skill, and twenty-two (19%) stated that they used their mobile device to access SMG knowledge articles or ICT Training YouTube channel.

4.2 Evaluation of the Measurement Model

Exploratory Factor Analysis (EFA) and Confirmatory Factor Analysis (CFA) are used to explain relationships among several observed variables using a smaller number of unobserved variables also known as latent variables or factors (Hair et al, 2006). The overall assessment was carried out using EFA, CFA, SPSS 20 and AMOS 25 tools to examine convergent and discriminant validity. Convergent validity is dependent on three indicators: 1) the reliability of each construct, 2) the item reliability of each measure (factor loading), 3) the average variance extracted (AVE). Constructs are considered to have convergent validity when the composite reliability (CR) exceeds the criterion of 0.70 and the average variance extracted is above 0.50 (Hair et al. 2006). Table 1 shows the factor loadings, the AVE, CR and the Cronbach Alpha values. All AVE's were above the 0.5 threshold and all CRs were above 0.7. Sixteen items were removed due to low loadings, cross loadings and optimising the reliability analysis. Thus, the results support the convergent validity of the scales. Additionally, all Alpha values are above the 0.7 threshold thus exhibiting good reliability (Nunnally and Bernstein, 1994).

Table 1. Results for the measurement model

Heading level	Example	Font size and style
Performance Expectancy	**1. INTRODUCTION**	13 point, bold
Effort Expectancy	**1.1 Printing Area**	13 point, bold
	1.1.1 Text	11 point, bold
Social Factors		
Facilitating Conditions		
Self-Directed		
Behavioural Intention		
Use		

The assessment of discriminant validity is the square root of the AVE for each construct compared with the inter-factor correlations between that construct and all the other constructs. If the AVE is higher than the squared inter-scale correlations of the construct, it shows good discriminant validity (Gefen et al. (2000); Hair et al. 2006). However, regarding this measurement model, the square root of the AVE for EE is less than its correlation with BIU and the square root of the AVE for PE is also less than its correlation with BIU. Therefore, according to Gefen et al. (2000) this measurement model is exhibiting poor discriminant validity. This means that some constructs are correlated with others that are designed to measure theoretically different concepts. See Table 2 for results.

Table 2. Results for the measurement model

	EE	SF	Use	FC	SD	PE	BI
EE	**0.830**						
SF	0.614***	**0.900**					
Use	0.779***	0.615***	**0.926**				
FC	0.291**	0.549***	0.300**	**0.837**			
SD	0.580***	0.367***	0.477***	0.292**	**0.793**		
PE	0.658***	0.783***	0.688***	0.510***	0.482***	**0.793**	
BIU	0.840***	0.792***	0.824***	0.465***	0.495***	0.842***	**0.906**

The square root of the average variance extracted is inserted diagonally and printed in bold. Off diagonal elements are the shared variance

† $p < 0.100$ * $p < 0.050$ ** $p < 0.010$ *** $p < 0.001$

Common Method Variance: The purpose of testing for common method variance (CMV) is to estimate to what degree biases exist. Common marker variable statistical technique was used in this study to estimate such variance. Lindell and Whitney (2001) recommend using variables with low correlations between observed variables as measures for the latent method variable. The results show that the constrained and unconstrained models are invariant. Therefore, failing to detect the presence of any specific response bias affecting the model.

4.3 Measurement Model Fit

Seven common model-fit measures were used to assess the model's overall goodness-of-fit. Chi-square mean/Degree of freedom ($\chi 2$/df), Incremental fit Index (IFI), Tucker Lewis Index (TFI), Comparative fit index (CFI), Root mean square error of approximation (RMSEA), Standard root mean square residual

(SRMR). Overall, the results of the proposed research model showed an adequate fit: (χ2/df 1.646., GFI 0.804, IFI .948, TLI .934, CFI .947, RMSEA .075, SRMR = .053).

Multivariate and outliers: A cook's distance analysis was carried out to determine if any multivariate influential outliers existed. There were no observed cases of a Cook's distance greater than 1. Most cases were less than 0.280, indicating no presence of influential outliers.

Multicollinearity: An examination of the Tolerance and Variance Inflation Factors (VIF) was carried out to assess multicollinearity. The multicollinearity does not exist in a regression model when the Tolerance value is greater than 0.1 and the VIF value is less than 10 (Field, 2009). The results of the Tolerance and VIF indicated that all Tolerance values were greater than 0.1, and the VIF values for all UTAUT constructs were less than 5. Thus, the assumption of the absence of multicollinearity was met.

4.4 Evaluation of Structural Model

The second step is to assess the structural model which includes testing the theoretical hypothesis and the relationships between the latent constructs. Seven common model-fit measures were used to assess the model's overall goodness-of-fit. Overall, the results of the proposed research model showed an adequate fit: (χ2/df 1.691., GFI .817, IFI .945, TLI .932, CFI .944. RMSEA .078, SRMR .0582). These results provided evidence that the model fit the data adequately. Thus, able to proceed to investigate the determinants, age and gender differences in mLearning adoption. Table 3 lists the path coefficients and their significance.

As expected, hypotheses (H1, H4, H7) representing the relationship among the main constructs (PE, EE, SI) to BIU were supported in this study. The hypothesis that was not supported was H10: SD to BIU. Self-Directed did not significantly predict behaviour intention to use mLearning (-0.03, n.s). Surprisingly, the data proved that FC did significantly predict behaviour intention to use mLearning. Thus, H13 was not supported.

Table 3. Structural model results

Path/Hypothesis	Beta	t-value	Results
PE → BIU (H1)	0.347**	3.244	Supported
EE → BIU (H4)	0.460***	5.590	Supported
SI → BIU (H7)	0.199*	2.160	Supported
SD → BIU (H10)	- .032	-0.504	Ns
FC → BIU (H13)	0.109†	1.822	Not Supported
FC → USE	-0.206	-2.690	Negative relationship
BIU → USE (H14)	0.960	10.659	Supported

Model fit indices: χ^2/df 1.691., GFI 0.817, IFI .945, TLI .932, CFI .944. RMSEA .078, SRMR = .0582

† p < 0.100 * p < 0.050 ** p < 0.010 *** p < 0.001 *ns* non-significant

The results of the analyses of gender and age differences are outlined in Tables 4 and 5 respectively, listing the path coefficients and their significance. Additionally, a multigroup comparison test was carried out via a chi-square difference test to test significance of moderation. This resulted in the p-value of the chi-square difference test to be significant.

Table 4. Structural model results (moderators male and female)

Path (Hypothesis)	Male Beta	Female Beta	Results
PE → BIU (H2)	-0.173	0.651***	Not supported. Stronger for Female staff than Male.
EE → BIU (H5)	0.749**	0.442***	Not supported. Stronger for Male staff than Female sta
SI → BIU (H8)	0.382*	-0.037	Not supported. Stronger for Male staff than Females
SD → BIU (H11)	0.056	-0.146	Not supported. No difference

† p < 0.100 * p < 0.050 ** p < 0.010 *** p < 0.001

Participants were divided into two groups: the older group consisted of ages greater than 30 years and the younger group with ages less than or equal to 30 years. A Multigroup comparison test was carried out via a chi-square difference test to test significance of moderation. It was observed that the p-value of the chi square difference test is statistically significant. Therefore, the model differs across the different groups (Younger staff and Older Staff).

Table 5. Structural model results (moderators younger staff and older staff)

Path	Older Beta	Younger Beta	Results/Interpretation
PE → BIU (H3)	0.426***	0.240	Supported. stronger for younger staff than older staff
EE → BIU (H6)	0.501***	0.248	Supported. Only significant for older staff
SI → BIU (H9)	0.097	0.895***	Not supported. Stronger for Younger staff than older staff
SD → BIU (H12)	-0.082	0.256*	Not supported. Stronger for Younger staff than older staff

† $p < 0.100$ * $p < 0.050$ ** $p < 0.010$ *** $p < 0.001$

Finally, R^2 value of the behavioural intention was 0.875 and that of the usage was 0.683. Translating these values into explanatory power, behavioural intention was 87.5% whilst use was 68.3%. This means that the explanatory power of this model is higher than Venkatesh et al. (2003) research reporting 70% explanatory power.

5. CONCLUSION

The purpose of this study was to use the UTAUT model as a theoretical framework to understand key factors that influences mLearning adoption at SMG. Due to the dearth of published research on the use of UTAUT in Museums, it can be assumed, this is the first assessment of the UTAUT model in relation to mLearning in the milieu of the Museum sector. The analysis of both the data captured and the UTAUT model was carried out using SEM. The findings from this study showed that there are age and gender differences that moderate the relationship between the UTAUT constructs. It was also found that the newly added self-directedness construct was not a predictor of behavior intentions to use mLearning at SMG. The conclusions in this research will help the diffusion of mLearning at SMG and across the museums, galleries, arts, academic, charitable and cultural heritage sector.

Numerous authors believe the future direction of research is motivated and dictated by mobile device applications. (Pereira and Rodrigues 2013; Lim and Churchill 2016). Lim and Churchill (2016) suggests that research should also focus on aspects of multimedia content, communication, digital storytelling, social networking and cloud computing.

Senior management at SMG are keen to explore machine learning capabilities as a way of automating many of the service desk processes.

The results and conclusion are limited and not intended to be exhaustive. Limitations exists in the interpretation of the findings thus suggestions throughout this study and specifically in the discussions section will require further research to confirm their validity.

This study used a single-time approach which was different from the research proposed by Venkatesh et al. (2008) where three measuring times of the same groups of samples were applied.

An inherent, limitation of the questionnaire is its static nature. Recipients can only answer the questions that researchers thought to ask. Therefore, it is acknowledged that further information may have been omitted.

REFERENCES

Anderson, J. C. and Gerbing D. W. (1988) Structural Equation Modeling in Practice: A Review and Recommended Two-Step Approach, *Psychological Bulletin* (103) 3, pp. 411-423.

Baumgartner, H. and Homburg, C. (1995) Applications of structural equation modelling in marketing research: A review. *International journal of research in Marketing.* 13, pp 139 -161

Beck, A. T. (1983) Cognitive therapy of depression: new perspectives. In P. J. Clayton & J. E. Barrett (Eds), *Treatment of depression: old controversies and new approaches* (pp. 265–290). New York: Raven Press.

Behera, S. K (2013) E- and M-Learning: A comparative Study. *International Journal on New Trends in Education and Their Implications*. Vol 4. (3) pp. 65 – 78

Chee, K. N., Yahaya, N., Ibrahim, N.H. and Hasan, M.N. (2016) Review of Mobile Learning Trends 2010-2015: A Meta-Analysis. *Educational Technology & Society, 20* (2), 113–126.

Field, A.P. (2009), *Discovering Statistics Using SPSS*, Sage, London

Gefen, D., Straub, D. and Boudreau, M, (2000) Structural Equation Modeling and Regression: Guidelines For Research Practice. *Communications of the Association for Information Systems*. Vol 4. (7)

Hair, J. F., Black, B., Babin, B. J., Anderson, R. E., and Tatham, R. L. (2006) *Multivariate Data Analysis* (6th Ed.) New Jersey: Pearson Prentice Hall

Hall, D., and Mansfield, R. (1995) Relationships of Age and Seniority with Career Variables of Engineers and Scientists, *Journal of Applied Psychology* Vol 60. (2). pp. 201-210

Hu, L-T and Bentler, P. M. (1999) Cutoff criteria for fit indexes in covariance structure analysis: Conventional criteria versus new alternatives. Structural Equation Modelling, Vol 6. (1) pp- 1 -55

Indrawati, R. M. and Chew, K.- W. (2010) "A Conceptual Model for Behavioral Intention to Use 3G Mobile Multimedia Services in Indonesia," Proceedings of the International Symposium on Information Technology, Kuala Lumpur.

Lave, J., and Wenger, E. (1991) *Situated Learning: Legitimate Peripheral Participation*. Cambridge: Cambridge University Press

Lim, C. P. and Churchill, D. (2016) Editorial: Mobile learning. Interactive Learning Environments, 24(2), 273-276. http://www.tandfonline.com/eprint/JzIGpwEKsJASCuqna6ZE/full. *Interactive Learning Environments*. 24. 273-276.

Lindell, M. K. and Whitney, D. J. (2001) Accounting for Common Method Variance in Cross-Sectional Research Designs. *Journal of Applied Psychology*. Vol.86 (4), 114 – 121

Livingstone, D. (2006) *Informal Learning: Conceptual Distinctions and Preliminary Findings. Counterpoints, 249, 203-227. Retrieved from http://www.jstor.org/stable/42979596*

Miller, J. B. (1976) *Toward a New Psychology of Women*, Beacon Press, Boston,

Minton, H. L., and Schneider, F. W. (1980) *Differential Psychology*, Waveland Press, Prospect Heights, IL,

Morris, M. G., and Venkatesh, V. (2003) Age Differences in Technology Adoption Decisions: Implications for a Changing Workforce, *Personnel Psychology. Vol 53. 2.* pp. 375-403

Nunnally, J. C., and Bernstein, I.H. (1994) *Psychometric theory (3rd Ed.).* New York: McGraw-Hill. Inc.

Pereira, O. R. E. and Rodrigues, J. J. P. C. (2013) Survey and Analysis of Current Mobile Learning Applications and Technologies, *ACM Computing Surveys,* Vol. 46, No. 2

Porter, L. J (1963) Job Attitudes in Management: Perceived Importance of Needs as a Function of Job Level, *Journal of Applied Psychology*. Vol 47. 2, pp. 141-148

Rhodes, S. R. (1983) Age-Related Differences in Work Attitudes and Behavior: A Review and Conceptual Analysis, *Psychological Bulletin.* Vol 93. (2) pp. 328-36

Rossett, A., and Marsahll, J. (2010) *E-learning:* What's old is new again. *Training and Development*, Vol.64 1 34 - 38.

Sposito, V. A., Hand, M. L., and Skarpness, B. (1983) On the efficiency of using the sample kurtosis in selecting optimal lpestimators. *Communications in Statistics-simulation and Computation*, 12(3), 265-272

Venkatesh, V., and Morris, M. G. (2000) Why Don't Men Ever Stop to Ask for Directions? Gender, Social Influence, and Their Role in Technology Acceptance and Usage Behavior, *MIS Quarterly*, Vol 24. (1), pp. 115-139

Venkatesh, V., Morris, M. G., and Ackerman, P. L. (2000) A Longitudinal Field Investigation of Gender Differences in Individual Technology Adoption Decision Making Processes, *Organizational Behavior and Human Decision Processes*. pp. 33-60

Venkatesh, V., Morris, M. G., Davis, G. B. and Davis, F. D. (2003) User acceptance of information technology: toward a unified view. *MIS Quarterly*, Vol 27, (3), pp 425–478

Wu, Y.- L., Tao, Y.- H. and Yang, P.- C. (2008) The Use of Unified Theory of Acceptance and Use of Technology to Confer the Behavioral Model of 3G Mobile Telecommunication Users, *Journal of Statistics & Management Systems*, Vol 11 (5), pp 919–94

MOBILE PERFORMANCE SUPPORT SYSTEM FOR TEACHERS AND PARENTS TEACHING FIRST GRADERS TO READ

Roberto Araya
Center for Advanced Research in Education, Institute of Education, Universidad de Chile
Periodista José Carrasco Tapia N° 75, Santiago, Chile

ABSTRACT

Teaching to read is a very complex task. There are two rival strategies, and while one of them is effective according to an extensive empirical evidence, many teachers and parents use the wrong strategy or an inefficient mix of them. In this paper we use an app that supports teachers in measuring students' progress and in communicating learning strategies with parents. It also supports parents to share their strategies to teach their children at home, and supports educational administrators to track students learning, in each one of the curriculum units, at each school, district and geographical region. In a semester the app was voluntarily adopted by 1,235 schools that tracked the progress of 30,158 students. We found a very rapid adoption of the app, a surprisingly big imbalance between the intended and implemented curriculum, a much lower student performance in writing than in reading and oral communication, and a strikingly great participation and enthusiasm of parents in creating videos to share them with other parents where they show playful strategies to teach reading to their kids.

KEYWORDS

Mobile, Cloud Computing, Pedagogical Approach, Social Networks

1. INTRODUCTION

Teaching to read is undoubtedly the most important task of the educational system. Today, a citizen who cannot read is completely marginalized. For this reason almost 100% of students learn to read. However, that was not always the case. In 1475 the literacy rate of Sweden was 1% and in England it was 5% (https://ourworldindata.org/literacy). Even though today in most countries practically everyone learns to read (more precisely almost 87% of the population is literate), many do not understand what they read or their comprehension is very weak. There are still several major challenges. There are two rival strategies to teach reading, which have been generating a pedagogic dispute for nearly a century, and have been described as the "reading wars". While one of them is effective according to empirical evidence, many teachers and parents use the wrong strategy or an inefficient mix of them. Thus, in 1997, the U.S. Congress asked the National Institute of Child Health and Human Development (NICHD), to work with the U.S. Department of Education in establishing a National Reading Panel that would evaluate existing research and evidence to find the best ways of teaching children to read. The National Reading Panel reviewed all the research available (more than 100,000 reading studies) on how children learn to read, and concluded that the best approach to reading instruction is one that incorporates explicit instruction in phonemic awareness, systematic phonics instruction, methods to improve fluency, and ways to enhance comprehension. However, the last Programme for International Student Assessment PISA 2018 (OECD, 2018a) study concluded that around the world, the share of 15-year-old students, in grade 7 and above, who reached a minimum level of proficiency in reading (at least Level 2 on the PISA scale) ranged from close to 90% in Beijing, Shanghai, Jiangsu and Zhejiang (China), Estonia, Macao (China) and Singapore, to less than 10% in Cambodia, Senegal and Zambia. Another recent report, Adams et al, 2020, concludes that "reading achievement isn't improving. Too many students—particularly students who are living in poverty or are of color—enter grade 3 unable to read or unable to read as well as they should."

One of the great pending challenges is that teachers and parents teach reading according to the effective strategies empirically demonstrated by those thousands of studies. While education ministries are increasingly designing evidence-based curricula and texts, these strategies are not always used in classrooms and homes. There is a big gap between the intended curriculum designed by the Ministry curriculum developers and the implemented and the attained curriculum on schools (OECD, 2018b). Moreover, there is a lack of on-time measurement instruments to inform principals, superintendents, curriculum developers and administrators of the Ministry of Education. In most countries, standardized measurements begin at the end of fourth grade, but this is too late to give timely feedback. In some countries there are measurements on samples of the population at the end of second grade, but they are also too late. They only measure a small sample of students due to the cost of measurement in students who still cannot follow the typical instructions of the regular standardized tests. The strategy required to achieve timely feedback is to be able to measure and monitor weekly progress of all first grade students.

On the other hand, parents' effort is critical for students learning outcomes (De Fraja et al., 2005). It is sometimes more critical than students' effort and school effort, and this is particularly true for elementary school boys. Moreover, parents' expectations are also critical. Given that parents of the lowest socioeconomic status (SES) segments have average expectations of attainment much lower than the average expectations of the rest of the parents (Araya et al., 2017, Child Trends Databank, 2015), then it is very important to engage parents of the low SES segment. Parents give enormous value to learning to read. What parents want and value (Zeehandelaar et al., 2013), is a strong core curriculum in reading and mathematics. However, according to Willingham (2015) parents have very little idea how their kids learn to read. They don´t think much about reading comprehension. They assume that if a kid can accurately say the words on the page out loud, then she is reading. They also don´t know how to motivate their kids to read.

Technology can help to support teachers to teach and implement the curriculum. There are several experimental and quasi-experimental studies that show the potential of Performance Support Systems (Araya, 2019). For example, in Araya et al. (2019), a yearlong RCT with 48 fourth grade classes showed half a year of extra learning in mathematics for the treatment condition that used a cloud based platform. However, after a systematic review and meta-analysis of numerous studies conducted comparing reading from paper and electronic sources, Clinton 2019, concludes that readers may be more efficient and aware of their performance when reading from paper compared to screens. Other studies show some positive impacts using smartphones. For example, Chee et al 2017, has tested impact of smartphone on students learning in small samples. They found higher scores on tests after four consecutive weeks of intervention. Thus the empirical evidence is mixed. In a recent study, the Asian Development Bank follows (Smart et al., 2018), concludes that all the evidence suggests that for most education systems—at least for the foreseeable future—digital resources will be used alongside traditional printed resources in what is often described as "blended learning".

In this paper, we propose a blended strategy, where only teachers, principals, educational administrators, and parents use their smartphones, but not students. Thus the contribution of this paper is to explore the impact of mobile technology when teachers, administration, and parents use it to teach students, to track their learning and to disseminate teaching strategies.

2. SMARTPHONES TO SUPPORT TEACHING TO READ

A major challenge in education is how to improve teaching. One possible strategy is the use of Performance Support Systems (Reynolds et al, 1995, Araya et al, 2015, Araya, 2019). This kind of systems provide real time support to users, similarly as waze or google maps support drivers to reach their location. In this paper we present the application for a semester of the ConectaIdeas Express app that was added to ConectaIdeas, a teaching platform. This is a Learning Managing Platform hosted in the cloud and that has proved on an RCT to be effective for teaching mathematics for fourth graders (Araya et al., 2019). The app supports teachers in the classroom to perform evaluation with quick questions, called exit tickets. These are formative assessments that give teachers a way to quickly understand how well their students comprehend the material they are learning during class time.

Figure 1. The ConectaIdeas Express app used by teachers to assess student learning on different activities all linked to official curriculum Learning Objectives

The app also allows teachers to have constant monitoring of each student learning and a concept map with the curriculum coverage. It displays a tree with the coverage and performance on the official curriculum Strands and Learning objective, as shown in figure 2. It also has a geographic information system that integrates a social network with its parents and with the rest of the school community in its district and region. Teachers manage the app, but parents can get maps and information at the course level (not individual student) on their smartphones.

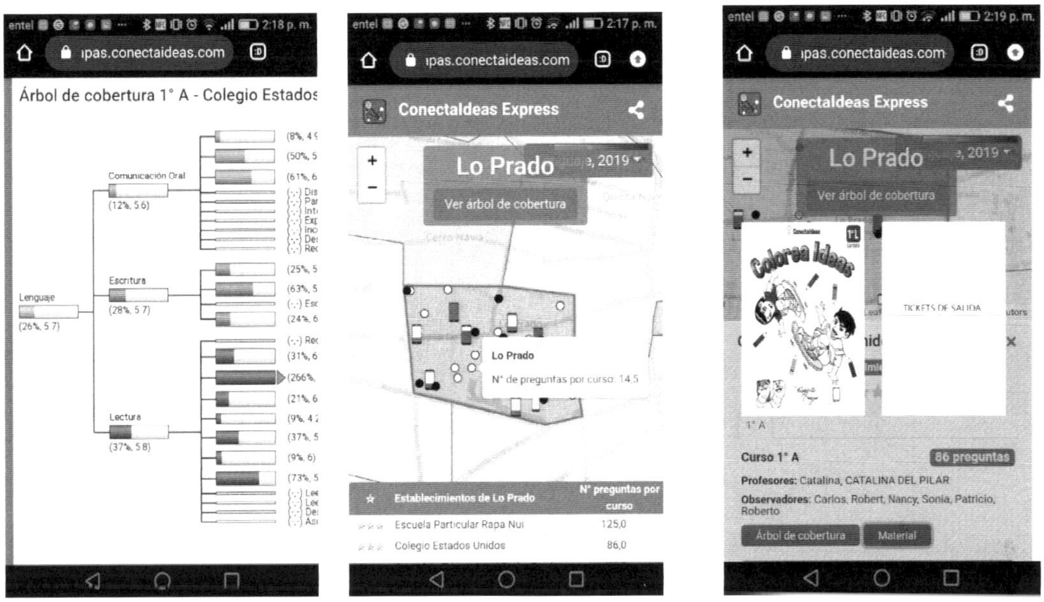

Figure 2. Left: a concept map tree showing each of the three strands with its coverage and performance, and each of the Leaning Objectives with its corresponding coverage and performance. Center: ConectaIdeas Express map with the schools of the Lo Prado district, and with a small smartphone showing the level of use of the app on each school. The activity of parents is also shown on this map. Right: material that each parent and kid can access on the place of his school on the map

The ConectaIdeas Express App allows teachers to use exit tickets without necessarily having to have an Internet connection at the time of the evaluation. Teachers can save the information on their smartphone and upload it later on, when they have Internet access.

The ConectaIdeas Express app was offered to schools on June 1st, 2019, to a universe of approximately 5,000 schools. Since the exit tickets loaded in the app were aligned to a specific textbook offered by the Ministry, and only 2,500 schools were effectively using that textbook according to a Ministry of Education Survey, then almost half of the potential schools adopted the app. Every week an e-mail was sent to schools principals and teachers describing the app and how to use it. By December 2019 1,235 schools adopted it. The adoption curve is shown in Figure 1. At the end of the year, 568,524 students´ answers were evaluated and registered by their teachers. The average number of exit tickets posed by teachers was 22. This means, that each teacher posted an exit ticket on 22 sessions. It is important to mention that July has two weeks of winter vacation and that there is also an extra week of vacation in September. Moreover, due to national strikes in October and November, 3 weeks were lost. This means, that on average each teacher used the app in two sessions per week.

In early December 2019, an online anonymous questionnaire was sent to 1,000 teachers and principals who had used ConectaIdeas Express. Among the questions was whether ConectaIdeas Express was easy to use. 86 responses were received. 90.5% of respondents replied that they agreed that it was easy to use.

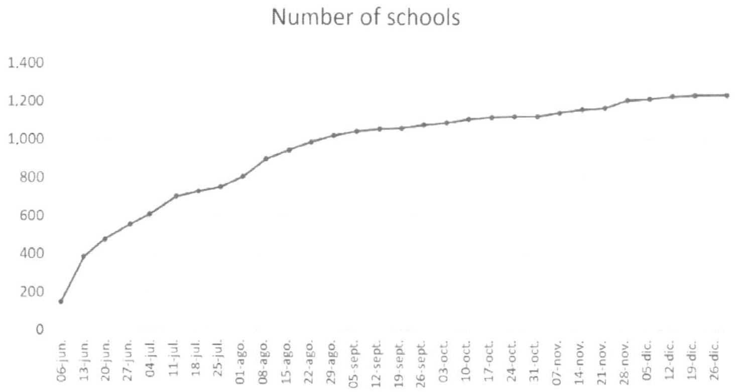

Figure 3. Number of schools that adopted the Mobile ConectaIdeas App from June to December 2019

One of the most surprising findings was the great imbalance in the learning objectives in the activities carried out by teachers. Out of the 26 Learning Objectives of the curriculum, 29.1% of the tickets posted by teachers correspond to the most used Learning Objective. Moreover, the most fundamental Learning Objectives, OA 10: "read independently and understand simple non-literary texts", was not used. Thus a remedial strategy was implemented in order to revert this situation. The Ministry of Education implemented A National Reading Day where schools were asked to do exit tickets that use that Learning Objective. This fact illustrate the benefit of on line monitoring. The use of the cloud monitoring system allowed Ministry officials to monitor in real time what was going on at the schools and detect a big gap between the intended and implemented curriculum, and therefore implement actions to revert part of this gap.

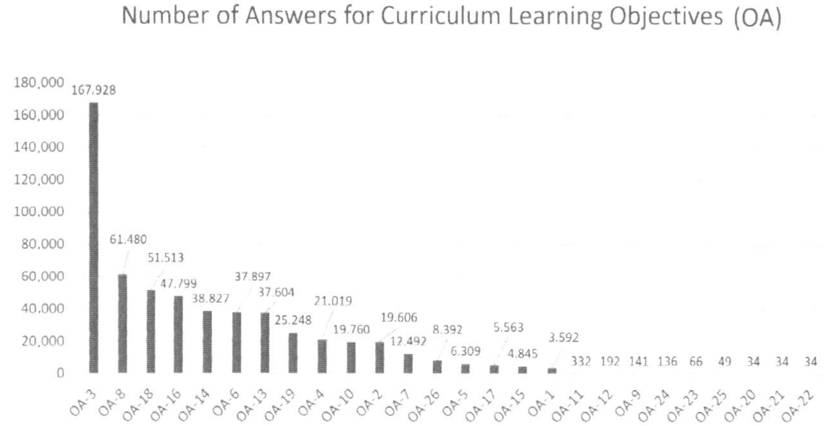

Figure 4. Number of students answers for each of the Learning Objectives (OA) of the first grade language curriculum

Most of the tickets posted by teachers belong to the Reading strand, and this was permanently so, as shown in figure 5. Writing was the strand where performance was the lowest as shown in Figure 6. Moreover, Learning Objective OA 13 "Experiment with writing to communicate facts, ideas and feelings", obtained significantly lower assessment than the rest of the Learning Objectives, as shown in Figure 7. An interesting finding is that on those classes where the teacher did more tickets, above the median, the performance in writing was 79%, which is higher than on the other classes where the performance was 77.9%. This difference is statistically significant. This difference was particularly higher in the Learning Objective OA 6 "Understand texts applying reading comprehension strategies".

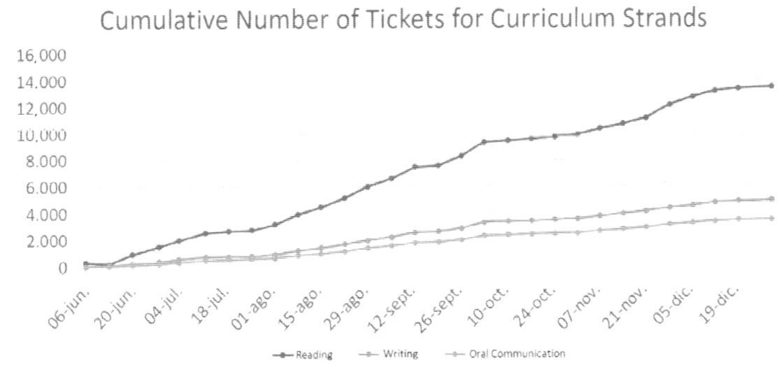

Figure 5. Accumulative number of question posed by the teachers by the three curriculum strands, reading, writing and oral communication. Each strand contains several Learning Objectives

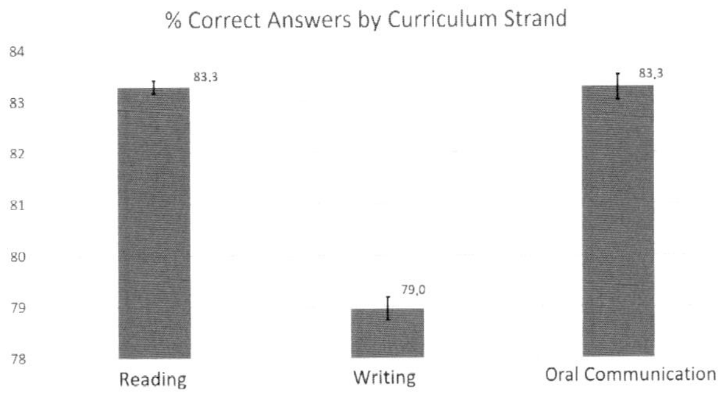

Figure 6. Percentage of correct answers for questions belonging to the three curriculum strands, reading, writing and oral communication

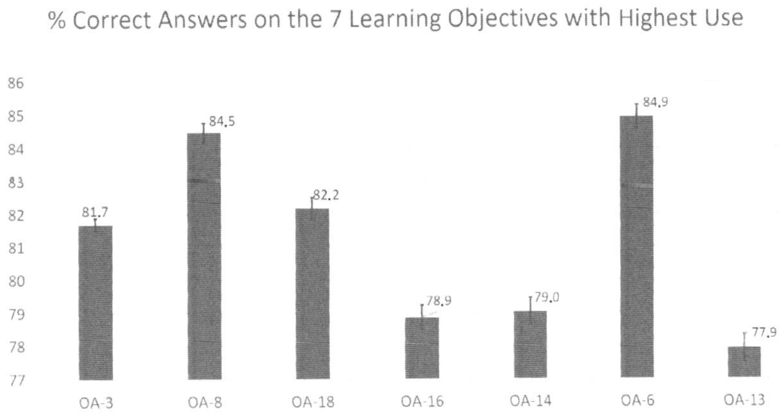

Figure 7. Percentage of correct answers for questions belonging to the most frequently used Learning Objectives

As mentioned before, from the data that was being gathered, authorities from the Ministry concluded that teachers practically were not asking questions to assess reading comprehension. Therefore, given the need to have an estimate of the level of the students´ reading comprehension by the end of the year, the Ministry of Education implemented a National Reading Day that was specifically designed to measure reading comprehension. Four exit tickets were designed, in which the text gave instructions to paint some drawings. The instructions on what to paint ad what color had to be read by the students. In this way it was constituted as a recreational and artistic activity, but which was basically a reading comprehension test. All tickets measured reading comprehension, more specifically the Learning Objective OA10: "Read independently and understand simple non-literary texts". 144 schools participated, and of these schools, teachers registered 9,808 student responses, corresponding to the 4 tickets. 87.33% of the answers were evaluated as correct by the teachers. The speed of the evaluation was highly valued in the Ministry of Education. Normally it takes about a year to have feedback with tests designed by the educational authorities. Additionally, in the country there is no government test for first graders. Thus this test was the first time ever a test was implemented for first graders in the country.

In order to attract and engage parents to support at home their kids' learning, videos of prototype activities were disseminated. These videos show strategies with games, dices and teddy bears to encourage phonemic awareness and reading comprehension. The games were recorded on videos and uploaded to the cloud together with an invitation to mothers, fathers and grandparents, to watch them. In two weeks, the videos had more than 4,000 views. The plan was to encourage parents to recreate the strategies at their homes, and also to modify the games and activities, and create new ones. It was also encouraged that they provided emotional support and motivation to their students, particularly to appreciate reading and writing. The idea was to get them to practice with their families with playful and social strategies. The goal was also to encourage parents to share their experiences and their inventions with other parents, and build a social network of parents of first graders. Thus a learning community between parents was created. They recoded short videos with their smartphones and uploaded to the ConectaIdeas map to share them. The Ministry of Education also implemented in a geographical region the First Breakfast with Parents for Reading. It was held in October 2019. 500 schools were invited to send one parent representing the school. Given the enormous interest of parents in participating that exceeded the capacity of the planned room, the Ministry of Education limited the participation to the first 160 schools that applied. Finally, 173 parents from different schools in the region attended the event, each one bringing their video recording. 98 videos were finally received and uploaded by their teachers to the ConectaIdeas map, as shown in figure 8. These videos show the implementation of the proposed strategies: 80 videos show mother and student, 48 videos show word segmentation, 47 videos show home-grown educational games, 26 videos show teddy bears or glove puppets, and 12 videos show games with magic boxes.

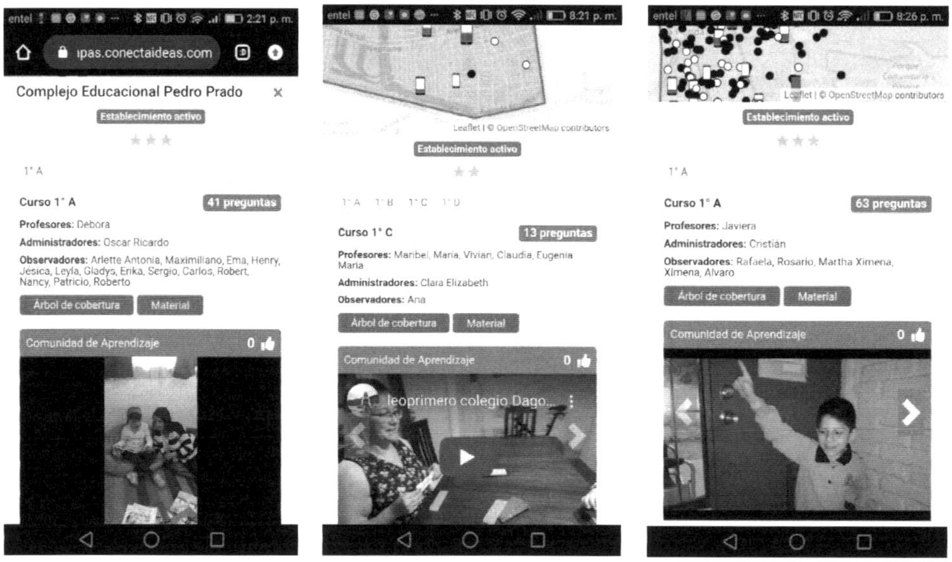

Figure 8. Screenshots of three videos designed and recorded by parents and uploaded on the ConectaIdeas map in order to share with other parents

According to Willingham, 2017, there are three levels in reading comprehension: extract ideas from sentences, connect ideas across sentences, and build a general idea of what a text is about. After the First Breakfast with Parents, new activities using a coloring book implemented these strategies, and particularly the strategy to connect ideas across sentences. The coloring book, shown in Figure 2 Right, is basically a list of exit tickets that the teacher can use. Several teachers and parents implemented them on classrooms and homes. We found that this is a very engaging mechanism for all the community. It is therefore a good tool for dissemination of strategies specially aimed to improve reading comprehension. However, much of this strategy is still work in progress.

3. CONCLUSION

After a semester 1,235 school voluntarily adopted mobile technology to support teaching to read to 30,158 students. This is a unique experience that shows the potential of mobile technology to teach reading to first graders. This is almost 50% of the schools that were effectively using the textbook to teach reading offered by the Ministry of Education. The ConectaIdeas Express app was designed to support that textbook. This fact shows a very fast adoption curve. On average, each teacher used for 22 sessions, posting exit tickets at the final part of the session. This means that it was used twice a week. A survey to teachers showed that they found it easy to use.

Parents also used the app to access information about the progress on the coverage of the curriculum and to record and share videos showing strategies that they implemented with their kids. The strategy of creating a community of parents to implement games in their homes, innovate them, and share them in the ConectaIdeas map, was very attractive. Surprisingly, it produced much more participation than expected.

A great benefit of the mobile app and of displaying the information in a geographical system with the advances in performance and curriculum coverage by school, district and region, was that it allowed early detection of large gaps between the intended curriculum and the implemented one. That allowed taking corrective actions. Other findings will allow for the adaptation of strategies, school textbooks, exit tickets and materials for the coming years. Almost 600,000 students´ answers were assessed, which made possible to detect Learning Objectives with much weaker performance than the other Learning Objectives. This information is very important to adapt strategies for new textbooks, materials and teacher professional development seminars.

This app and its implementation show that using mobile technology in teaching reading from first grade is a great opportunity for effective improvement. This is a blended strategy, where teachers, principals, educational administrators, and parents use their smartphones to track students´ learning and share their teaching experiences. In 2020 the Ministry of Education has already started implementing it also for second grade.

ACKNOWLEDGEMENT

Support from ANID/ PIA/ Basal Funds for Centers of Excellence FB0003 is gratefully acknowledged, and from María Jesús Honorato from the Curriculum Unit of the Ministry of Education of Chile.

REFERENCES

Adams, M.; Fillmore, L.; Goldenberg, C.; Oakhill, J.; Paige, D.; Rasinski, T.; Shanahan, T., 2020. *Comparing Reading Research to Program Design: An Examination of Teachers College Units of Study*

Araya, R.; Gormaz, R.; Bahamondez, M.; Aguirre, C.; Calfucura, P.; Jaure. P.; Laborda, C. 2015. ICT supported learning rises math achievement in low socio economic status schools. 10th European Conference on Technology Enhanced Learning. Lecture Notes in Computer Science, Volume 9307, pp 383-388. Springer.

Araya, R., Gormaz, R., Ulloa, O., 2017. For which socioeconomic segments are parental expectations of educational attainments more sensitive to their children performance? Proceedings of the 6th International Conference on Sustainability, Technology and Education, Sydney, Australia, pp 51-58. http://www.iadisportal.org/digital-library/for-which-socioeconomic-segments-are-parental-expectations-of-educational-attainment-more-sensitive-to-their-children-performance

Araya R., 2019. Teacher Training, Mentoring or Performance Support Systems?. In: Nazir S., Teperi AM., Polak-Sopińska A. (eds) Advances in Human Factors in Training, Education, and Learning Sciences. AHFE 2018. Advances in Intelligent Systems and Computing. Springer, Cham. Vol 785, pp 306-315.

Araya, R.; Arias Ortiz, E.; Bottan, N.; Cristia, J., 2019. Does Gamification in Education Work? Experimental Evidence from Chile. IDB WORKING PAPER SERIES Nº IDB-WP-982 Inter-American Development Bank

Chee, K.; Yahaya, N.; Ibrahim, N., 2017. Effectiveness of mobile learning application in improving reading skills in Chinese language and towards post-attitudes. *International Journal of Mobile Learning and Organisation* 11(3): 210-225

Child Trends Databank, 2015. *Parental expectations for their children's academic attainment*. Online at: http://www.childtrends.org/?indicators=parental-expectations-for-their-childrens-academic-attainmen

Clinton, V. 2019, Reading from paper compared to screens: A systematic review and meta-analysis. *Journal of Research in Reading.* Vol 42. Issue 2: 288-325

De Fraja, G.; Oliveira, T.; Zanchi, S, 2005. Must Try Harder. Evaluating the Role of Effort in Educational Attainment. Centre for Economic Policy Research Discussion Paper No. 5048

National Reading Panel, 2000. *Teaching Children To Read: An Evidence-Based Assessment of the Scientific Research Literature on Reading and Its Implications for Reading Instruction*

OECD, 2018a. *PISA 2018 Results. What Students Know and Can Do Vol I.* OECDiLibrary.

OECD, 2018b, Future of Education and Skills 2030: Curriculum Analysis. Bridging curriculum design and implementation, 8th Informal Working Group (IWG) Meeting. Online at: https://www.oecd.org/education/2030-project/contact/Bridging_curriculum_redesign_and_implementation.pdf

Reynolds, A.; Araya, R. 1995. *Building Multimedia Performance Support Systems*. McGraw-Hill, New York.

Smart, A.; Jagannathan, S. 2018, *Textbook Policies in Asia Development, Publishing, Printing, Distribution, and Future Implications*. Asian Development Bank

Willingham, D., 2017. *The Reading Mind: A Cognitive Approach to Understanding How the Mind Reads*. Jossey-Bass.

Willingham, D., 2015. *Raising Kids who Read. What Parents and Teachers Can Do*. Jossey-Bass.

Zeehandelaar, D. and Winkler, A., 2013. *What Parents Want: Education Preferences and Trade-Offs*. Thomas B. Fordham Institute.

CONCEPTUALIZING MOBILE DIGITAL LITERACY SKILLS FOR EDUCATORS

Farshida Jahoor[1], Adele Botha[2] and Marlien Herselman[2]
[1]*University of South Africa, Preller St, Muckleneuk, Pretoria, South Africa*
[2]*CSIR, University of South Africa, Meiring Naudé Road, Brummeria, Pretoria, South Africa*

ABSTRACT

With mobile phones as a near pervasive technology amongst the youth, their use in classroom practice are often considered particularly daunting by the teaching fraternity. Many teachers qualified in the so-called 'pre PC' era, and do not consider themselves on technology par with their students. Their students on the other hand are growing up in an era of technology immersion. In order to enact the 'loco parentis' role often required, these educators need to be equipped with mobile digital literacy skills; often neglected in, amongst other, Teacher Professional Development interventions. The purpose of this paper is conceptualize mobile digital literacy skills for educators in using mobile technology in formal education. The research exapts the 'best-fit' framework synthesis of Carroll et al. (2013) from the health domain, towards this end. The strategy is operationalized through two phases. Phase 1 identifies the Ng (2013) digital skills model as *a priory* framework. Phase 2 utilizes the categories presented in Phase 1 to guide the classing of purposefully selected literature towards conceptualizing mobile digital literacy skills for educators using mobile technology in formal education. The literature considered was identified in accordance with Grant et al. (2014) description of a systematized scoping review. The contribution of this paper lies in its outcomes to identify and classify literacy skills for mobile technologies. These identified skills can further guide interventions aimed at educational mobile phone use.

KEYWORDS

Mobile Digital Literacy Skills, Mobile Devices, Literacy, Digital Literacy

1. INTRODUCTION

The number of mobile technology users have increased considerably, not only South Africa, but across the world (ITU, 2018), making mobile ICT the world's fastest growing technology. The perceived availability of the technology and the established user base present several developmental opportunities (Van Biljon & Renaud, 2017). As mobile Information and Communication Technology (ICT) continues to permeate the market (Chang & Hwang, 2018), the ability to navigate the technology becomes even more important (Bartikowski, Laroche, Jamal, & Yang, 2018). This state of affairs has created a conundrum within the education domain in South Africa (Mabila, Biljon, & Herselman, 2017) where educators are supplied with technology, that they are expected to meaningfully utilize in their classroom practice, in support of 21st century teaching and learning (Finn-Stevenson, 2018). However, ICT education initiatives have been noted to have failed due to a lack of a focus on, amongst other factors, the digital literacy skills (Mabila et al., 2017). The lack of skills pose a challenge for educators to successfully integrate mobile technologies into classrooms (Yu, Lin, & Liao, 2017).

This paper endeavors to conceptualize mobile digital literacy skills towards eventually enabling the articulation of the mobile digital literacy skills needed by educators using mobile technologies in formal education. The perspective of *formal education* highlights the active teaching and learning activities that are associated with classroom practice. As such, this paper prioritizes specific instances where mobile technology is used in educational specific contexts, although not necessarily as an exclusive focus to answer the research question: What constitutes mobile digital literacy skills for educators in formal education?

2. METHOD

This paper adopts the 'best-fit' framework synthesis of Carroll, Booth, Leaviss, and Rick (2013) towards conceptualizing mobile digital literacy skills for educators when embarking on using mobile technology in their classroom practices. The technique presents a method to extend on existing published research artifacts, in the form of models frameworks or theories, conceived within sufficiently similar context. The 'best fit' framework synthesis is considered suitable for this study as it entails a moderately rapid, transparent and pragmatic process whereby purposefully selected literature can be scrutinized at the hand of *a priory* research artifact. The systematic method for identifying suitable frameworks and subsequent thematic analysis enables both *artifact* and *literature synthesis* outcomes that are "reproducible and correspond to a shared reality" (Carroll et al., 2013, p. 1). This paper enacts the best-fit framework synthesis through the identification of a suitable digital literacy model as a relevant research artifact that can be abstracted to themes, which forms the *a priori* framework for a systematized scoping review as outlined by Grant and Booth (2009). A systematized scoping review is envisioned to cover the breath of the literature available while providing a systematic, transparent method in its identification and selection.

The methodology followed in this paper is then operationalised in two phases. Firstly, a literature synthesis that involves the identification of *a priori* themes against which to map literature from purposefully selected studies in the second phase. The identification and selection of *a priori* framework that would present the themes is outlined in section 3, the thematic synthesis at the hand of the themes is detailed in section 4. Due publication constraint, a full literature overview is not feasible and only a literature synthesis is presented in both section 3 and 4.

3. *A PRIORY* FRAMEWORK

In selecting a suitable framework, relevant and well-cited articles documenting research artifacts such as frameworks, models and theories for mobile digital literacy skills were sought in academic journals, as indicated in Table 1. As per year of publication, articles from 2000 to 2018 were included. Some older articles were incorporated as they were highly cited by other publishing researchers or were often viewed.

Table 1. Identifying a priory framework

	Systematised scoping review to select a priory framework
Keywords	Digital, Literacy, Digital skills, Framework
Literature review method	Systematized Scoping
Databases used	Scopus, IEEE Xplore, Wiley Online Library, Web of Science, Science Direct
Inclusion and exclusion principles	Only publications written in English were used; Studies referring to the components of digital skills were used; Studies including frameworks and models of digital skills were used; and Studies involving PC-centric skills were excluded
Number of papers used	30

The literature suggests that reading and writing were adequate literacy proficiencies a few decades ago and certainly sufficient to distinguish the educated in society (Zheng, Yim, & Warschauer, 2018). Lankshear and Knobel (2008) argue that this, however, is no longer the case. Technology has given rise to new literacies, involving different sets of skills and abilities to perceive and manage information. Markauskaite (2007) further notes that practical skills are a very important aspect of digital literacy. At the same time these is consensus that the notion of digital literacy refers to more than the mere operation of a technological device (Parry, Eikhof, Barnes, & Kispeter, 2018; Sadaf & Johnson, 2017; Zapata, 2018; Zheng et al., 2018).

Several approaches have been used to unpack the idea of digital literacy. Some authors regard digital literacy as a group of literacies (Eshet-Alkalai, 2004; Eshet-alkalai & Chajut, 2009; Jisc, 2015; Parry et al., 2018; Sadaf & Johnson, 2017; Zapata, 2018; Zheng et al., 2018), while others are proponents of a component view of digital literacy (Ferrari, 2008; Gilster, 1997; Schreuers, Quan-Haase, & Martin, 2017). This research identified the digital literacy model of Ng (2012) as the most appropriate as it manages to combine most of the published literacies and/or components into a single digital literacy model. The themes identified and their conceptual relations suggests that digital literacy is facilitated by the intersection of technical, cognitive and social-emotional perceptions. The three dimensions are briefly outline in Table 2.

Table 2. A priory framework for educator digital skills (Ng, 2012)

Dimension	Literacy	Description
Technical dimension	Operational Literacy; Reproduction Literacy; Branching Literacy; Social networking functional literacy	Technical and functional expertise of ICT in daily use.
Cognitive dimension	Information Literacy; Reproduction Literacy; Branching Literacy; Online etiquette literacy; Cyber safety Literacy	Critical thinking for digital information.
Social-emotional dimension	Social-emotional literacy; Social networking functional literacy; Online etiquette literacy; Cyber safety Literacy	Use internet appropriately.
All dimensions	Critical Literacy	Applicable to all dimensions

Ng (2012) has argues that the dimensions of digital literacy are very much applicable to mobile devices. The digital literacy model of Ng (2012) is then selected as a scaffold against which the literature examined in the following section (section 4) can be brought together and organized.

4. SYSTEMATISED SCOPING REVIEW

The literature review scrutinized the phenomena of Mobile Information and Communication Technology (ICT), and ICT in the education domain as framed by the *a priory* framework themes outlined in Table 2.

Table 3. Summary of search criteria for literature review

	Mobile Information and communication Technology (ICT)
Keywords	Mobile ICT, Connectivity, Networks, Adoption model, Mobile digital literacy skills
Literature review	Systematised Scoping
Databases used	Information systems research, INFORMS journal of Computing and MIS Quarterly: Management Information systems, Web of Science, Science Direct
Inclusion and exclusion principles	Only publications written in English were used; Studies referring to the components of Mobile Digital Literacy skills were included; Studies looking at mobile technology in Africa were considered; and Uptake of technology in non-African rural areas were excluded.
N° of papers	70

The following narrative highlights some of the most relevant literature towards synthesizing a conceptualization of mobile digital literacy skills of educators using mobile technology formal education.

Mobile technologies have evolved over the years, from specific devices created for either communication or information access, to a powerful mixed device supporting both *information access* and *communication* (Chipangura, 2016; Walls, 2017). Mobile technologies are described as computing devices that are portable due to their smaller size (like a cell phone or smartphone) and can include tablets, laptops and netbooks (Valk, Rashid, & Elder, 2010). Within this understanding, mobile digital literacy is seen as a subset of digital literacy. This view is supported by Hansen (2018) and Ng (2013). Digital literacy is described as progressive and adaptive and builds on initial skills which lead to the adaptation of new and emerging mobile devices requiring mobile digital literacy skills (Ng, 2012). Clark, Coward, Rothschild et al. (2017) agree and concede that the experience of using a mobile device differs to that of any other technological device. The *European Information Society* supplied a brief definition of mobile digital literacy skills as an individual's ability to use mobile devices to manipulate digital data and to interact (Martin, 2018). Despite the significant amount of research has been carried out on digital literacy and digital literacy skills, mobile digital literacy skills is yet to be comprehensively articulated (Hansen, 2018). Many of the published authors affirm that the available digital literacy frameworks have failed to incorporate a mobile-centric orientation (Clark et al., 2017; Ng, 2012).

Van Biljon and Kotzé (2007) proposed a Mobile Phone Technology Adoption Model (MOPTAM) depicts the *determining* and *mediating* factors in mobile technology uptake and use. Van Biljon and Kotzé (2007) categorized the following six determining factors: Social influence, these conditions refer to the social burden placed on individuals, based on the opinions and beliefs of other people or groups. This category includes social influences and perceived usefulness and ease of use; Facilitating conditions refers to mobile phone infrastructure which comprises of: system services, cost of system services and cost of handset; Perceived usefulness as the degree to which an individual believes in the benefits of a mobile device; Perceived ease of use which is described as the degree to which an individual believes that using the device will be effortless; Attitude involves the negative or positive associations of an individual with a targeted behavior; and the behavioral intention, that involves perceived performance while interacting with a mobile device.

The three mediating factors that determine mobile phone usage, are (Van Biljon & Kotzé, 2007): Personal factors that include an individual's personal preferences and/or beliefs regarding the benefits of technology. Therefore, relative advantage, compatibility, intricacy, image, trust and observability are considered; Demographic factors denoting an individual's age, gender, education level and technological expertise and ability; and the Socio-economic factors that include variables like job status, occupation and earnings.

Together these determining and mediating factors affect the actual usage of a device (Van Biljon & Kotzé, 2007). Additionally it can be argued that improvements in mobile devices have led to a further increase in the number of users (Mushi, Jafari, & Ennis, 2018). In support of this, Chipangura (2016) mentions that many South Africans prefer acquiring a more feature enabled smartphone which has resulted in a decreased demand for feature phones. The increase in smartphone usage could be due to two factors. Firstly, the increased broadband network coverage reaching more or less 90% of South Africa (Chipangura, 2016) and, secondly, the reduction in the price of smartphones due to competitive pricing of devices (Kende, 2015). Poushter (2016) feels that the proper adaptation and use of mobile technology is currently the crucial factor in human progress. This leads to Sharples, Sánchez, Milrad, and Vavoula (2009) asking why people take to using mobile technologies. The following listed benefits of mobile technology use go a long way in answering Sharples et al. (2009) question:

- It is easy to use and requires only one hand engagement (Rashevska & Tkachuk, 2018).
- Functionalities are rich and devices have many sensors, therefore many more abilities (Casey & Babu, 2016).
- It is smaller and ubiquitous (Bagot, Matthews, Mason et al., 2018).
- It does not require lengthy boot up and shut down (Paily, 2016).
- It facilitates easy access to applications, like checking e-mails and shopping online (Casey & Babu, 2016).
- A very suitable personal device that keeps track of meetings etc. and thus helps one to organise his/her life (Mabila et al., 2017).

The literature further suggests that learners are embracing mobile devices, so much so that they prefer group facilitated learning through social media platforms like Facebook and WhatsApp (Aventurier, 2014; Blodgett, 2017; Kasemsap, 2017). Rodriguez and Igartua (2018a) strongly agree and note that social group education thrives due to quick response times and easy sharing of resources (Blodgett, 2017). Other scholars suggested that learners prefer e-mail as a method of communication with their educator (Krish & Salman, 2018; Savić, 2018). This preference was as a result of its formality, record being kept of conversations and ability to ask more detailed and comprehensive questions (Krish & Salman, 2018).

Despite the listed benefits, users need to have some knowledge of safety and security guidelines when using mobile devices (Chew, Cheng, & Chen, 2018; Collins & Halverson, 2018; Kluzer, 2015). Several precautions have been listed to safeguard mobile devices and their owners (Chew et al., 2018; Collins & Halverson, 2018; Kluzer, 2015).

Further to these selected highlights, the selected papers' examination for relevant Mobile digital literacy skills for the use of mobile technologies, led to the additional identification and classing according to the categories identified in the a priory framework selected in Section 3. The ordered skills are presented in Table 4 with the literature that supports it, and the dimensions and categories used to synthesize this conceptualization of Mobile Digital Literacy skills

Table 4. Identified and classed Mobile Digital Literacy skills as obtained from the literature study

Dimensions: Digital Literacy Model	**Category of Digital literacy skills (Ng, 2012)**	**Mobile digital literacy skills for the use of mobile technologies**	**Support from Literature**
Technical dimension	Operational literacy	Getting started with a mobile device	(Martin, 2018)
		Personalization of one's device	(Kelly & Minges, 2012)
		Underpinnings – basic skills to operate a device	(Jere, Thinyane, Boikhutso, & Ndlovu, 2013); (Kelly & Minges, 2012); (Pan, 2012); (Brown & Mbati, 2015); (Caudill, 2007)

Dimensions: Digital Literacy Model	Category of Digital literacy skills (Ng, 2012)	Mobile digital literacy skills for the use of mobile technologies	Support from Literature
		Understanding mobile hardware operation, affordances and specifications of a device	(Kelly & Minges, 2012); (Brown & Mbati, 2015); (Caudill, 2007); (Martin, 2018)
		Using basic functionalities on a mobile device to organize one's life	(Ventimiglia & Pullman, 2016); (Kelly & Minges, 2012); (Sharon, 2003); (Rashevska & Tkachuk, 2018)
		Adaptability	(Brown & Mbati, 2015)
		Navigation - use of fingers to navigate	(Kelly & Minges, 2012); (Pan, 2012); (Bagot et al., 2018)
		Application management	(Casey & Babu, 2016); (Kelly & Minges, 2012); (Hausknecht & Kaufman, 2018)
		Securing one's device and its contents	(Kluzer, 2015); (Paasch & Duchene, 2012); (Hicks & Turner, 2013); (Voogt, Erstad, Dede, & Mishra, 2013)
Social-emotional dimension	Social-emotional literacy	Understanding the internet platform	(Clark et al., 2017); (Saxena, Gupta, Mehrotra et al., 2017)
		Use the internet to search information	(Chipangura, 2016); (Qadir, Gordon, Tan et al., 2018)
	Social networking functional literacy	Use of social networks for collaborative learning and teamwork	(Rodriguez & Igartua, 2018b); (Zhang, 2018)
		Being part of online groups	(Krish & Salman, 2018)
		Sharing and storing of information –cloud computing	(Mitrovic, 2017)
		Using social networks for professional growth and collaboration	(Nagel & Verster, 2012); (Aventurier, 2014; Mayisela, 2013); (Bansal & Joshi, 2014); (Rodriguez & Igartua, 2018a)
		Communication	(Nagel & Verster, 2012); (Chipangura, 2016); (Harper, 2003; Jones & Flannigan, 2006); (Kelly & Minges, 2012); (Dahlstrom, Walker, & Dziuban, 2013); (Martin, 2018)
	Online etiquette Literacy	Conduct and demeanour over the internet	(Voogt et al., 2013); (Dhir, Kaur, Jere, & Albidewi, 2012); (Chew et al., 2018)
	Cyber Safety Literacy	Being safe in the online world	(Kluzer, 2015); (Chew et al., 2018)
Cognitive dimension	Reproduction Literacy	Dealing with graphics, video and animation	(Kelly & Minges, 2012); (Dhir et al., 2012)
		Content recreation	(Dhir et al., 2012)
		Word processing and electronic spreadsheets	(Martin, 2018)
	Branching Literacy	Multidimensional skills at sourcing information	(Chipangura, 2016)
		Developing a connection between different forms of information	(Mabila et al., 2017); (Russell, Rawson, Freestone et al., 2018)
		Having visual and media knowledge	(Dhir et al., 2012)
	Information Literacy	Background knowledge in acquiring information	(Mabila et al., 2017); (Russell et al., 2018)
Literacy for all dimensions	Critical Literacy and other literacies like financial literacy and work around literacy		(Van Biljon & Kotzé, 2007); (Astill, 2017); (Supachayanont, 2011)

The table 4 provides an initial conceptualization of Mobile digital literacy skills for the use of mobile technology as identified from literature, framed by the *a priory* framework constituted by the digital literacy model of Ng (2013).

5. CONCLUSION

In this paper, a conceptualization of mobile digital literacy skills towards eventually enabling the articulation of the mobile digital literacy skills needed by educators using mobile technologies in formal education is resented and the research question (What constitutes mobile digital literacy skills for educators in formal education?) answered (Table 4). The authors paper exapted the 'best-fit' framework synthesis of Carroll et al. (2013) from the health domain, towards conceptualizing mobile digital literacy skills for educators when embarking on using mobile technology in their classroom practices. Table 4 suggests a conceptualization of mobile digital literacy skills needed by an educator. This will, going forward, in its turn, be used as an updated a priory framework to explore a nuanced conceptualization framed specifically by the activities of the educator within their classroom practice.

As it currently stands however, the conceptualization can serve as a Meta level guide for future training programmers designed for educators. Educators and experts developing courses for ICT in schools may also benefit from this study, as they seek to enhance their skills to heighten the success of implementing mobile technologies in formal education. This study further provide educators with a list of skills to assess themselves in terms of implementing mobile technology in the classroom.

REFERENCES

Astill, J. (2017). Beefing up mobile-phone and internet penetration in Africa. *The Economist.*

Aventurier, P. (2014). *Academic social networks: challenges and opportunities.* Paper presented at the 7th UNICA Scholarly Communication Seminar.

Bagot, K., Matthews, S., Mason, M., Squeglia, L., Fowler, J., Gray, K., . . . Godino, J. (2018). Current, Future and Potential Use of Mobile and Wearable Technologies and Social Media Data in the ABCD Study to Increase Understanding of Contributors to Child Health. *Developmental cognitive neuroscience.*

Bansal, T., & Joshi, D. (2014). A study of students experiences of WhatsApp mobile learning. *Global Journal of Human-Social Science Research.*

Bartikowski, B., Laroche, M., Jamal, A., & Yang, Z. (2018). The type-of-internet-access digital divide and the well-being of ethnic minority and majority consumers: A multi-country investigation. *Journal of Business Research, 82*, 373-380.

Blodgett, J. (2017). Taking the class out of the classroom: Libraries, literacy, and service learning *The Experiential Library* (pp. 43-52): Elsevier.

Brown, H., & Mbati, L. S. (2015). Mobile Learning: Moving Past the Myths and Embracing the Opportunities. *16*(2), 115-115.

Carroll, C., Booth, A., Leaviss, J., & Rick, J. (2013). "Best fit" framework synthesis: refining the method. *BMC medical research methodology, 13*(1), 37. doi:10.1186/1471-2288-13-37

Casey, M., & Babu, A. (2016). *Game of Phones: Deloitte's Mobile Consumer Survey. The Africa cut 2015/2016.* . Retrieved from https://www2.deloitte.com/content/dam/Deloitte/za/Documents/technology-media-telecommunications/ZA_Deloitte-Mobile-consumer-survey-Africa-300816.pdf

Caudill, J. G. (2007). The Growth of m-Learning and the Growth of Mobile Computing: Parallel developments. *International Review of Research in Open and Distance Learning, 8*(2).

Chang, C.-Y., & Hwang, G.-J. (2018). Trends of mobile technology-enhanced medical education: a review of journal publications from 1998 to 2016. *Int. J. Mobile Learning and Organisation, 12*(4), 373.

Chew, S. W., Cheng, I.-L., & Chen, N.-S. (2018). Exploring challenges faced by different stakeholders while implementing educational technology in classrooms through expert interviews. *Journal of Computers in Education, 5*(2), 175-197.

Chipangura, B. (2016). A Framework for providing mobile centric services to students at higher education institutions: The case of open distance learning.

Clark, M., Coward, C., Rothschild, C., Reynal, l. d., & Richter, B. (2017, 2017). *Towards a Mobile Information Literacy framework: Rethinking Information Literacy in a Mobile Era.*

Collins, A., & Halverson, R. (2018). *Rethinking education in the age of technology: The digital revolution and schooling in America*: Teachers College Press.

Dahlstrom, E., Walker, J., & Dziuban, C. (2013). *ECAR study of undergraduate students and information technology*. Retrieved from www.educause.edu/ecar:

Dhir, A., Kaur, P., Jere, N., & Albidewi, I. A. (2012). *Understanding mobile phone battery-human interaction for developing world a perspective of feature phone users in africa.* Paper presented at the Future Internet Communications (BCFIC), 2012 2nd Baltic Congress on.

Eshet-Alkalai, Y. (2004). Digital literacy: A conceptual framework for survival skills in the digital era. *Journal of Educational Multimedia and Hypermedia, 13*(1), 93-106.

Eshet-alkalai, Y., & Chajut, E. (2009). Changes Over Time in Digital Literacy. *12*(6).

Ferrari, A. (2008). *Digital Competence in Practice : An Analysis of Frameworks*. Retrieved from www.jrc.ec.europa.eu:

Finn-Stevenson, M. (2018). *Schools of the 21st century: Linking child care and education*: Routledge.

Gilster, P. (1997). Digital literacy. The thinking and survival skills new users need to make the internet personally and professionally meaningful.

Grant, M. J., & Booth, A. (2009). A typology of reviews: an analysis of 14 review types and associated methodologies. *Health Information & Libraries Journal, 26*(2), 91-108.

Hansen, J. J. (2018). Digital literacy–cognitive strategies, genre skills and situated practice *Designing for Learning in a Networked World* (pp. 138-157): Routledge.

Harper, V. (2003). The digital divide (DD): A reconceptualization. *Association for the Advancement of Computing in Education (AACE), 11*(1), 96-103.

Hausknecht, S., & Kaufman, D. (2018). *Increasing digital literacy skills of older adults through a digital storytelling project-based course.* Paper presented at the EdMedia+ Innovate Learning.

Hicks, T., & Turner, K. H. (2013). No longer a luxury: Digital literacy can't wait. *English Journal, 6*, 58-65.

ITU. (2018). *Achieving universal and affordable Internet in the least developed countries* (9789261254513). Retrieved from https://www.itu.int/en/ITU-D/LDCs/Pages/ICTs-for-SDGs-in-LDCs-Report.aspx:

Jere, N. R., Thinyane, M., Boikhutso, T., & Ndlovu, N. (2013). *An assessment of ICT challenges in rural areas: ICT experts vs rural users views: a case of the Siyakhula Living Lab.* Paper presented at the Proceedings of the South African Institute for Computer Scientists and Information Technologists Conference.

Jisc. (2015). *Digital students are different.* Retrieved from https://drive.google.com/file/d/%0A0B4y3qNoTbFdYd0ttdEx1STVyeDRFOGdvMVhkeWhMdjZYcVBR/view?pli¼1 (

Jones, B. R., & Flannigan, S. (2006). Connecting the Digital Dots : Literacy of the 21st Century. *Workforce, 29*(2), 8-10. doi:Article

Kasemsap, K. (2017). Digital storytelling and digital literacy: Advanced issues and prospects *Deconstructing the Education-Industrial Complex in the Digital Age* (pp. 151-171): IGI Global.

Kelly, T., & Minges, M. (2012). *Maximizing Mobile.*

Kende, M. (2015). *Global Internet Report 2015: Mobile Evolution and Development of the Internet*: Internet Society.

Kluzer, S. (2015). Guidelines on the adoption. 1-28.

Krish, P., & Salman, Q. (2018). Politeness in Email Communication Among Arab Postgraduate Students in a Malaysian Public University. *e-Bangi, 11*(2).

Lankshear, C., & Knobel, M. (2008). Concepts, Policies and Practices (Vol. 30, pp. 29-29): Peter Lang.

Mabila, J., Biljon, J. V., & Herselman, M. (2017). A sustainability framework for mobile technology integration in schools . The case of resource- constrained environments in South Africa. *The Journal of Community Informatics, 13*(2), 59-86.

Markauskaite, L. (2007). Exploring the structure of trainee teachers' ICT literacy: the main components of, and relationships between, general cognitive and technical capabilities. *Educational Technology Research and Development, 55*(6), 547-572.

Martin, J. P. (2018). *Skills for the 21st century: Findings and policy lessons from the OECD survey of adult skills.* Retrieved from

Mayisela, T. (2013). The potential use of mobile technology: enhancing accessibility and communication in a blended learning course. *South African Journal of Education, 33*(1), 1-18.

Mitrovic, Z. (2017). *The impact of cloud computing on the role of an IT department: a case study of a higher education institution in the Western Cape.* Cape Peninsula University of Technology.

Mushi, R., Jafari, S., & Ennis, A. (2018). Measuring Mobile Phone Technology Adoption in SMEs: Analysis of Metrics *Technology Adoption and Social Issues: Concepts, Methodologies, Tools, and Applications* (pp. 1546-1557): IGI Global.

Nagel, L., & Verster, M. (2012). *A student-grown Facebook group in an architecture class: Seed or weed.*

Ng, W. (2012). Can we teach digital natives digital literacy? *Computers and Education, 59*(3), 1065-1078. doi:10.1016/j.compedu.2012.04.016

Ng, W. (2013). Conceptualising mLearning Literacy. *International Journal of Mobile and Blended Learning, 5*(1), 1-20. doi:10.4018/jmbl.2013010101

Paasch, C., & Duchene, F. (2012). Exploring Mobile / WiFi Handover with Multipath TCP Categories and Subject Descriptors. *Cellular Networks: Operations, Challenges, and Future Design (CellNet)*, 1-6. doi:10.1145/2342468.2342476

Paily, M. U. (2016). [Information and communication technology].

Pan, Y. (2012). Portable tablet computing device with a low power operation mode as a media player: Google Patents.

Parry, R., Eikhof, D. R., Barnes, S.-A., & Kispeter, E. (2018). *Development, supply, deployment, demand: Balancing the museum digital skills ecosystem. First findings of the 'One by One' national digital literacy project*.

Poushter, J. (2016). *Smartphone Ownership and Internet Usage Continues to Climb in Emerging Economies*. Retrieved from

Qadir, J., Gordon, S., Tan, J., Chiaraviglio, L., Wu, J., & Zhang, W. (2018). *A Sustainable Connectivity Model of the Internet Access Technologies in Rural and Low-Income Areas.* Paper presented at the Smart Grid and Innovative Frontiers in Telecommunications: Third International Conference, SmartGIFT 2018, Auckland, New Zealand, April 23-24, 2018, Proceedings.

Rashevska, N., & Tkachuk, V. (2018). Technological conditions of mobile learning in high school. *arXiv preprint arXiv:1808.01989*.

Rodriguez, -. d.-D. I., & Igartua, J.-J. (2018a). Skills of digital literacy to address the risks of interactive communication *Information and Technology Literacy: Concepts, Methodologies, Tools, and Applications* (pp. 621-632): IGI Global.

Rodriguez, d.-D. I., & Igartua, J.-J. (2018b). Skills of digital literacy to address the risks of interactive communication *Information and Technology Literacy: Concepts, Methodologies, Tools, and Applications* (pp. 621-632): IGI Global.

Russell, F., Rawson, C., Freestone, C., Currie, M., & Kelly, B. (2018). Parallel Lines: A Mixed Methods Impact Analysis of Co-Curricular Digital Literacy Online Modules on Student Results in First Year Nursing. *College & Research Libraries*.

Sadaf, A., & Johnson, B. L. (2017). Teachers' Beliefs About Integrating Digital Literacy Into Classroom Practice: An Investigation Based on the Theory of Planned Behavior. *Journal of Digital Learning in Teacher Education, 33*(4), 129-137.

Savić, M. (2018). Lecturer perceptions of im/politeness and in/appropriateness in student e-mail requests: A Norwegian perspective. *Journal of Pragmatics, 124*, 52-72.

Saxena, P., Gupta, S. K., Mehrotra, D., Kamthan, S., Sabir, H., Katiyar, P., & Prasad, S. S. (2017). Assessment of digital literacy and use of smart phones among Central Indian dental students. *Journal of Oral Biology and Craniofacial Research*.

Schreuers, K., Quan-Haase, A., & Martin, K. (2017). Problematizing the digital literacy paradox in the context of older adults' ICT use: Aging, media discourse, and self-determination. *Canadian Journal of Communication, 42*(2), 1.

Sharon, M. (2003). an Introduction To Mobile Technologies and services. *Machine Learning, 2010*(June), 9128-9128.

Sharples, M., Sánchez, I. A., Milrad, M., & Vavoula, G. (2009). Mobile learning Small devices, big issues (pp. 20-20).

Supachayanont, A. (2011). *Workaround as a craft skill of the computerised paper production process.* University of St Andrews.

Valk, J.-H., Rashid, A. T., & Elder, L. (2010). Using mobile phones to improve educational outcomes: An analysis of evidence from Asia (Vol. 11, pp. 117-140).

Van Biljon, J., & Kotzé, P. (2007). *Modelling the factors that influence mobile phone adoption.* Paper presented at the Proceedings of the 2007 annual research conference of the South African institute of computer scientists and information technologists on IT research in developing countries.

Van Biljon, J., & Renaud, K. (2017). *Harnessing both Information and Knowledge Visualisation to Represent a Community of Practice: Depicting the South African ICT4D Researcher Community*.

Ventimiglia, P., & Pullman, G. (2016). From Written to Digital: The New Literacy. *Educause Review, 51*(2).

Voogt, J., Erstad, O., Dede, C., & Mishra, P. (2013). Challenges to learning and schooling in the digital networked world of the 21st century. *Journal of Computer Assisted Learning, 29*(5), 403-413. doi:10.1111/jcal.12029

Walls, E. (2017). *The perceived relation between ICTs and social good.* University of Southampton.

Yu, T.-K., Lin, M.-L., & Liao, Y.-K. (2017). Understanding factors influencing information communication technology adoption behavior: The moderators of information literacy and digital skills. *Computers in Human Behavior, 71*, 196-208. doi:http://dx.doi.org/10.1016/j.chb.2017.02.005

Zapata, G. C. (2018). The Role of Digital, Learning by Design Instructional Materials in the Development of Spanish Heritage Learners' Literacy Skills *Multiliteracies Pedagogy and Language Learning* (pp. 67-106): Springer.

Zhang, L. (2018). Automatic Traffic Scheduling for Internet Connectivity Failures.

Zheng, B., Yim, S., & Warschauer, M. (2018). Social media in the writing classroom and beyond. *The TESOL Encyclopedia of English Language Teaching*, 1-5.

MOBILE LEARNING IN OUTDOOR SETTINGS: A SYSTEMATIC REVIEW

Johan Stymne
Stockholm University, Department of Computer and Systems Sciences/DSV
SE-164 07 Stockholm, Sweden

ABSTRACT

Learning with mobile technology, or mobile learning, is gaining more and more interest in education. One example is mobile learning in outdoor settings, where mobile technology can support students' interaction with the physical environment. To understand how mobile technology has been used in learning activities in outdoor settings, a systematic review was carried out. A number of reviews on mobile learning and on specific sub-areas such as language learning or computer education have been published in scientific journals and conferences. So far, however, no systematic review has focused on mobile learning in outdoor settings. To address this problem and to guide the review the following research questions were posed: "Which are the educational subjects and educational levels in mobile learning in outdoor settings?" and "What types of technologies and methods for data collection and annotation are used in mobile learning in outdoor settings?". In total 87 articles were included in this review. The conclusions include that biology was the most common subject, primary or elementary school the most common educational levels, GPS was the major technology used for positioning and navigation, AR was the most common technology used for augmenting the outdoor learning environment, and taking photos and taking notes was the most common methods for data collection in outdoor settings. Building on the conclusions of this review and on previous reviews, suggestions are made for future research.

KEYWORDS

Mobile Learning in Outdoor Settings, Mobile Learning, Outdoor Learning, Systematic Review, State of the Art

1. INTRODUCTION

Mobile phones can be used for learning that is contextualized, making the physical environment, together with the temporal, social, and cultural environments relevant in learning activities (Frohberg, Göth, & Schwabe, 2009; Sharples, Taylor, & Vavoula, 2007; Tan, et al., 2018). One type of mobile learning, where these different environments, and especially the physical environment, can be included in learning activities, is mobile learning in outdoor settings.

Rikala (2015) has proposed that: "the aim of mobile learning should be to offer new opportunities for learning that extend learning beyond the traditional teacher-led and classroom-bound approaches. Learners with mobile devices can go into the field, interact with other people, and gain concrete knowledge instead of sitting in the classroom and listening to a teacher." (p.69). One step towards this aim, could be to review how mobile learning has been used in outdoor settings.

So far, two reviews of mobile learning in general have been published by Frohberg et al. (2009) and Wingkvist & Ericsson (2011). These reviews were intended to cover the whole research field. Frohberg et al. (2009) focused their analysis of 102 research projects on five dimensions: context, tools, control, communication, subject and objective. Wingkvist & Ericsson (2011) reviewed 114 articles from the World Conference on Mobile and Contextual Learning (mLearn) 2005, 2007 and 2008, focusing their analysis on research purpose and research method. With the growth of the research field of mobile learning these general reviews are giving way for more specific reviews. In recent years, reviews on different aspects of the mobile learning research field are appearing, such as Almeida & Araújo Jr (2016) focusing on science and mathematics, Crompton et al. (2016) focusing on science, Anohah et al. (2017) focusing on computer education, Kukulska-Hulme and Viberg (2018) focusing on second language acquisition, Crompton et al. (2017) focusing on educational levels from pre-kindergarten to grade 12, and Suárez et al. (2018) focusing on mobile inquiry-based learning. Tan et al. (2018), reviewed studies on mobile inquiry-based learning, however only from two countries: The Netherlands and Singapore. So far there has been no systematic review focusing on mobile learning in outdoor settings. In identifying gaps in previous research, Crompton et al.

(2017) also suggested that there is a need for more reviews on mobile learning: "Further reviews are needed to build on this study and add to the paucity of research in this area." (p. 61).

This article presents a systematic review of research where mobile phones and other mobile devices have been used to support contextualized learning in outdoor settings. This may be of interest to the mobile learning research community as it identifies gaps in current research on mobile learning in outdoor settings.

To summarise, there have been a number of reviews on mobile learning in general and on specific subject areas such as second language acquisition or on specific learning approaches such as inquiry-based learning, however no systematic review has focused specifically on mobile learning in outdoor settings.

To address this problem and to guide the review and analysis the following research questions are posed:

- Which are the educational subjects and educational levels in mobile learning in outdoor settings?
- What types of technologies and methods for data collection and annotation are used in mobile learning in outdoor settings?

2. BACKGROUND

Many descriptions and definitions of mobile learning have been suggested, and as the research area and the mobile technologies have evolved, so have the definitions. Sharples et al. (2007) suggests a definition of mobile learning as: "the processes of coming to know through conversations across multiple contexts amongst people and personal interactive technologies". The definition is adopted to add focus to this review.

In reviewing research on outdoor learning, Rickinson et al. (2004), describes one category of outdoor learning activities as "fieldwork and outdoor visits", giving examples of outdoor settings such as: "...field study centres, nature centres, farms, parks or gardens.". These examples of outdoor settings are in line with the focus of this review.

In a review of the use of mobile learning in science, Crompton et al. (2016) reviewed 49 articles from 2000 onwards. Among the results they presented were science area, educational level, countries of study, and types of mobile devices. The most common science area was life science (67%), including for example biology. The most common educational level was elementary school (53%) followed by high school (22%). Taiwan (43%), followed by USA (16%) were the most common countries. Mobile phones and PDAs were the most common mobile devices (30% each). 15% was reported as mobile devices in general, digital camera made up 9%, iPad 5%, and handheld, tablet and iTouch had a share of 4% each. In the discussion they note that the specific type of mobile phone or PDA was rarely mentioned in the articles, or even just mentioned as mobile device or handheld. Crompton et al. (2016) suggest that: "...those interested in doing future research regarding the use of mobile technologies need not focus on the specific type of mobile device, but rather on the multifunctionality and accessibility of the device." (p. 158). Crompton et al. (2017) reviewed 113 articles on mobile learning from pre-kindergarten to grade 12 (PK-12), from 2010 to 2015. The results show, for example, that the most common subject area was science (56%), followed by literacy (21%), and mathematics (10%). The most common educational level was elementary school (46%), followed by middle school (29%), and high school (19%). The most common mobile device was mobile phone (34%), followed by PDA (22%), tablet (16%), iPad (11%), ebook (2%), and iPod (1%). Taiwan (35%) was the most common country, followed by Singapore (9%), and USA (8%).

Crompton et al. (2017; 2016) present clear results on the educational contexts of mobile learning in science and mobile learning in PK-12 education, and which mobile devices are used. There is a knowledge gap, however, in which technologies are used apart from mobile devices. There is also a knowledge gap in what the educational subjects and educational levels are for mobile learning in outdoor settings.

Suárez et al. (2018) reviewed 62 studies on mobile inquiry-based learning from 2006 to April 2016. They extracted data in five categories: direct instruction, access to content, data collection, peer-to-peer communication, and contextual support. In their results, location guidance was described as part of the direct instruction category. Location guidance, by using for example GPS, RFID or QR codes, was reported in 27 of the studies. Digital artifacts triggered by GPS and AR was reported as fixed content, as part of the access to content category. Fixed content was reported in 25 of the studies. For the data collection category, capturing multimedia data or taking notes was described as cooperative data collection. Cooperative data collection was reported in 57 of the studies. In a meta-analysis they mapped the five categories to six types of agency supported by the mobile technology in inquiry-based learning. One result of the review and meta-analysis is an overview of what kind of learner agency can be supported by different parts of a mobile inquiry-based learning activity.

Suárez et al. (2018) present results on how technologies like GPS, AR and taking notes on mobile devices are used in mobile inquiry-based learning. They present their results in their five categories. There is a knowledge gap, however, in what technologies are used, reported separately, and for mobile learning in outdoor settings. A systematic review could contribute to filling these knowledge gaps.

3. METHOD

The PRISMA statement (Liberati, et al., 2009) gives guidelines for reporting systematic reviews of evaluations of interventions. This systematic review follows Liberati et al. (2009) in that it presents which information sources were used, search strategy, study selection, and data collection process. The information sources that were used were research databases and conference proceedings. The search strategy used both keyword search and manual search. The study selection used six selection criteria and three inclusion and exclusion criteria. The data collection process used eight categories for data extraction.

3.1 Database Selection and Search Strategy

Database searches were carried out using ERIC via EBSCOhost, Scopus and DBLP. The Title, Abstract and Keyword fields were included in this search. As a complement the main conferences focusing on mobile learning were selected for free text search: World Conference on Mobile and Contextual Learning (mLearn), and the International Conference on Mobile Learning.

The search strategy used was a combination of keyword search using databases, manual search and reference list search. Two sets of keywords were used in the keyword search, mobile device-related keywords and outdoor learning-related keywords. The mobile device-related keywords were identified from previous mobile learning reviews: Frohberg et al. (2009), Wingqvist & Ericsson (2011), and Crompton et al. (2017; 2016), and the outdoor learning-relaed keywords were identified from outdoor learning reviews: Rickinson et al. (2004), and Fiennes et al. (2015).

As the articles should include both mobile technology and learning in outdoor settings the search was done using the following combination of mobile technology related and outdoor learning related keywords:

- ERIC, Scopus (Title, Author keywords, Abstract): ("mobile learning" OR m-learning OR "mobile phone*" OR "mobile device*" OR "mobile technolog*" OR smartphone OR handheld OR pda* OR "augmented reality") AND ("outdoor * learning*" OR "outdoor * lesson*" OR "outdoor * education*" OR "field trip*" OR excursion* OR adventur* OR "nature visit*" OR bushcraft*).
- DBLP (Title, Author keywords, Abstract): Manual combination of the keywords.
- World Conference on Mobile and Contextual Learning (Full text), International Conference on Mobile Learning (Title, Author keywords, Abstract): Manual combination of the outdoor learning-related keywords without wildcards.

3.2 Selection Criteria

The overall focus for the review was: "Original empirical research on the use of mobile learning in outdoor settings". The articles were published between 2004 and 2019. This timeframe was chosen because the first studies on mobile learning in outdoor settings identified were published in 2004, and the selection includes articles published until December 2019. The geographical scope was international. All educational levels were included, ranging from pre-kindergarten to higher education including postgraduate level. Articles from all countries were included in the search, however only articles published in English were included in the selection. Only published articles that had been peer-reviewed were included.

3.2.1 Inclusion and Exclusion Criteria

- For articles reporting on the same empirical study, only the last published article was included in the review.
- Included articles needed to present results from empirical tests with representative learners using some mobile technology. This means that articles presenting results from tests with colleagues, or focusing on performance, technical functionality or usability of a system without also focusing on mobile learning were excluded.

- Only articles presenting studies where some aspect of the mobile technology, hardware or software, was designed for a specific learning activity were included. Studies using off-the-shelf mobile technology or with apps not intended for specific learning activities were excluded. Studies using laptop computers were also excluded.

3.3 Study Selection

643 articles were identified through database search and manual search: ERIC (118), Scopus (414), DBLP (18), World Conference on Mobile and Contextual Learning (63), International Conference on Mobile Learning (11). After duplicates removal and screening 145 articles remained. In the end, 87 articles met the criteria for inclusion and were included in this review.

3.4 Data Extraction

The following data was extracted from the published articles: name of study, educational subject(-s), educational level(-s), country, mobile device(-s), technology used for positioning or navigation, technology used for augmenting the outdoor learning environment, and data collection or annotation method(-s). Each of the extracted data is described in Table 1. The database with extracted data and full references can be accessed from here: http://johan.blogs.dsv.su.se/data/.

Table 1. Description of extracted data

Data	Description
Name	Name of study, or where not available, Name of project or system or course
Educational subject(-s)	Educational subject(-s)
Educational level(-s)	Pre-kindergarten, kindergarten and pre-school (typical age 1-6 years old), primary school or elementary school (6-12) secondary school or middle school (12-16), high school (16-18), higher education (18+)
Country	Country where the empirical study took place
Mobile device(-s)	Mobile phone, PDA, Tablet
Technology used for positioning or navigation	GPS, QR, RFID, WIFI, Compass, Numerical code
Technology used for augmenting	AR (Augmented Reality), 3D model, Image recognition
Method(-s) for data collection or annotation	Photo, Notes, Audio, Video, Probe

The name of the study was not always reported in the articles. In those cases the name of the project, the name of the system, or the name of the course was extracted.

The educational levels differ from country to country. That is why two or more levels can belong to the same category in the data extraction phase. Differences in educational levels are also the reason why typical ages are given instead of exact ages.

4. RESULTS

To give a backdrop to the results, the number of articles per year and per country are presented. The number of articles per year on mobile learning in outdoor settings has increased, from two articles, which was the lowest number, in 2004, 2006 and 2007 to nine, which was the highest number, in 2015 and 2018.

The top seven countries or regions to publish on mobile learning in outdoor settings were (number of articles in parenthesis): Taiwan (26), UK (7), Sweden (6), USA (6), Germany (5), Singapore (5), and Finland (4). Out of the 87 articles in this review, 30% were from Taiwan. The articles from Taiwan were published between 2005 and 2019. The articles from the UK were published from 2004, however the last article was published in 2012. The articles from Sweden were published between 2008 and 2015, and from USA between 2011 and 2018. The articles from Germany were published between 2005 and 2018, from Singapore between 2007 and 2015, and from Finland between 2012 and 2018.

There were articles from 16 more countries or regions: Greece (3), Israel (3), Japan (3), Brazil (2), Hong Kong (2), Italy (2), Portugal (2), Spain (2), Australia (1), Austria (1), Czech Republic (1), Estonia (1), Indonesia (1), Ireland (1), Norway (1), and South Africa (1).

4.1 Educational Subjects and Educational Levels

The five most common subjects in the reviewed articles were (number of articles in parenthesis): biology (38), history (14), mathematics (9), language (7), geography (5) and geology (5) (see Table 2). The biology subject, reported in 38 articles, was much more common than any of the other subjects. Subjects reported in between 1-4 articles were (number of articles in parenthesis): natural science (4), local culture (3), orientation (3), science (2), health education (2), physics (2), sustainability (2), tourism (2), archaeology (1), computer science (1), economy (1), information and communication technology (1), pedagogy (1), and technology (1).

Table 2. Subjects, number of articles and years of publication

Subject	Number of articles	Years of publication
Biology	38	2004-2019
History	14	2008-2019
Mathematics	9	2006-2019
Language	7	2008-2015
Geography	5	2005-2013
Geology	5	2008-2019

Biology was also the only subject reported on in articles from the first year of the review until the last year, 2004-2019. History, mathematics and geology were represented until 2019, while language and geography were represented in the middle of the timeframe for the review: 2008-2015 and 2005-2013.

Primary school or elementary school was the most common educational level with 49 articles, see Table 3. It was more common than secondary school or middle school with 22 articles and higher education with 18 articles. No articles were from pre-kindergarten, kindergarten and pre-school.

Table 3. Number of articles and educational levels (one article from 2009 had both primary and middle school students and one article from 2019 had both primary and secondary school students).

Year	Number of articles	Pre-kindergarten, kindergarten and pre-school	Primary or elementary school	Secondary or middle school	Higher education
2004-2019	87	0	49	22	18

4.1.1 Country or Regional Comparison

One difference between countries or regions was the subject reported in the articles. For example, the most common subject in Taiwan was biology. The subject was studied in 16 out of the 26 articles from Taiwan. The second most common subject in Taiwan, history was studied in four out of the 26 articles. Biology was also the most common subject in Germany, Singapore and Finland. In Sweden the most common subject was mathematics and in USA the most common was natural science. In UK biology and language were as common, studied in two articles each.

Another difference between countries was the educational level of participating students. For example, the most common educational level in Taiwan was elementary school. Elementary school was reported in 23 out of the 26 articles. Primary or elementary school was also the most common in Sweden, USA, Singapore and Finland. Secondary school was the most common in UK and in Germany. Higher education was not the most common educational level in any of the top seven countries, however it was the second most common educational level in Taiwan, UK, USA, Germany, and Finland. All students from higher education were undergraduate students; no students were from the graduate level.

One last difference between countries or regions was the size of student groups, ranging from one student, learning individually, to nine students in a group. Out of the top seven countries or regions, the most common group size in Taiwan and Singapore was one student, corresponding to individual learning. This group size was used in 20 out of the 26 articles from Taiwan. The second most common group size for Taiwan was five students in each group. This group size was used in four of the 26 articles. In UK and USA the most common group size was two students, in Sweden it was three students and in Germany and Finland it was two or three students.

4.2 Mobile Devices

Mobile phones were the most common mobile devices, see Table 4. The use of PDAs has decreased, going from 18 in the first eight years between 2004 and 2011 to four in the last eight years between 2012 and 2019. However, the use of mobile phones has increased in the same time period, going from 17 between 2004 and 2011 to 32 between 2012 and 2019. The use of tablets has also increased, going from two between 2004 and 2011 to 20 between 2012 and 2019.

Table 4. Number of mobile phones, PDAs and tablets used in the articles (two or more mobile devices in six articles)

Year	Number of articles	Mobile phone	PDA	Tablet
2004-2019	87	49	22	22

Mobile phones are used in much the same way as PDAs in mobile learning, and have gradually replaced them. DVD or smart watch was not part of the data extraction, however DVD was used as mobile device in one of the reviewed articles. Smart watch was not used in any of the reviewed articles.

4.3 Positioning or Navigational Technologies

GPS was the most common technology used for positioning or navigation to learning material in outdoor settings, see Table 5. It was reported in 46 articles, published between 2004 and 2019. The second most common technology was QR codes, with 17 articles, published between 2007 and 2018.

Table 5. Positioning or navigational technology used, with number of articles and years of publication

Positioning or navigational technology	Number of articles	Years of publication
GPS	46	2004-2019
QR	17	2007-2018
RFID	7	2007-2019
WIFI	3	2005-2008
Compass	3	2012-2019
Numerical code	2	2008 and 2015

The third most common technology was RFID, with 7 articles, published between 2007 and 2019. WIFI networks were used in three articles, published in 2005 and 2008, and compass was used in three articles, published in 2012, 2015 and 2019. Numerical codes to type in manually were used for positioning or navigation in two articles, published in 2008 and 2015.

In 20 articles, no technology was used for positioning or navigation. In 55 articles one technology was used for positioning or navigation. 12 articles used more than one. No articles used three or more technologies for positioning or navigation.

4.4 Augmenting Technologies

AR was the most common technology used for augmenting the outdoor learning environment, see Table 6.

Table 6. Augmenting technology used, with number of articles and years of publication

Augmenting technology	Number of articles	Years of publication
AR	14	2009-2019
3D model	9	2008-2019
Image recognition	3	2005-2012

AR was used in 14 articles published between 2009 and 2019. The second most common technology was 3D models, with 9 articles, published between 2008 and 2019. The third most common technology was Image recognition, with 3 articles, published between 2005 and 2012.

4.5 Methods for Data Collection or Annotation

Taking photos and taking notes were the most common methods used by the students for data collection or annotation, see Table 7. Taking photos was used in 40 articles, published between 2005 and 2019. Taking notes was used in 20 articles, published between 2005 and 2018. The third most common method was recording audio, with 13 articles, published between 2008 and 2018. The fourth most common method was recording video, with 10 articles, published between 2008 and 2019. The fifth most common method was probing, for example by using specific devices for measuring water quality, air temperature or carbon monoxide. Probes were used in 6 articles, published between 2004 and 2018.

Table 7. Methods for data collection or annotation, with number of articles and years of publication

Methods for data collection or annotation	Number of articles	Years of publication
Photo	40	2005-2019
Notes	20	2005-2018
Audio	13	2008-2018
Video	10	2008-2019
Probe	6	2004-2018

5. DISCUSSION AND CONCLUSION

One interpretation of the increasing number of articles published per year is that the research interest in mobile learning in outdoor settings is still growing. In the first few years of this review, there were only two and three studies published on mobile learning in outdoor settings, whereas in the last few years of the review there were between five and nine studies published each year.

Most of the articles in this review were from Taiwan. This confirms the results of the review of mobile learning in science by Crompton et al. (2016), who found that Taiwan was the most common country of study. It also confirms the results of Crompton et al. (2017), who reviewed mobile learning in PK-12 education, finding that Taiwan had the most publications. One difference was that the second most common country of study in this review was UK compared to USA in second place in Crompton et al. (2016) and Singapore in Crompton et al. (2017). Notable is that UK has the second highest number of articles published on mobile learning in outdoor settings, even though the last publication from UK is from 2012.

The first research question: "*Which are the educational subjects and educational levels in mobile learning in outdoor settings?*" can be answered with the following: The most common educational subject for mobile learning in outdoor settings was *biology* followed by *history* and *mathematics*. That biology was the most common subject is in line with Crompton et al. (2016). The most common educational level for mobile learning in outdoor settings was *primary or elementary school*. This confirms the results of Crompton et al. (2017; 2016). There are differences between countries or regions regarding common subjects, educational levels, and group sizes in mobile learning in outdoor settings. In five of the top seven countries biology was the most common subject. In Sweden mathematics was most common and in USA natural science was most common. In five of the top seven countries primary or elementary school was the most common educational level. In UK and Germany secondary school were the most common. In Taiwan, UK, USA, Germany, and Finland higher education was the second most common educational level. In five of the top seven countries groups of two to three students was the most common. In Taiwan and Singapore individual learning was the most common.

The second research question: "*What types of technologies and methods for data collection and annotation are used in mobile learning in outdoor settings?*" can be answered as follows: *Mobile phones or PDAs* were the most common mobile devices. This confirms the results of Crompton et al. (2017; 2016). The use of tablets has increased during the last eight years. *GPS* was the most common technology for positioning or navigation, reported in 46 articles, followed by *QR codes* (17), and RFID (7). That positioning or navigation was common in outdoor mobile learning activities is in line with the results of Suárez et al. (2018), in describing location guidance as being common in mobile inquiry-based learning. *AR* was the most common technology for augmenting the outdoor learning environment, reported in 14 articles. Finally, *taking photos*, reported in 40 articles, followed by *taking notes* (20), and *recording audio* (13), were the most common data collection or annotation methods. This is also in line with the results of Suárez et al. (2018), who describe cooperative data collection as being common in mobile inquiry-based learning.

A number of gaps have been identified in this review. First, the most common subject was biology. Future studies of mobile learning in outdoor settings may focus on other subjects further down the list. Second, all of the articles had students from primary or elementary school to higher education. Studies of mobile learning in outdoor settings in pre-kindergarten, kindergarten or pre-school are needed. Third, mobile phones were the most common devices. Tablets were increasingly being used. Studies using smart watches are still lacking. Fourth, few studies used two technologies for positioning or navigation and no articles used three or more. Future studies could support the whole range from small-scale to large-scale navigation and positioning by using two or more technologies, available in new mobile phones. Fifth, in many studies students took photos and notes by using mobile devices or other mobile technology. Only ten articles reported that video was used for data collection, and six articles reported that probes were used. More studies could use video or probes for data collection.

This study has a number of limitations. Even though the review method was applied in a thorough way, one limitation is that there may be articles fulfilling the inclusion criteria that were not identified through the database and manual search. Another limitation is that no inter-rater reliability check has been performed. One last limitation is that only articles published in English were included in the review.

REFERENCES

Almeida, R. R., & Araújo Jr, C. F. (2016). Mobile Learning in Science and Mathematics Teaching: A Systematic Review *Mobile and Blended Learning Innovations for Improved Learning Outcomes* (pp. 277-296): IGI Global.

Anohah, E., Oyelere, S. S., & Suhonen, J. (2017). Trends of mobile learning in Computing Education from 2006 to 2014: A systematic review of research publications. *International Journal of Mobile and Blended Learning (IJMBL), 9*(1), 16-33.

Crompton, H., Burke, D., & Gregory, K. H. (2017). The use of mobile learning in PK-12 education: A systematic review. *Computers and Education, 110*, 51-63.

Crompton, H., Burke, D., Gregory, K. H., et al. (2016). The Use of Mobile Learning in Science: A Systematic Review. *Journal of Science Education and Technology, 25*(2), 149-160.

Fiennes, C., Oliver, E., Dickson, K., et al. (2015). The existing evidence-base about the effectiveness of outdoor learning. *Institute of Outdoor Learning: London, UK.*

Frohberg, D., Göth, C., & Schwabe, G. (2009). Mobile Learning projects - a critical analysis of the state of the art: Original article. *Journal of Computer Assisted Learning, 25*(4), 307-331.

Kukulska-Hulme, A., & Viberg, O. (2018). Mobile collaborative language learning: State of the art. *British Journal of Educational Technology, 49*(2), 207-218.

Liberati, A., Altman, D. G., Tetzlaff, J., et al. (2009). The PRISMA statement for reporting systematic reviews and meta-analyses of studies that evaluate health care interventions: Explanation and elaboration. *PLoS Medicine, 6*(7).

Rickinson, M. (2004). *A review of research on outdoor learning*: Field Studies Council.

Rikala, J. (2015). Designing a mobile learning framework for a formal educational context. *Jyväskylä studies in computing*(220).

Sharples, M., Taylor, J., & Vavoula, G. (2007). A Theory of Learning for the Mobile Age. In R. Andrews & C. A. Haythornthwaite (Eds.), *The SAGE handbook of e-learning research*. Thousand Oaks, Calif.: SAGE Publications.

Suárez, Á., Specht, M., Prinsen, F., et al. (2018). A review of the types of mobile activities in mobile inquiry-based learning. *Computers & Education, 118*, 38-55.

Tan, E., Rusman, E., Firssova, O., et al. (2018). *Mobile Inquiry-based Learning: Relationship among levels of inquiry, learners' autonomy and environmental interaction*. Paper presented at the World Conference on Mobile and Contextual Learning 2018. Retrieved from https://www.learntechlib.org/p/184919

Wingkvist, A., & Ericsson, M. (2011). A Survey of Research Methods and Purposes in Mobile Learning. *International Journal of Mobile and Blended Learning (IJMBL), 3*(1), 1-17.

EXPLORATION OF VIDEO E-LEARNING CONTENT WITH SMARTPHONES

Stefan Räbiger, Tuğberk Dalkılıç, Alperen Doğan, Buket Karakaş, Berk Türetken and Yücel Saygın
Faculty of Engineering and Natural Sciences, Sabancı University, Istanbul, Turkey

ABSTRACT

Nowadays computer users prefer to learn or complement their studies with video materials. While there are many video e-learning resources available on the internet, video sharing platforms such as YouTube which provide these resources, do not structure the presented material in the prerequisite order. Furthermore, they do not track the background of the users when recommending the next material to watch. Our aim is to overcome this limitation of the existing video on demand systems. In this paper we describe the architecture of the e-learning system that we are developing which allows users to search and watch video materials organized with respect to their background and presented in prerequisite order. One of the key features of our e-learning platform is to enable users to explore the video content with mobile devices. We propose a new visual metaphor based on lists for mobile devices which reflect the prerequisite graph structure, utilizing the limited screen size more effectively.

KEYWORDS

e-Learning, Visualization, Mobile Learning, Visual Metaphor

1. INTRODUCTION

Nowadays students spend more time with mobile devices. Due to the high popularity of mobile devices, particularly smartphones, it is natural to provide learners access to learning material through mobile devices. We also observed that students tend to use video sharing platforms such as YouTube to find course supplementary materials or to learn new topics. However, video sharing systems are not designed to present video content with a coherent structure following the prerequisite order, also their personalization mechanisms are not tailored to take the academic background of their users into account when presenting material. For example, one can search on YouTube for a specific topic and a list of videos is returned in response to a query. As expected, the returned list of videos is good in terms of relevance with a lot of alternative materials. However, the user background is not considered by such systems except for the general interests identified by the previously watched videos. Also, the order of the recommendations by the video sharing platforms, suggesting what to watch next, does not follow the prerequisite order among the video content. In order to overcome these limitations of video sharing platforms, we are developing a new platform and a mobile app which acts as an interface to present the video learning materials in an order reflecting the prerequisite relationships. Our platform has a server component which contains a pool of concepts that we call micro-topics. The micro-topics form the learning space and they are organized in a graph structure with prerequisite relationships acting as a knowledge base. The mobile app component on the other hand acts as an interface for the user to search for video e-learning content for specific topics. The requested e-learning content is enriched with the prerequisites which are prefetched from the video sharing platform as a subgraph and displayed to the user on the mobile device. We have integrated the popular video sharing platform YouTube into our system; however, other video sharing platforms can also be used as the source for the video learning material.

In this paper, we describe the architecture of the general system and the mobile interface which maps the subgraph of video learning content with prerequisite information on a limited screen size. Screen size imposes constraints on the user interface since the screens of mobile devices are smaller than those of desktop computers and laptops. In our context this implies that the information conveyed by the graph must also be conveyed on mobile devices. To accomplish this goal, we propose a new visual metaphor based on lists which presents to learners only a small subset of the graph at a time, while still allowing learners to traverse the entire graph. This innovative list representation of the subgraph conveys the same information as the graph, utilizing the limited screen size more effectively, and allows easy interaction with the user to enable navigation in the graph through the mobile device. Initial user studies show that the mobile interface has the potential of being adopted by the students who would like to use existing resources in video sharing platforms.

2. RELATED WORK

The most relevant areas for our paper are existing e-learning platforms and how graphs are visualized on mobile devices. While the former one motivates the need for building a new e-learning platform, the latter one outlines why it is necessary to consider alternative metaphors for visualizing graphs on mobile devices with small screens.

2.1 E-learning Platforms

To the best of our knowledge, there are no other platforms which enable users to view existing learning material from popular video sharing platforms in an organized way. Existing systems are based on traditional courses and they transform these courses into massive online open courses where learners enroll in an online environment. Learners either register to those systems and enroll in the courses or they prefer to search general video sharing platforms for instructional videos. Our aim in this work is to enable learners to utilize the existing resources freely but in an organized way.

Popular e-learning platforms include Coursera, edX, and Udemy amongst others. However, these platforms adopt a "one size fits all" approach in the sense that a course is taught by displaying the same learning materials in the same order to different learners. This lack of content adaptation to individual learners is problematic since individuals learn differently. Splitting learning materials into smaller blocks (e.g. into micro-topics) is one method to adapt content to learners. This idea is commonly used in microlearning (Buchem & Hamelmann, 2010), which was proposed as a new learning paradigm to teach new concepts to employees, who are only available for a limited amount of time at work. It is based on the idea of spaced learning, i.e. instead of teaching knowledge in one session, it is stretched over a longer period by providing materials that cover smaller topics, which has been shown to improve long-term memorization results of employees in randomized clinical trials (Cecilio-Fernandes et al., 2018). Various microlearning platforms exist, such as Auzmor (https://auzmor.com/learn/), Axonify (https://axonify.com/microlearning-platform/), Oplift (https://ocasta.com/oplift/products/engage), and Qstream (https://qstream.com), but they all neglect at least one of the following aspects: content adaptation, multiple learning materials per micro-topic, gamification, or content is provided by experts only. Furthermore, memorization does not imply a broader understanding of key concepts. And employees are the target audience of microlearning platforms which is reflected in their business models as accessing the content costs money. In contrast, our e-learning platform will combine the adaptive features of microlearning platforms and the openness of e-learning platforms. In addition, our platform will implement more methods to make the content adapt to learners such as giving them the freedom to choose the order in which they want to learn the different materials as long as this order does not violate any prerequisite relationships.

2.2 Graph Visualizations on Mobile Devices

Different methods exist to display graphs on mobile devices such as smartphones and tablets. On smartphones, which are our primary concern since learners tend to own smartphones instead of tablets, the authors of (Kister et al., 2017) combined the screens of multiple devices to display different regions of a graph. In our context this is not applicable since we cannot expect learners to possess multiple devices. In (Du et al., 2017), the authors evaluated different graph visualizations on single smartphones and noted that having to explore large parts of a graph increases the difficulty of completing the task as an extensive amount of panning and zooming interactions must be performed by users. This is also the reason why we propose an alternative visual metaphor based on lists. For tablets, on the other hand, it is feasible to provide visualizations that utilize a graph metaphor, e.g. (Drochtert & Geiger, 2015).

3. ARCHITECTURE AND IMPLEMENTATION

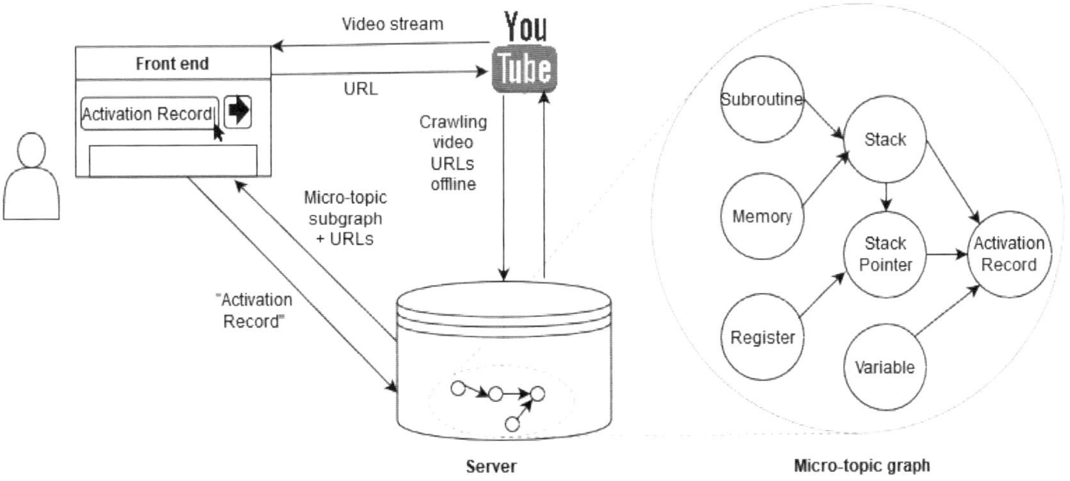

Figure 1. Architecture of the e-learning platform

E-learning platforms have become very popular over the last years since they allow individuals to acquire new skills. However, they all suffer from the lack of content adaptation because they address a topic by splitting it up into smaller blocks, to which we refer as micro-topics. Learners must then complete the list of learning materials in a fixed order, where the same set of learning materials is used for all learners. This does not consider the fact that individuals learn differently. In order to overcome this limitation, we are in the process of building an adaptive e-learning platform which provides different learning materials for micro-topics and which adjusts the order in which micro-topics will be covered. The order will only be constrained by prerequisites, i.e. if a micro-topic is required for understanding a more advanced one, it must be completed first. Since there could be arbitrarily many of such prerequisite constraints, we visualize them in a graph, to which we refer as micro-topic graph.

The client server architecture of our e-learning platform is depicted in Figure 1. The micro-topic graph, which serves as the key data structure, is stored on the server and is constructed offline. Initially, a set of micro-topics is automatically extracted from text documents such as books or slides according to (Wang et al., 2016). To understand in which order these micro-topics are to be processed by learners, we infer pairwise prerequisite relationships between the topics. This imposes a partial order on the micro-topic graph since directed edges are inserted between micro-topics if one is a prerequisite for another one. To compute these relationships, for the respective micro-topics, we crawled the subtitles of relevant YouTube videos and their corresponding URLs which are then stored in the database on the server side. The subtitles correspond to the text documents used for determining the pairwise prerequisites (Talukdar & Cohen, 2012) using a method similar to (Liang et al., 2016). We refer to this graph as the micro-topic graph, in which learners may proceed with any micro-topic for which they satisfy all prerequisites. Given a micro-topic m, all the incoming edges of m are coming from direct prerequisites.

All remaining operations are performed in real time. Whenever a learner wants to learn about a micro-topic, she submits a query through the front end, which is a mobile device in this case, and the query is then sent to the server for processing. The server queries the micro-topic graph to return the subgraph which contains the requested micro-topic and its prerequisites as a list of JSON objects, where each micro-topic contains additional metadata like URLs to multiple YouTube videos and which of those should be recommended to be watched first by the learner, i.e. their rankings.

Periodically, the server updates the URLs that should be recommended for a learner to initially watch based on her previous interactions with the e-learning platform. For example, as shown in Figure 1 in the sample micro-topic graph on the right-hand side, suppose a learner wants to learn about the micro-topic "Stack" and enters this subject in the search bar in the front end. Then the server will return the micro-topics "Subroutine", "Memory" and "Stack", where the former two are the only prerequisites for the latter. The query result will also include URLs to relevant YouTube videos for all three micro-topics, which were already stored on the server. For each of the micro-topics, multiple URLs for different learning materials are included which caters to the fact that individuals learn differently and might prefer different explanations. When the learner clicks on one of the returned micro-topics in the front end, the mobile device will open the respective URL to stream the video given that a learner satisfies all prerequisites to play this video. Part of the metadata for each micro-topic is also which of the video URLs should be displayed to a learner, but she is free to choose a different one.

YouTube as a video platform could be replaced by any other platform, but since it is the most popular one, we have decided to integrate it into our platform. We use YouTube videos instead of Wikipedia for inferring prerequisite relationships between micro-topics since some of them could be explained from different perspectives. Therefore, merging multiple related YouTube videos instead of using one Wikipedia entry yielded more robust results in our preliminary experiments. Another reason in favor of YouTube is that for some micro-concepts there are no entries in Wikipedia, while there are entries on YouTube.

3.1 Exploration of Micro-Topics on Mobile Devices using a List Metaphor

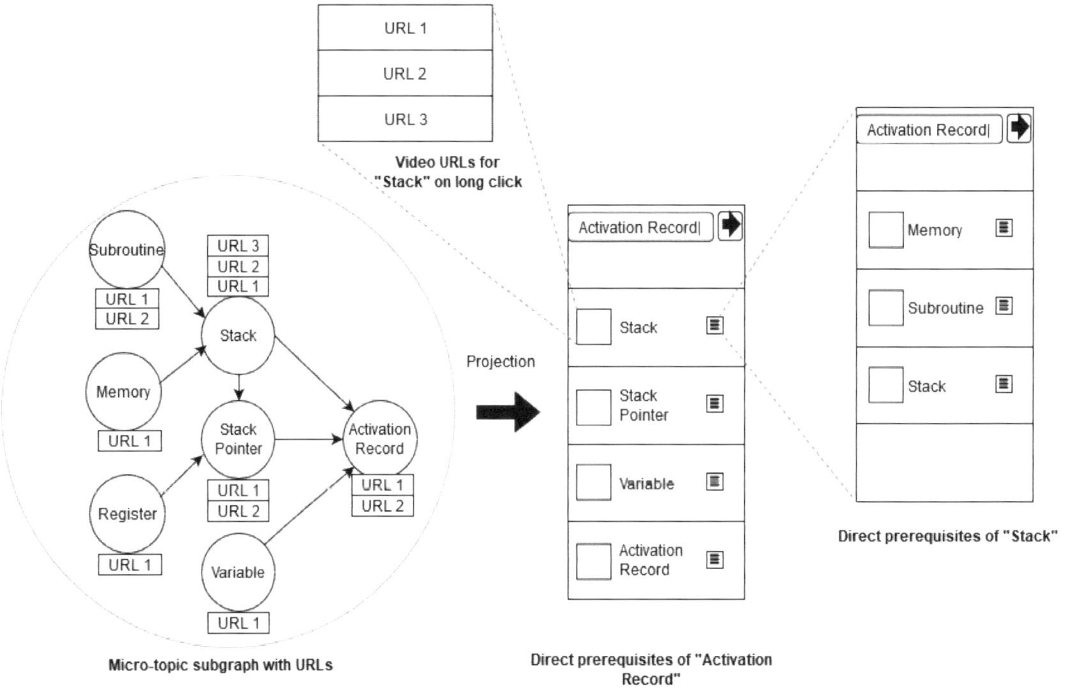

Figure 2. Mapping the micro-topic subgraph to the list metaphor on mobile devices

Given that the respective micro-topic subgraph, shown in Figure 2, was returned by the server for the topic "Activation Record" to the front end, the visualization of this subgraph depends on the type of front end. While computers have enough space to display an interactive graph, mobile devices, especially smartphones, lack it. Hence, a graph is not the best visual metaphor on mobile devices as it wastes space. Instead, we propose to use a metaphor based on lists which utilizes the limited space more effectively and avoids panning and zooming operations. This means that the micro-topic subgraph must be projected to this list according to Figure 2, where the desired micro-topic ("Activation record" in this case) is displayed at the bottom of the list and all direct prerequisites ("Stack", "Stack Pointer", "Variable") precede it in an arbitrary order as there cannot be a prerequisite relationship among direct prerequisites. This resembles a YouTube playlist where items at the top of the list will be played first. Long clicking on any micro-topic displays a list of available videos for that topic from which the learner may choose.

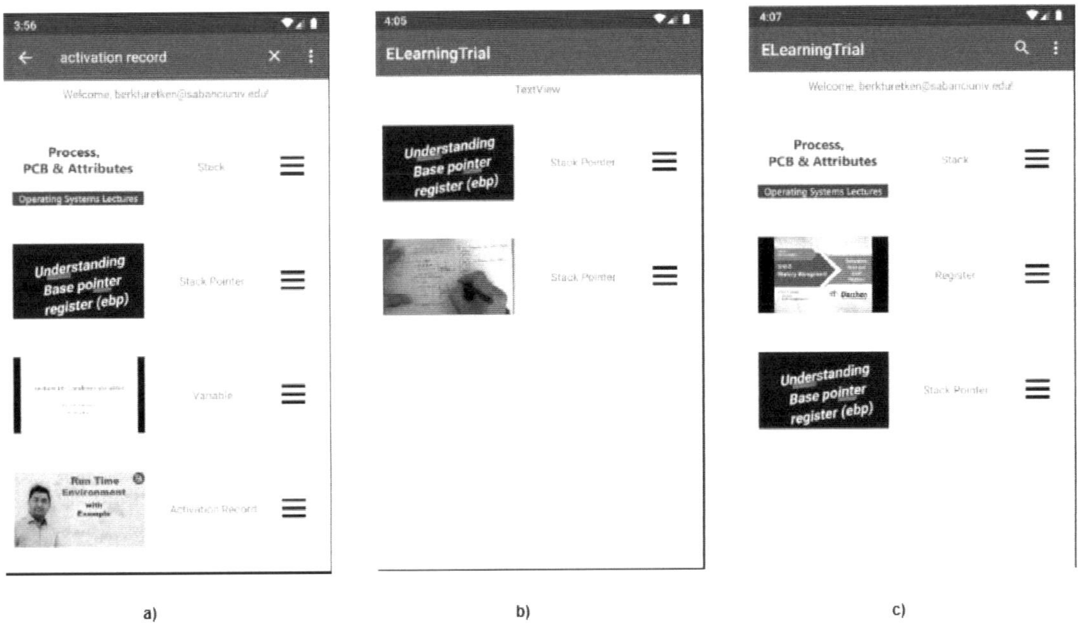

Figure 3. Screenshots of the prototype. In a) the learner searched for "Activation Record". After long clicking on the video thumbnail of "Stack Pointer", a list of available videos for this micro-topic is displayed. In c) the learner clicked in a) on the hamburger icon of "Stack Pointer" to see its direct prerequisites, which are "Stack" and "Register"

We implemented a prototype of our metaphor in Android as shown in Figure 3. Initially, a learner wants to learn about the micro-topic "Activation Record" from a course on operating systems (which makes it easier to follow our running example) and enters it in the search bar at the top. As a result of this query, the micro-topic subgraph with video URLs from Figure 2 is returned by the server and is visualized in Figure 3a using our proposed list metaphor. For each micro-topic it displays a thumbnail of the most suitable video, that was determined by the server from the video URLs which were collected offline for that topic. The micro-topic the learner wants to complete, "Activation Record" is shown at the bottom of the list and the direct prerequisites "Stack", "Stack Pointer", and "Variable" must be finished prior to that which is indicated by them being ranked higher in the playlist. When long clicking on the video thumbnail of "Stack Pointer", the list with available videos for that topic pops up allowing the learner to select a different video. This is illustrated in Figure 3b. When clicking on the hamburger icon at the right hand side of "Stack Pointer", its direct prerequisites are displayed as a playlist with "Stack Pointer" being the last entry indicating that both its prerequisites, "Stack" and "Register", must be completed first. From this view they may return to Figure 3a at any time.

4. PRELIMINARY EVALUATION RESULTS

We performed a preliminary user study which assessed a) how well our proposed metaphor for mobile devices conveys the same information as a graph, b) how intuitive learners find the interactions, and c) any suggestions for improvement. Overall, 9 students from our university participated in this study and before starting the experiment, they were all given a short introduction about the available functionalities in the user interface and how they can be accessed. The information that was provided in that step will be explained by a tutorial in the actual mobile app but is not implemented yet. To address a), we asked them afterwards to perform three tasks that cover the different aspects of graphs, namely in which order a learner should watch micro-topics given the playlist (a.1), navigating the micro-topics through direct prerequisites (a.2), and changing learning materials (a.3). The original survey questions for the three tasks are listed below:

a.1) Indicate in which order (from 1 to n, where n is watched at the end) you would watch the videos when you searched for "Activation Record".

a.2) Which videos should you watch before watching the video about "Stack"? Please write the names down.

a.3) How many videos exist for the topic "Stack"? Please write down the number.

For b), participants rated our visual metaphor on a Likert scale from 1-5, where higher scores correspond to more positive feedback. After a) and b) participants suggested improvements for the user interface in the survey. Successful solutions to a.1), a.2), and a.3) were awarded with a score of 1 if participants used Any successful solution of a task from a) was awarded with a score of 1, while a correct solution using a different way to achieve the correct result was counted as 0.5; otherwise it was counted as 0. With 9 participants, the scores for each of the three tasks in a) could be at most 9. The results are depicted in Table 1.

Table 1. Success rate of the 9 volunteers to solve the different tasks using the list metaphor

Task number	Task goal	Score
a.1	Determine micro-topic order	9/9
a.2	Micro-topic navigation	9/9
a.3	Changing learning materials	4.5/9

While participants were successful in navigating through the micro-topics and in understanding in which order to watch the videos, they encountered problems when having to select a different video for micro-topic. Roughly half of the participants failed to complete this task correctly.

For b), our metaphor was generally perceived positively which is reflected in an average score of 3.9 (out of 5). In terms of c), the lower score for changing learning materials was reflected in the comments we received. Participants shared different ideas on how to make this task more intuitive. The most frequently suggested improvement was replacing long click events by swipe actions. Other suggestions involved adding more visual feedback for completed videos with progress bars like in YouTube.

5. CONCLUSION

In this paper we have introduced a novel visual metaphor based on lists which allows learners to explore different micro-topics and their prerequisites. By focusing on the visualization of direct prerequisites of a micro-topic only, the small screen size is utilized effectively, and learners will not get overwhelmed with information even if there are hundreds of thousands of micro-topics in the graph. Moreover, no panning or zooming interactions are required to navigate through the micro-topics as opposed to a graph. However, as we stated before, our e-learning platform is still under development and the same holds for our mobile application. The metaphor needs to be refined to convey additional information such as which micro-topics learners had already completed in the past, which micro-topics are not accessible yet due to unsatisfied prerequisites, etc. The feedback from the preliminary study will also be incorporated. Once this is implemented, we will conduct a more extensive user study to evaluate if the positive feedback from our preliminary study for our proposed visual metaphor is confirmed.

ACKNOWLEDGEMENT

The authors would like to thank all participants of the preliminary user study for their constructive feedback to improve the user interface.

REFERENCES

Buchem, I., & Hamelmann, H. (2010). Microlearning: a strategy for ongoing professional development. *eLearning Papers*, *21*(7), 1-15.

Cecilio-Fernandes, D., Cnossen, F., Jaarsma, D. A., & Tio, R. A. (2018). Avoiding surgical skill decay: a systematic review on the spacing of training sessions. *Journal of surgical education*, *75*(2), 471-480.

Drochtert, D., & Geiger, C. (2015). Collaborative magic lens graph exploration. In *SIGGRAPH Asia 2015 Mobile Graphics and Interactive Applications* (pp. 1-3).

Du, F., Cao, N., Lin, Y. R., Xu, P., & Tong, H. (2017, May). isphere: Focus+ context sphere visualization for interactive large graph exploration. In *Proceedings of the 2017 CHI Conference on Human Factors in Computing Systems* (pp. 2916-2927).

Kister, U., Klamka, K., Tominski, C., & Dachselt, R. (2017, June). GraSp: Combining Spatially-aware Mobile Devices and a Display Wall for Graph Visualization and Interaction. In *Computer Graphics Forum* (Vol. 36, No. 3, pp. 503-514).

Liang, C., Wu, Z., Huang, W., & Giles, C. L. (2015, September). Measuring prerequisite relations among concepts. In *Proceedings of the 2015 conference on empirical methods in natural language processing* (pp. 1668-1674).

Talukdar, P. P., & Cohen, W. W. (2012, June). Crowdsourced comprehension: predicting prerequisite structure in wikipedia. In *Proceedings of the Seventh Workshop on Building Educational Applications Using NLP* (pp. 307-315). Association for Computational Linguistics.

Wang, S., Ororbia, A., Wu, Z., Williams, K., Liang, C., Pursel, B., & Giles, C. L. (2016, October). Using prerequisites to extract concept maps from textbooks. In *Proceedings of the 25th acm international on conference on information and knowledge management* (pp. 317-326)

VIRTUAL REALITY AND ITS IMPACT ON LEARNING SUCCESS

Thomas Keller, Elke Brucker-Kley and Christian Wyder
ZHAW School of Management and Law
Winterthur, Switzerland

ABSTRACT

For elementary schools, the question arises as to whether the use of Virtual Reality (VR) can lead to better learning success for pupils. A field experiment was chosen as the methodology for investigating this question. A total of 82 pupils from four first and third secondary school classes were available for this field experiment. They were randomly assigned to a group per class, taking gender into account. Both groups attended a pre-test one week before the respective course unit in order to identify any previous knowledge. One week after the course unit, both groups again completed the post-test. The tests were designed in such a way that equal weight was attached to each learning objective of the learning units. During the evaluation, the individual learning success, i.e. the difference between the post-test and the pre-test, was calculated for each pupil. No significant differences in learning success between the traditional and the VR based units could be found. However, the VR learning unit showed a positive effect on the learning success and was widely accepted by the pupils. From an methodological point of view it is very difficult to design equivalent learning units and to compare them fairly.

KEYWORDS

Field Experiment, Learning Success, Virtual Reality

1. INTRODUCTION

Keller et al (2018) designed a learning unit on micro plastics supported by virtual reality technology. In this work he describes in detail the procedure from the motivation, the choice of a suitable learning content, the design and creation of the learning unit as well as an evaluation round with experts and students of a secondary school class in Switzerland. As essential artifacts, a procedure model for the creation of VR learning units as well as the VR learning unit on micro plastics emerged from his work. (Glauser & Keller, 2018)

This paper is a continuation of Keller's work. However, the continuation does not concentrate on a revision of the VR course unit, but on a detailed evaluation of the influence of this VR course unit on the learning success of secondary school students. This continuation is useful because in (Keller et al., 2018) only an evaluation with a small sample have been made. In addition, the focus of his evaluation was on the learning unit itself and no systematic survey was carried out on the influence on learning success. (Glauser & Keller, 2018)

This paper presents the results of a field experiment that was conducted to measure the influence on learning success. Learning success is defined as the increase in knowledge which has taken place and which is influenced by the learning unit and which is measured against the learning objectives defined in the learning unit. This means that a learning success has taken place when at least one or more learning objectives can be achieved by pupils who were not achieved before the unit.

2. SCIENTIFIC CONTRIBUTION

As already mentioned above, Glauser (2018) did not measure the influence of the VR learning unit on learning success. Furthermore, he points out that further, longer-term studies must be carried out in this regard (Glauser & Keller, 2018). This also implies that such studies must be carried out with larger samples. Glauser also recommends that educational institutions carry out further pilot experiments in order to develop a further understanding of the application (Glauser & Keller, 2018).

This work can make a concrete contribution here by carrying out the VR course unit micro plastics with a larger sample and comparing it with a control group. Another reason for the investigation with the VR course unit micro plastics in the Swiss secondary school is that the general positive results of digital game-based course units must not be generalized. Hays (2005) explicitly formulates this warning on the grounds that the existing studies give only a fragmented picture in this respect. Hew and Cheung (2010) point out that the results are strongly dependent on sociocultural factors. The implementation of the VR course unit micro plastics in the concrete context of the Swiss secondary level therefore makes sense and leads to new knowledge.

Looking at the literature on the subject of learning in immersive virtual worlds, there is a few other research in this field. If one looks at the literature, it is noticeable that all studies attest to the positive effects of the implementation of VR learning units. All (2016) writes that the positive effects are proven and Mikropulos and Natsis (2011) claim in their conclusion that by the end of the decade (2020) VR technology is mature and suitable for educational applications. Merchant et al. (2014) also come to this conclusion by writing that VR learning units are quoted as "quite effective". At the same time pointing out the various limitations of the studies in the subsequent sentence. However, most of these studies don't deal with immersive VR.

This picture can be seen in all three meta-studies mentioned. The main limitations addressed relate to the type of learning unit, the conduct of the study, the documentation of the procedure and the results. In concrete terms, the following frequently criticized points on the effectiveness of game-based virtual learning units could be identified in the literature:

- Some studies do not contain an exact description of the implementation of the learning unit. It is unclear which variables were used and the statistical information is not adequate (Merchant et al., 2014). Generally insufficient documentation of the procedure and implementation of the course unit. (Clark et al., 2016)
- The feedback within the learning unit as well as between the instructor and the trial participant is insufficiently documented and does not allow any conclusions to be drawn about the influence on learning success. (Merchant et al., 2014)
- No control group was implemented for the study or the control group was not exposed to an alternative learning unit (All et al., 2016). The learning unit of the control group was not equivalent in content. (Hays, 2005)
- The methodological approach to the creation of groups and the allocation of learning units was judged insufficient. (All et al., 2016)
- The scientifically correct methodological approach of the study was criticized. For example, there was no pre-test or the post-test was performed too early after the course unit. (All et al., 2016)
- There are no statements in the studies as to how far sustainable learning success has taken place. (Mikropoulos & Natsis, 2011)
- Missing description of how the relevant influences on learning success between the different groups are kept constant. (All et al., 2016)

At this point the comment of Mikropoulos and Natsis (2011) should be mentioned that there are only a few studies that explicitly document a positive relationship with immersive VR systems. This in turn confirms the above statement that the type of implementation is not always described in detail. Thus, the metastudy by All et. al. (2016) does not reveal whether the VR learning units are fully immersive.

The metastudy by Merchant et al. (2014) is clearer in this regard. It focuses primarily on desktop-based virtual reality systems, i.e. it does not contain any studies with fully immersive systems. Of the 53 studies carried out by Mikropoulos and Natsis (2011), only just 16 concerned fully immersive systems.

Considering the above points of criticism as well as the small number of existing studies explicitly dealing with fully immersive VR systems, a relevant contribution to science can be made within the scope of this work. However, the points of criticism suggest that rigor in methodology must also be given. The rigorousness according to Hevner (2004) describes a methodically correct and scientifically adequate procedure. In order to guarantee rigor, attention must be paid to documenting the procedure and the results as specifically as possible, taking the above points of criticism into account.

Under these circumstances, it is understandable that in many studies no concrete statements on the effectiveness of VR learning units can be found. If such statements are available, they are often very vaguely formulated. A good example of this can be found in the work entitled "the effectiveness of instructional games". Hays writes here in his conclusion: "...research has shown that some games can provide effective learning..." (Hays, 2005). As already quoted above, Merchant (2014) writes "quite effective". Mikropoulos (2011) writes in this regard that it is difficult to make statements about the extent to which a learning defect has taken place and the knowledge can later be retrieved and demands that further studies be carried out. Hew and Cheung (2010) go even further here and call for studies that query the learning effect and the available knowledge up to one year after the course unit. Although this time span cannot be covered within this work, a statement on the effectiveness of the VR course unit can be made by implementing a control group and a suitable test setting.

The last point to be mentioned here is the topic of the VR course unit, where a contribution to science can be made. In addition to the small number of immersive VR units, Mikropoulos (2011) also mentions that of the 53 studies only 13 do not come from the fields of mathematics or science. From the later explanations it becomes clear that science refers to topics such as the structure of atoms and the reaction between two atoms. Here, the VR course unit micro plastics (Keller et al., 2019), which takes place in a lake, a laboratory and a barbecue area, certainly offers an exciting change, not only for science, but also for the pupils.

Based on the above mentioned points this work can make a relevant contribution to science. This is especially the case if the rigor of the procedure is guaranteed and the documentation is specific enough.

3. RESEARCH OBJECTIVE

For this research work learning with the help of games in virtual worlds is thus defined as a specific subject area. A literature research on this topic shows that this kind of learning leads to promising results. Thus, in his meta-study on the empirical investigation of studies on EVEs, Mikropoulos (2011) concludes that both teachers and pupils are very positive about virtual learning units in education. This statement coincides with the evaluation of the VR course unit micro plastics by Keller (2018), who concludes that all pupils perceived the VR course unit as motivating.

As already mentioned, the subject literature contains many positive statements regarding the influence of VR learning units on learning success. However, many points of criticism can also be identified with regard to the studies conducted. For example, All et al. (2016) point out that in many studies too little methodological precision was applied or that the documentation of the implementation of the learning unit is insufficient. Furthermore, Hays (2005) writes in his study on the effectiveness of game-based learning that the results of such studies cannot be generalized under any circumstances.

For the teachers of the Swiss elementary school, the concrete question is whether VR learning units can lead to positive learning success in their concrete learning environment.

Hypothesis 1: The VR course unit micro plastics (Keller et al., 2019) has a positive influence on the learning success of the pupils.

Hypothesis 2: The VR learning unit micro plastics has a bigger influence on the learning success of the pupils compared to a traditional learning unit based on "paper and pencil"[1].

Learning success is defined as the increase in knowledge which has taken place and which is influenced by the learning unit and which is measured against the learning objectives defined in the learning unit. This means that a learning success has taken place when at least one or more learning objectives can be achieved by pupils who were not achieved before the unit.

4. THE FIELD EXPERIMENT

The field experiment consists of a pre-test, a post-test, a course unit with VR and a course unit based on a conventional teaching method. Both units have the same learning objectives.

Four classes from a secondary school were available for this field experiment. All four classes are level A, with two in the first year and two in the third (TABLE I). The focus in selecting the classes was on the

[1] https://drive.switch.ch/index.php/s/qCXBcYIJi5ZIMol

same level. Although the influence of age must be taken into account in the evaluation, the teachers do not consider the age difference to be very influential. In this case, this has to do with the subject matter, as the VR course unit could also be carried out with sixth grade pupils.

Table 1. List of classes and number of pupils

Class	total	females	males
1c	18	12	6
1d	20	9	11
3b	22	15	7
3c	22	14	8

Two types of group allocation are suggested in the literature, random allocation of pupils or classes. The preferred option would be the allocation of pupils, recognizing that this is difficult to achieve in the school and class context. The allocation according to classes is easier, but has several disadvantages. For example, an entire class could be shaped by the teaching style of its class teachers. If an experiment is conducted across several schools, other differences such as city, country, poorer quarter or richer quarter could also have an influence. (All et al., 2016)

Since all test persons for this experiment are from the same school and locality, this factor can be weighted slightly lower. Nevertheless, the attempt was made to take a middle course. For the allocation of the groups, each class was randomly assigned to a group separately for pupils. For example, approximately half of each class absolved the VR course unit and the other half the classical course unit. Technically, this was solved by allocating a random number (according to normal distribution) per pupil. These numbers were then divided into medians and assigned to each half of a group.

In the end, 39 pupils were assigned to the VR course unit and 43 to the classical course unit. The gender distribution is graphically shown in Figure 1 below. On the left the absolute values are shown, on the right the relative values.

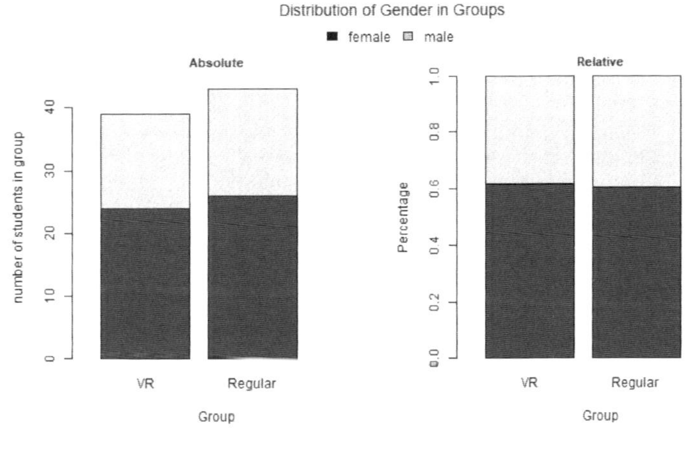

Figure 1. Distribution of gender in groups

5. RESULTS

To evaluate the dataset[2], the results of the pre- and post-tests as well as the information from the individual schedules were converted into tables and imported into the statistical software R-Studio. The application of a statistical test in itself does not yet give any indication as to whether there are significant differences between two samples. For this purpose, a significance level must be determined by the researcher. The significance level can also be described as the probability of error (Kraft & Landes, 1996). Based on the selected significance level, the P value of the test is considered. If the P value is below the selected significance level,

[2] The complet set of raw data including the R-scripts are available at https://drive.switch.ch/index.php/s/ffrZ6Qbj3BTJm6z

significant differences can be assumed. This means that the differences between the samples examined do not seem to be random (Bortz & Schuster, 2010). For statistical analyses, the 95% significance level is often chosen. Stigler argues that this is probably due to Fisher because it can reliably show effect sizes even with small sample sizes. (Stigler, 2008)

For this reason, the 95% significance level is chosen in each of the following studies in this paper.

5.1 Overview

A simple overview of the results of the pre- and post-test is shown in Figure 2. The graph allows a comparison of the results per class and contains the data for both groups.

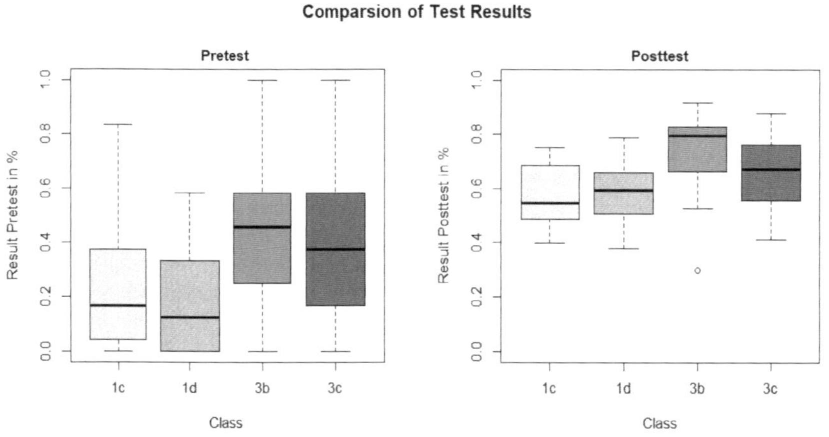

Figure 2. Comparison of test results

If one compares the results of the pre-test and the post-test in Figure 2, it becomes apparent that the results of the pre-test scatter much more strongly than those of the post-test. Furthermore, the medians are visibly lower in the pre-test than in the post-test. It is exciting that both third classes scatter between 0 % and 100 % in the pre-test. This means that some don't know anything, others are already very well informed about the topic of micro plastics. Since nobody reached 100% in the post-test, this also leads to negative learning successes. This is probably due to the fact that the pre-test and the post-test differ with regard to the questions.

It is also noticeable that the two first and the two third grades each behave similarly. Class 3b seems to have the most knowledge after the post-test. However, this is easy to understand, as the class has the highest median in the pre-test. Otherwise, it can probably be assumed that most pupils have achieved a learning success. The small variance of the post test suggests that both learning units were effective.

5.2 Hypothesis 1

The first hypothesis claims that the VR learning unit has a positive influence on learning success. This means that the students have more knowledge about the topic after the VR unit and can retrieve it. The hypothesis can be accepted if the results of the pre- and post-test differ significantly.

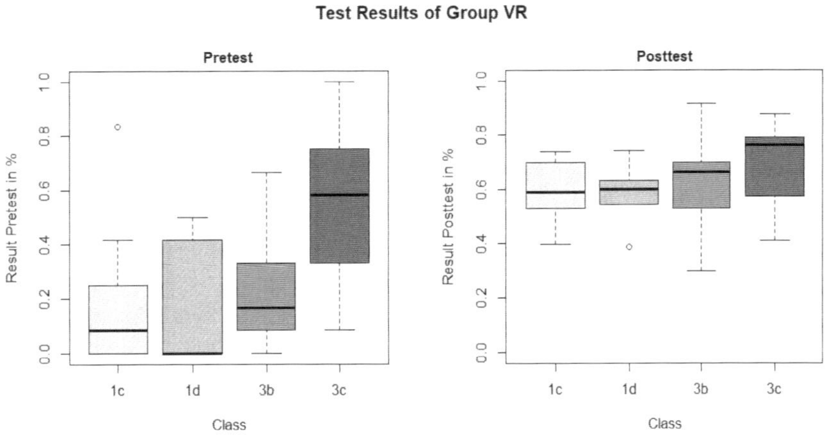

Figure 3. Test result of group VR

The mean value of the results of the post-test is twice as high as in the pre-test. The median of the post-test is even three times higher with half the variance. To compare the results of the pre-test and post-test of the VR learning unit group, these are visualized for each class in Figure 3.

The result of the Wilcox test shows that the results of the pre- and post-test of the VR unit group differ significantly. This can be read from the P-value, which is lower than the defined significance level of 0.05. Hypothesis 1 can thus be accepted, i.e. the application of a VR learning unit leads to a positive learning success.

5.3 Hypothesis 2

The second hypothesis says that a VR learning unit leads to a bigger learning success than a classical learning unit. For the hypothesis to be accepted, the learning success of the VR group must be significantly greater than the learning success of the classical learning unit group. Figure 4 below shows the achieved learning successes (referred to as "gain" in graphics) per group and class as box plots.

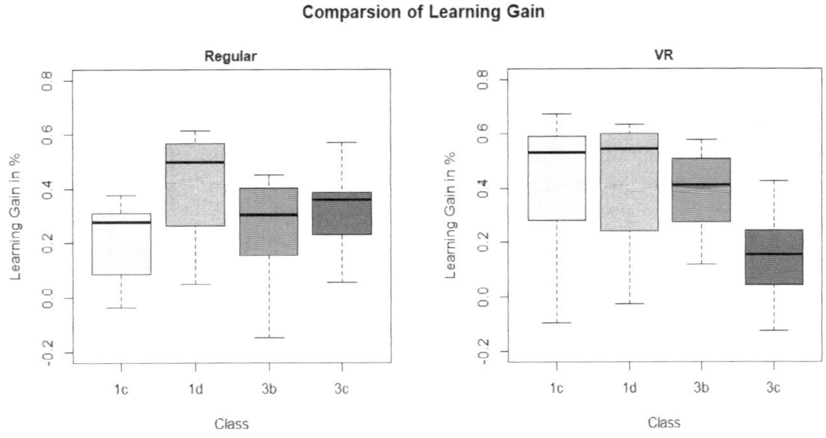

Figure 4. Comparison of learning gain

Looking at Figure 4, it is not clear whether the VR or the traditional learning unit leads to better results. If one compares the learning outcomes between the classes and groups, one sees that the VR unit leads to slightly higher average results, but that the dispersion is also somewhat larger. An exception is class 3c, which has on average completed less well in the VR unit. A possible explanation for the worse result of class 3c is that class 3c already achieved the highest average in the pre-test and therefore already had a lot of previous knowledge.

The average of the VR unit's learning success across all classes is just 2% higher than that of the regular unit. Conversely, the median is slightly lower. For a concrete statement, however, a statistical test is required. First, the distribution of the learning success must be determined. For this purpose, the data of the learning success is compared with a theoretical normal distribution. A normal distribution can be assumed if the data points shown in Figure 4 follow as closely as possible the straight line in the middle of the grey confidence interval.

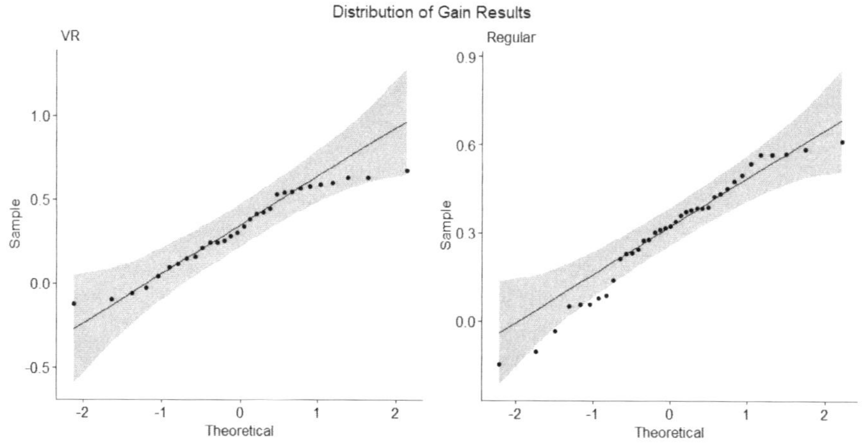

Figure 5. Distribution of gain results

According to Figure 5, a normal distribution can be assumed. However, there are also some data points that are quite far away from the straight line. Another possibility to examine a data set for normal distribution is the Shapiro test. (Bortz & Schuster, 2010)

The calculation of the P values by the Shapiro test confirms that a normal distribution can be assumed for the learning success of the VR group as well as for the classical learning unit. This means that the T-test is suitable for testing differences between groups. The Levene test can be used to test the equal distribution of variances (Universität Zürich, 2018). The P-value of the Levene test is greater than 0.05, which means that there are no significant differences between the variances of the learning success of the two groups (Dormann, 2013). Thus, all criteria for the application of the T-test are given.

The calculation of the P-value of the T-test shows a value greater than 0.05, i.e. there are no significant differences between the learning success of the VR group and the traditional learning unit. It follows that the second hypothesis, that the VR unit is better than the classical unit, cannot be inferred.

5.4 Further Perceptions

During the implementation of the VR learning unit it was noticed that there are large differences in how intuitively students move in the VR learning environment. This leads to the question of whether this has an influence on the result, i.e. the learning success. The variable "intuitive behavior" does not exist, but it may be assumed that students who play lots of video games can move more intuitively in a virtual environment. This variable was also collected during the execution and the result of the evaluation is shown in Figure 6.

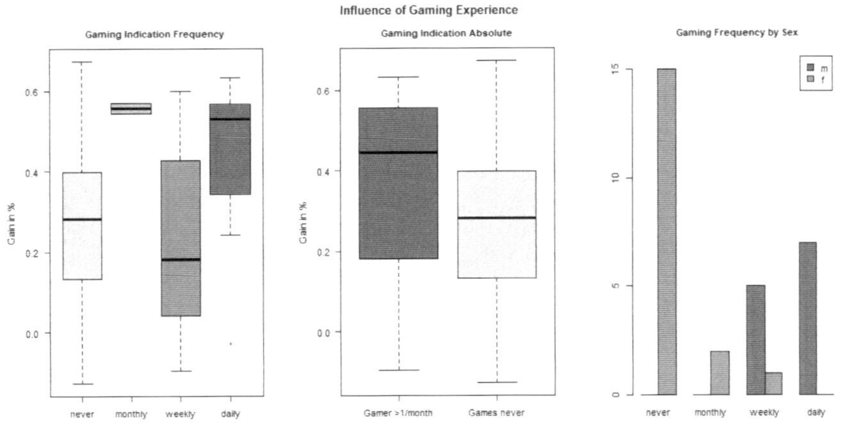

Figure 6. Influence of gaming experience

The middle box plot in Figure 6 shows a similar variance for both groups, but the median is about 15% higher for groups that play video games at least once a month or more. However, a significant influence of experience with video games cannot be confirmed.

Figure 6 also shows that all pupils have indicated that they play video games at least once a week. For female students, the opposite is true, with the majority saying that they never play video games. This leads to the next question as to whether gender has any influence on the result of the VR group. Figure 7 below shows the learning success and the results of the pre- and post-tests per group.

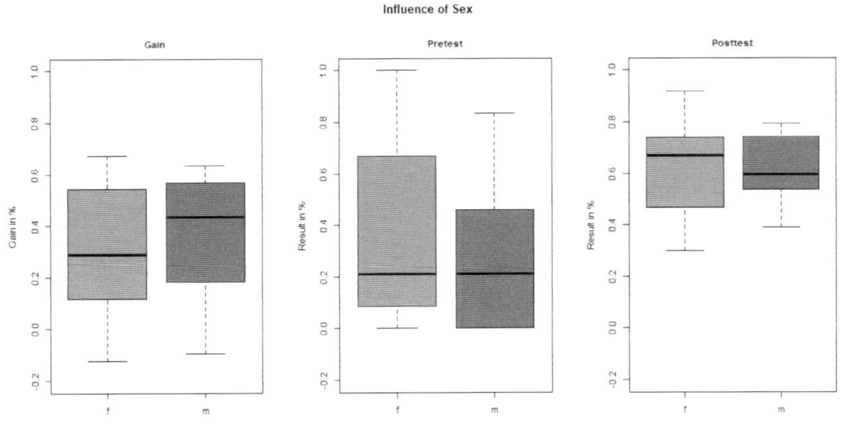

Figure 7. Influence of gender

The male pupils have a median which is about 15% higher than the one of female pupils. If one also considers the overall results of the pre- and post-tests, it can be seen that the male pupils were slightly worse than the female pupils. In addition, the variance of the male pupils is somewhat lower, which indicates that there are fewer male pupils with very poor learning outcomes than among the female pupils. However, the statistical test shows that gender does not lead to significant differences.

6. CONCLUSION

As a result of this work, it can be stated that the research question initially formulated can be confirmed. The implementation of the VR course unit micro plastics has led to a positive learning success. However, no evidence could be found for the assumption that the VR learning unit leads to bigger learning success than with a traditional teaching method in the context of this field experiment.

The VR unit seems to evoke very different feelings in the pupils. Most of them enjoy the technology and are curious. However, there are also some who either have great reservations beforehand or experience a feeling of fear or discomfort during the learning unit. While this confirms that a VR session has the potential to convey very personal content, it also means that these feelings may have a negative impact on the learning success of individual pupils. This also includes the observed factor of intuition, i.e. how easy or difficult it was for individual pupils to navigate within the VR unit. These factors were not collected in the context of this field experiment, which is why further statements in this respect are not possible. A further confirmation for this influence could be the larger scatter of the VR learning unit compared to the traditional learning unit. This would explain that there are greater differences in learning success within the VR group.

In this field experiment the learning unit had to be abandoned by four female students. Hence, the learning content could not be conveyed and furthermore the pupils left the learning unit with negative feelings. It is assumed that this effect will diminish with the future pervasion of the technology. A VR learning unit would become something "normal" and "known".

REFERENCES

All, A., Nuñez Castellar, E. P., & Van Looy, J. (2016). Assessing the effectiveness of digital game-based learning: Best practices. *Computers & Education*, *92–93*, 90–103. https://doi.org/10.1016/j.compedu.2015.10.007

Bortz, J., & Schuster, C. (2010). *Statistik für Human- und Sozialwissenschaftler* (7., vollständig überarbeitete und erweiterte Auflage). Springer.

Clark, D. B., Tanner-Smith, E. E., & Killingsworth, S. S. (2016). Digital Games, Design, and Learning: A Systematic Review and Meta-Analysis. *Review of Educational Research*, *86*(1), 79–122. https://doi.org/10.3102/0034654315582065

Dormann, C. F. (2013). Das Lineare Modell: T-Test und ANOVA in R. In C. F. Dormann, *Parametrische Statistik* (pp. 209–223). Springer Berlin Heidelberg. https://doi.org/10.1007/978-3-642-34786-3_12

Glauser, P., & Keller, T. (2018). *Einsatz von Virtual Reality an der Schweizer Volksschule*. https://drive.switch.ch/index.php/s/jnO5w4a8aozjlKt

Hays, R. T. (2005). *The Effectiveness of Instructional Games: A Literature Review and Discussion:* Defense Technical Information Center. https://doi.org/10.21236/ADA441935

Hevner, A. R., March, S. T., Park, J., & Ram, S. (2004). *Design Science in Information Systems Research*. 32.

Hew, K. F., & Cheung, W. S. (2010). Use of three-dimensional (3-D) immersive virtual worlds in K-12 and higher education settings: A review of the research: Use of 3-D in K-12 and higher education. *British Journal of Educational Technology*, *41*(1), 33–55. https://doi.org/10.1111/j.1467-8535.2008.00900.x

Keller, T., Glauser, P., & Brucker-Kley, E. (2018). *Virtual Reality at secondary schools: First resulsts*. 53–60. http://www.iadisportal.org/digital-library/virtual-reality-at-secondary-school-%C2%96-first-results

Keller, T., Hebeisen, A., Glauser, P., & Turnheer, L. (2019). Neue Lehrkonzepte an Schulen – Einsatz von Virtual Reality. *Neue Lehrkonzepte*. https://neuelehrkonzepte.ch/

Kraft, M., & Landes, T. R. (1996). *Statistische Methoden: Eine Einführung für das Grundstudium in den Wirtschafts- und Sozialwissenschaften* (3., durchges. und aktualisierte Aufl). Physica-Verl.

Merchant, Z., Goetz, E. T., Cifuentes, L., Keeney-Kennicutt, W., & Davis, T. J. (2014). Effectiveness of virtual reality-based instruction on students' learning outcomes in K-12 and higher education: A meta-analysis. *Computers & Education*, *70*, 29–40. https://doi.org/10.1016/j.compedu.2013.07.033

Mikropoulos, T. A., & Natsis, A. (2011). Educational virtual environments: A ten-year review of empirical research (1999–2009). *Computers & Education*, *56*(3), 769–780. https://doi.org/10.1016/j.compedu.2010.10.020

Stigler, S. (2008). Fisher and the 5% Level. *CHANCE*, *21*(4), 12–12. https://doi.org/10.1080/09332480.2008.10722926

Universität Zürich. (2018, August 13). *Methodenberatung Universität Zürich—Wilcoxon Test*. Wilcoxon-Test. https://www.methodenberatung.uzh.ch/de/datenanalyse_spss/unterschiede/zentral/wilkoxon.html

M-LEARNING FOR THE RECRUITMENT AND SELECTION OF HUMAN TALENT. CASE: INTERVIEW

Paula Asto Machaca and Luis Alfaro Casas
Universidad Nacional de San Agustín de Arequipa, Arequipa, Perú

ABSTRACT

The job interview within the recruitment and selection process is a very important activity for both the candidate and the company that requires staff. In order to improve the preparation of the job applicant, many artificial intelligence techniques together with emerging technologies could be used. This paper presents a mobile learning application with two modules for learning and practice using textual case-based reasoning to improve system performance. The document describes the architecture of the design of the system, implementation, and evaluation of mobile learning system. The results of the evaluation show that the mobile learning system is technically feasible, didactic effective and user-friendly.

KEYWORDS

Mobile Learning, Case-Based Reasoning, Textual Case-Based Reasoning, Competency-Based Interview

1. INTRODUCTION

The labor demand of the software industry has grown exponentially. It is being reflected in the increase in jobs in online platforms. Analyzing seventeen online job portals according to the five common jobs a systems engineer could do (Analyst, Project Manager, Administrator, Architect, Developer), we select 3 positions with more job offers for study purposes, Developer, Analyst, and Administrator. In Peru, systems engineering and computer science careers are considered one of the highest-paid and many young graduates belong to this family. This reality encourages the employability of more people in the IT field and the great importance of the job interview is reflected, which is the technique most used in the recruitment and selection of human talent in companies (Blasco 2004). The job interview is usually the most relevant filter in the incorporation of adequate personnel for the positions that are required in a given organization. On the other hand, mobile learning associated with artificial intelligence techniques is among the most popular technologies, whose importance has been driven by the growth of mobile device use, emerging as a useful tool for education in general. However, far too little attention has been paid to the use of these emerging technologies in the recruitment and selection process of human talent.

The aim of this paper is to discuss an m-learning system to prepares the applicant with fundamental notions of the interview and provides a selection of cases using artificial intelligence techniques and emerging technology tools to facilitate this task. The remaining part of the paper is organized as follows. A brief review of the state-of-the-art in this paper is explained in Section 2. Details of the methodology are described in Section 3. Results with the experiment settings are introduced in Section 4. Conclusions and some future works are presented in Section 5.

2. STATE-OF-THE-ART

Employers seek certain skills and aptitudes in their workers to play the desired role in a company, but in many cases, desired expectation is not found (Najwa Azmi et al. 2018), this problem contributes to the unemployment problem of recent engineering graduates, people who do not have enough experience required by the industry or in many cases do not have the confidence to be able to face a job interview due to lack of knowledge or nervousness, among others factors. The use of interviews in the recruitment and selection of personnel (RSP) (Blackman 2009) is very common because they help in the classification of suitable persons. This practice is not only based on knowledge but on attitudes and/or psychological states. The job interview is an extensive and complex field, for that reason, this study works based on competency-based interviews (McClelland 1973).

The preparation of the candidate towards an interview can be carried out through many technological tools, one of them that shows the greatest potential is mobile learning. This is because mobile phone screens are more versatile than laptops, desktop computers, and televisions. As they are almost always at hand, it means that they are seen in more times and places than other screens (Bridger 2017), have characteristics at any time, any place and can be applied in any profession or activity (Ally 2007) (Traxler 2007) (Alrasheedi and Capretz 2015) (Yorganci 2017) (Hamdani 2013).

There here are several mobile educational platforms, both in the initiative and in developed applications for M-learning (Gnana et al. 2017), but few investigations have been found that focus on supporting this part of the research. Smart teaching can make use of case-based reasoning (CBR) because the best way to learn is through identity learning, where the student identifies with the case presented (Facer et al. 2004), and thanks to the CBR the system can select similar cases from a new entry. CBR is based on the use of historical data as cases or experiences to predict a solution to the current problem, and consists of four phases: RECOVER the most similar cases, REUSE the information and knowledge in these cases to solve the problem, REVIEW the solution proposal and CONSERVE the solution to solve similar cases in the future (Abutair and Belghith 2017) (Aamodt and Plaza 1994). In the case of text handling, a CBR variant called case-based textual reasoning is used. In most of the works consulted on this topic (Elhalwany et al. 2014) (Gerhana et al. 2017) (Ahmed et al. 2008) (Weber et al. 2005) (Delany and Bridge 2006) describes a process for text preprocessing steps that includes filtering, tokenization, and derivation, with certain variants to increase effectiveness, this subprocess is included in the life cycle of the CBR life.

3. METHODOLOGY

3.1 System Features

Education teaching processes generally consist of theory and practice, but when both notions are connected, there are disputes, however, educational coherence depends on this relationship. Addressing the field of theoretical-practical relations from the didactic is complicated because the subject is ambiguous and elusive, the problem is to recognize the contribution that each one makes to the teaching action (Álvarez 2012). Didactics is a theoretical-practical science because it is essentially about what, how and when to teach, the didactic necessarily implies the practical, and the intervention of the practice demands the technological and artistic theory (technique). For this reason, the M-learning system consists of two modules that will help to better structure the topic and provide the information presented in a simple way.

Theory module Composed by the set of basic concepts of a job interview, distributed and organized to motivate the user's self-learning.

Practical module Includes a selection of cases formulated for a job interview by competencies, applying textual case-based reasoning for the evaluation of the answers entered by the user.

3.2 Architecture

The system is built with the Google UI toolkit called flutter that allows creating mobile applications compiled natively to Android and IOS from a single code base, using services offered by firebase such as database, authentication, and storage. The implementation of the system was done using the bloc pattern as a design architecture, which helps in the management of the state and in the access to the data from a central place of the project. The bloc pattern consists of blocs, a bloc is created for each function that is added, and since the flutter is based on the creation of widgets, it is possible to add or delete a widget with a block behind it, without having to worry about affect the code and system in general, it helps the project to be scalable and readable, separating the user interface from the logical part.

The architecture consists of two important parts. The first part is the mobile client which is mainly composed of the interface, models, repository, util, and blocs that connect the client to the server. The second part is the server which is based on firebase and google libraries that make the backend or system services possible to develop (see Figure 1).

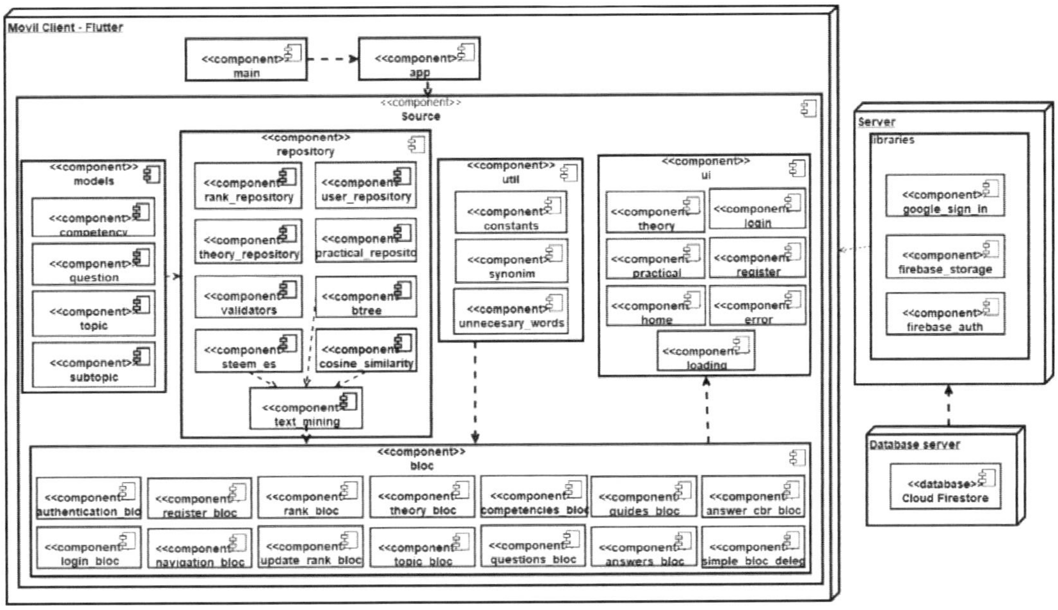

Figure 1. Component diagram representing the architecture of the M-learning system

3.3 Theory Module

In the theory module, the concepts of the interview are distributed by grouping them according to the bibliography consulted (see Table 1). The objective of this module is to motivate the user's self-learning. According to the research conducted by Bourgeois, the use of levels to obtain different ranges as the user learns more about a particular subject is a learning strategy used to motivate through rewards called rewards-based learning (Bourgeois et al. 2016).

Table 2. General interview concepts for the theory module grouped according to the bibliography consulted

Group	Group
Interview	Interview phases
Interview format	Types of interview
Competency-based Interview	Practical suggestions
Case study	

In the M-learning system, the user can see their progress on the application's home screen. The topics they have consulted will be easily viewed as complete once they have finished. The system is programmed in order to the user can pass levels and reach the rank of "Grand Master of Knowledge in Interviews", which would indicate that they reviewed, completed and/or learned all the topics proposed in the theory module. The ranges that are being considered are described in Table 2.

Table 2. Distribution of ranges by levels proposed for the theory module of the M-learning system

Rank	Level	Rank	Level	Rank	Level	Rank	Level
Beginner	Level 1	Silver	Level 3	Platinum	Level 5	Heroic	Level 7
Bronze	Level 2	Gold	Level 4	Diamond	Level 6	Grand Master	Level 8

3.4 Practical Module

A survey of software companies in the region of Arequipa in Peru was carried out, in order to measure the level of importance they consider for the set of competencies defined after an analysis of several documents that relate the skills that an engineer must have, in the three selected positions (Analyst, Administrator, and Developer). The levels of importance are measured according to the Likert scale from 1 to 5, where the lowest value represents nothing important and the highest value in very important, the five competencies best classified by position are selected by comparing the sums of the values obtained in the survey, which gives a total of eleven competitions (see Table 3).

Table 3. Selection of competencies more ranked by position by adding the levels of importance that the competencies for the positions that a systems engineer can play according to the companies surveyed in Arequipa, Peru

Competency	Developer	Analyst	System Administrator
Teamwork	47	**51**	**51**
Leadership	37	43	**53**
Permanent learning	**53**	46	46
Verbal communication	44	**49**	47
Decision making	40	45	**49**
Delegation	38	42	48
Analytical ability	**49**	**48**	45
Pressure tolerance	45	45	45
Planification and organization	47	**50**	48
Innovation/Creativity	**48**	47	46
Emotional control	41	46	44
Autonomy/Initiative	36	42	**49**
Responsibility	**52**	**49**	**52**
Change/Adaptability	43	45	42
Use of technology	**50**	44	45
Systemic thinking	46	43	44
Mastery of skill and techniques	43	45	44
Resource management	40	41	44
Understand the system by viewing the full picture	46	47	49
Proactive role with administration	35	42	46

A dataset of more than 350 questions, with useful notes which serve as a guide for the user to answer a question, and more than 400 responses of the competencies selected for the practical module were organized to form the initial database of cases. The implemented system shows the competencies in a grid list with the alternative of selecting the number of questions desired by the user to practice (See Figure 2). In practice, the questions are shown in sequence, a guide can be selected by the user in order to get help about how to solve the practice questions or, in other cases, the user can skip the question to continue with the next one.

To give the user freedom and comfort and ensuring user practice, there is no restriction that the question should be answered before moving on to the next one. Feedback from the response entered by the user is processed by text mining and textual-CBR; The purpose of this process is to show the user a response similar to the one entered in order to analyze, observe and make a constructive criticism that serves as a reference to face a job interview.

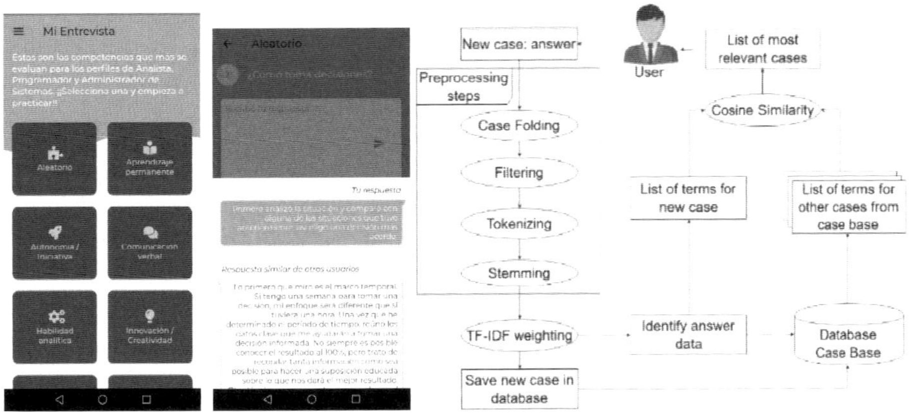

Figure 2. The practical module of the M-learning system. (left) Competencies selected are listed. (center) Feedback of the response entered by the user with a selected response using data mining and textual CBR is shown. (right) Workflow diagram of the process of recovering text data characteristics for textual cases

The application of artificial intelligence in the system is given in the practice module, where textual case-based reasoning is applied to the response entered by the user. The process workflow Textual-CBR (See Figure 2) is detailed below:

- New case: A response entered by the user to the case question presented in the M-learning system.
- Preprocessing steps:
  - Case Folding: Converts text to lowercase and removes strange characters. Only letters from a to z including ñ are considered since the native language of the test subjects in Spanish.
  - Filtering: Eliminates unnecessary words and replaces the remaining words compared with a B-tree of selected synonyms.
  - Tokenizing: Generate a list of single and significant words to be processed.
  - Stemming: Change the word into its base, eliminating prefixes, suffixes, and affixes (the Spanish Porter stemming algorithm is used).
- TF-IDF: TF-IDF is a method that works to weigh the term. TF (Frequency term) is the word weighting (term) that is based on the calculation of the number of words that appear in a document or case. IDF (Reverse Document Frequency) is the word weighting (term) that is based on the calculation of the number of words that appear in all documents or cases.
- Identify response data: Look for possible answers in the database for the case entered.
- Cosine Similarity: When the list of terms for the new case and other cases in the database are ready, a comparison is made with the cosine similarity to select a list of cases for the response. The cosine similarity is used to calculate the relevance approach to querying a document.
- List of most relevant cases: After comparing all cases with similarities, some cases are selected to show the user as feedback and suggestion, because in a job interview is difficult to talk about a correct response.

Tracking the preprocessing steps are useful for data mining of the response provided by the user and the responses found in the database. The answer is stored in the database for the recovery of a similar case with a later entry.

4. RESULTS

A questionnaire was used to evaluate the usability of the M-learning system and demonstrate whether it could be usable for the end-user, where tasks are evaluated with respect to the use of the theory and practice module, user satisfaction (Enriquez y Casas 2013) (López et al. 2017), as well as user confidence to face a job interview after using the system.

Statistical demographic data. - The evaluation was made to 28 people; the population is made up of students and graduates. 54% of the total are graduates, which indicates a greater predisposition to be evaluated in a job interview soon. According to gender data, the majority of the population surveyed belong to the male group (See Figure 4).

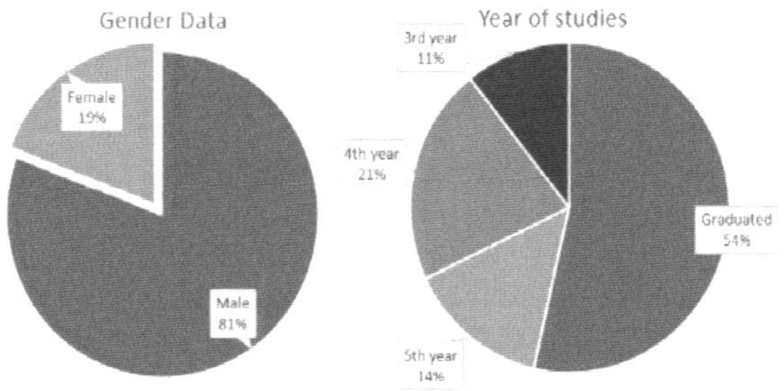

Figure 4. Statistical Demographic Data in the evaluation of the system m-learning

Task: Interact with the theory module. - The results obtained from the analysis of task 1 were positive, there is a high approval rate for this module (See Figure 5). It can be shown that most users have learned concepts about the job interview. We can affirm that the module fulfills its main objective. In the survey, a question was asked to verify the maximum range reached by each user to analyze the willingness to use the system, 21.4% of the population surveyed reached the beginner rank, indicating that they did not deepen or explore the module theory in greater detail, while more than 78% reached higher levels. The low inclination to the use of the theory module by a small part of the population could be due to several reasons, one of them could be that the system does not fit the individual's learning style. There are currently several investigations that indicate the importance to adjust the system to the learning style of an individual, this could be considered for future work.

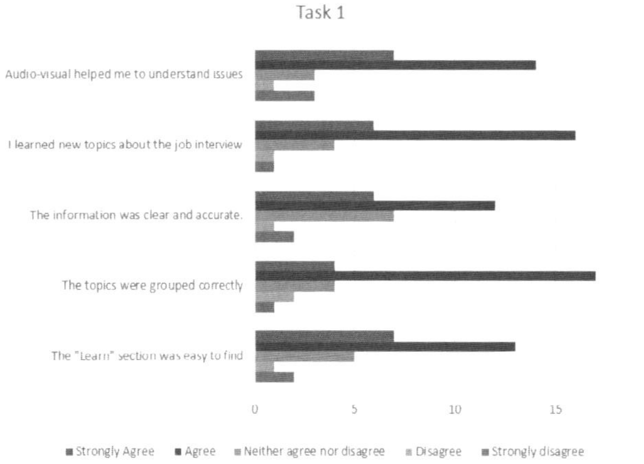

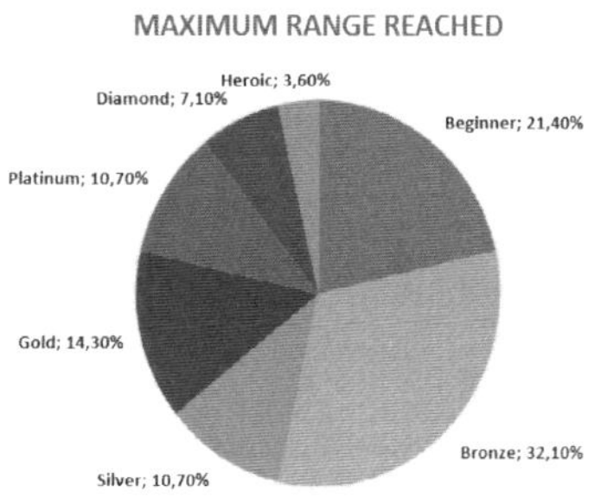

Figure 5. (first image) Evaluation of task 1: interact with the theory module (second image) Maximum range reached

Task 2: interact with the practical module. - The practical module had a high approval rate, that is, this module had more reception than the theory module. A large percentage of people evaluated indicated that the similar response offered by the system was very useful for analyzing and/or improving their response. We can affirm that the use of artificial intelligence techniques (CBR) in mobile learning can improve user learning and be a powerful tool.

The satisfaction of use. - The most prominent feature positively evaluated is the ease of use of the system, obtaining approval of 85.71%. Nevertheless, there is a small part of the survey population that is undecided towards the use of the application (See Figure 6).

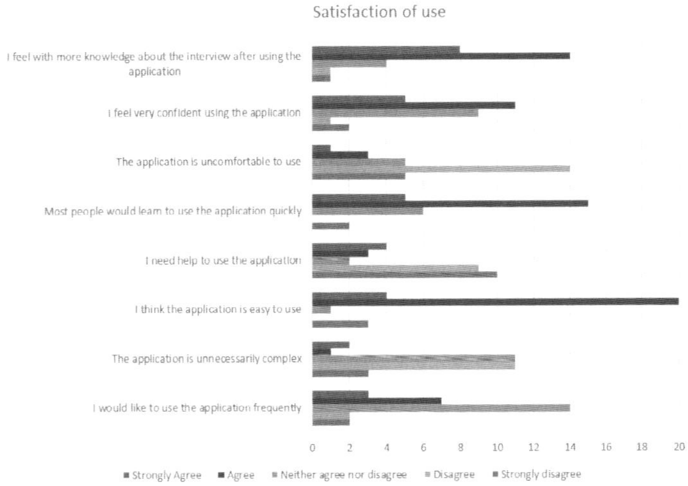

Figure 6. Evaluation of satisfaction of use

Positive effects. - One of the positive effects observed after the evaluation of the system was that a large part of the people evaluated felt that their level of confidence to face a job interview increased significantly after interacting with the system. This fact indicates that the M-learning system helps the applicant to gain more confidence to face a job interview. This will be a factor that plays an important role in a person's behavior when applying to a job. However, there are many other factors that could influence an interview, which could be taken into account for future work.

5. CONCLUSION AND FUTURE WORK

The increasing use of mobile devices and their characteristics at any time and any place make it an attractive tool for the user, developers, and researchers interested in M-learning. The application of textual reasoning based on cases helps to improve the processes of practice using cases that give a new approach to teaching.

It has been shown that the application of mobile technologies with artificial intelligence support allows the preparation of candidates for a better recruitment interview and selection of human talent, favoring learning, practice and providing them with more confidence.

Regarding future work, the following are proposed:

To future work, add the functionality of adapting the system to the user according to their learning styles through an evaluation test, in order to increase motivation and user interest in the system. Integrate emerging technologies as virtual, augmented or mixed reality for the practice process, simulating a real interview with a virtual realist interviewer. Integrate pedagogical agents that help guide the user to perform complex tasks and guide them through the platform.

ACKNOWLEDGMENT

We would like to thank UNSA-Investiga for the support provided for the development of this research work and the National University of San Agustin de Arequipa - UNSA for providing me with so many opportunities and enriching myself in knowledge.

REFERENCES

Aamodt, A. and Plaza, E., 1994. Case-Based Reasoning: Foundational Issues, Methodological Variations, and System Approaches. *AI Communications*, vol. 7, no. 1, pp. 39–59.
Abutair, H.Y.A. and Belghith, A., 2017. Using Case-Based Reasoning for Phishing Detection. *Procedia Computer Science*, vol. 109, pp. 281–288.
Agreda, S.A., 2016. Nuevos retos en el reclutamiento y selección de personal: perspectivas organizacionales y divergencias éticas. *Boletín Informativo CEI*, vol. 1.
Ahmed, M.U. et al, 2008. Case-based Reasoning for Diagnosis of Stress Using Enhanced Cosine and Fuzzy Similarity. *Transactions on Case-Based Reasoning for Multimedia Data*, vol. 1, pp. 128–144.
Al-Ismail, M. et al, 2017. Effects of personality traits and preferences on M-learning. *International Journal of Information Technology*, vol. 9, no. 1, pp. 77–86.
Ally, M., 2007. Guest Editorial - Mobile Learning. *The International Review of Research in Open and Distributed Learning*, vol. 8, no. 2.
Alrasheedi, M. and Capretz, L.F., 2015. An Empirical Study of Critical Success Factors of Mobile Learning Platform from the Perspective of Instructors. *Procedia - Social and Behavioral Sciences*, vol. 176, pp. 211–219.
Álvarez, C.Á., 2012. La relación teoría-práctica en los procesos de enseñanza-aprendizaje. *Educatio Siglo XXI*, vol. 30, no. 2, pp. 383–402.
Blackman, M., 2009. *The effective interview*. Oxford University Press.
Blasco, R.D., 2004. Reclutamiento, selección de personal y las tecnologías de la información y de la comunicación. *Revista de Psicología del Trabajo y de las Organizaciones*.
Bourgeois, A. et al, 2016. How motivation and reward learning modulate selective attention. *Progress in Brain Research*, vol. 229, pp. 325–342.
Bridger, D., 2017. *Neuro design: neuromarketing insights to boost engagement and profitability*. London: Kogan Page.
Delany, S.J. and Bridge, D., 2006. Textual case-based reasoning for spam filtering: a comparison of feature-based and feature-free approaches. *Artificial Intelligence Review*, vol. 26, nos. 1–2, pp. 75–87.
Elhalwany, I. et al, 2014. Enhancements to knowledge discovery framework of SOPHIA textual case-based reasoning. *Egyptian Informatics Journal*, vol. 15, no. 3, pp. 211–220.
Enriquez, J.G. and Casas, S.I., 2013. Usabilidad en aplicaciones móviles. *Informe Científico Técnico UNPA*, vol. 5, no. 2, pp. 25–47.
Facer, K. et al, 2004. Savannah: mobile gaming and learning?: Mobile gaming and learning. *Journal of Computer Assisted Learning*, vol. 20, no. 6, pp. 399–409.
Gerhana, Y.A. et al, 2017. The implementation of K-nearest neighbor algorithm in case-based reasoning model for forming automatic answer identity and searching answer similarity of algorithm case. *2017 5th International Conference on Cyber and IT Service Management (CITSM)*, p. 1–5.
Gnana, A.A. et al, 2017. Mobile application for m-learning. *International Journal of Advanced Research in Computer Science*, vol. 8, no. 3, pp. 313–316.
Hamdani, D.S.A., 2013. Mobile Learning: A Good Practice. *Procedia - Social and Behavioral Sciences*, vol. 103, pp. 665–674.
Lopez, C.M.R. et al, 2017. Guía metodológica de pruebas especializada en control y calidad de aplicaciones móviles fundamentados en la norma ISO 9241-11 Ergonomic requirements for office work with visual display terminals (VDTS) 2016. *Memorias de Congresos UTP*, pp. 70–82.
Mcclelland, D.C., 1973. Testing for competence rather than for 'intelligence.' *American Psychologist*, vol. 28, no. 1, pp. 1–14.
Najwa Azmi, A. et al, 2018. Competencies of Engineering Graduates: What are the Employer's Expectations? *International Journal of Engineering & Technology*, vol. 7, no. 2.29, p. 519.
Traxler, J., 2007. Defining, Discussing and Evaluating Mobile Learning: The moving finger writes and having writ .... *The International Review of Research in Open and Distributed Learning*, vol. 8, no. 2.
Weber, R.O. et al, 2005. Textual case-based reasoning. *The Knowledge Engineering Review*, vol. 20, no. 3, pp. 255–260.
Yorganci, S., 2017. Investigating Students' Self-Efficacy and Attitudes towards the Use of Mobile Learning. *Journal of Education and Practice*, vol. 8, pp. 181–185.

SHORT PAPERS

MOBILE LEARNING IN HIGHER EDUCATION

Petra Bauer[1,3], Christine Kolb[3] and Jasmin Bastian[2,3]
[1]*Dr.*
[2]*Jun.-Prof. Dr.*
[3]*Department of Educational Studies, Johannes Gutenberg University Mainz, Germany*

ABSTRACT

Mobile technologies are an important part of our daily life and we carry them with us all the time. Mobile learning is already used in informal and non-formal learning but in the context of formal learning, it is not much used, yet. The constant availability of learning content and integration in digital networks inspire new methods and concepts in the field of learning and teaching. Furthermore, more emphasis on learners is required, to understand how they are already using mobile devices to support their learning and to encourage their active participation in mobile learning in formal settings. This paper presents some of the work of the ERASMUS+ funded MINE project which has brought together lecturers and learners from a range of European institutions to help develop competencies for active mobile learning in higher education.

KEYWORDS

Mobile Learning, Higher Education, International Project, Learning Scenarios

1. INTRODUCTION

The use of mobile learning in Higher Education should also increase the participation of the learner in the learning process. Within this project, a curriculum for university teachers was developed to prepare university teachers with the competencies they need to implement mobile learning in their teaching. However, students also need some preparation, because many of them are not used to or do not have the competencies required to use mobile learning. Therefore, a second curriculum for students was developed within this project. The aim was to produce open educational resources (OER) in this process, to be used for mobile learning, but there will also be practical examples of mobile learning, which can be easily adapted for different contexts and subjects. The strategic partnership also included an intensive program. This was held as part of the MINE Project, at which the emerging curricula were explored by university teachers and students to help them develop their own competencies in mobile learning. All relevant documents and results of this project are published under the creative commons license. This paper presents selected scenarios of mobile learning in the context of higher education.

2. MOBILE LEARNING

Mobile learning is defined by the use of different mobile devices such as smartphones, tablets, and notebooks and also by the use of free and open knowledge resources (Gikas 2013). Besides, the development of an open feedback culture and new forms of performance assessments are important components (Sung 2016). In the area of formal learning at university, there is a need for pedagogic scenarios to encourage educators to use these new technologies (Hochschulforum Digitalisierung 2015). Farley (2015) suggests that educators will need to move beyond didactic approaches still frequently found in higher education. Social constructivist approaches have been advocated, along with the development of communities of practice to support educators (Cochrane 2012).

Taking into account this context, the European teaching and research project "MINE - Mobile Learning in Higher Education" aims to increase the use of mobile technologies in higher education and contribute to the development of teaching and learning scenarios in this field.

3. TEACHING AND LEARNING ACTIVITIES

Teachers in higher education need to care not only about what they are teaching but also about how they are mediating the topics. The pedagogical scenarios were evolved in order to address the views of learners and teachers in creating a context where active learning can happen. As Traxler and Crompton (2015) point out, mobile devices present great challenges to education systems. In higher education, the use of technology to enhance teaching and learning is a topic increasingly spoken about but which still needs further implementation in practice. These scenarios are examples of practices that have already been developed by the participants in the MINE project and they intend to show that mobile learning is not just about mobile technologies but above all about pedagogy.

3.1 Mobile Learning Scenarios

From the perspective of higher education, a wide range of different learning scenarios can be used, starting from individual mobile learning units to virtual teaching. In our project work, the partners of the MINE Project developed and applied different mobile learning scenarios in their work with students at the universities. Examples for these scenarios are videos, weblogs, online survey tools, e-portfolios, collaborative learning tools and wikis.

3.1.1 Video

Videos are everywhere. We could say that they have been one of the dominant forms of media consumption in the last few decades. They are an integral part of our everyday life and we consume them through different kinds of media. Entertainment and learning are the main things we draw from them. Producing and distributing videos has become increasingly easy and popular. Since the digital revolution and the invention of the internet we are moving away from single made and expensive film production with big studios involved in private and individual video making. Sharing and producing has become so easy that in some cases video platforms like YouTube have replaced traditional television as we know it. A big part of those videos is not only for entertainment purposes but also for education. Millions of tutorials, "how-to", taped lessons have been uploaded and the number of informally learning students is rising accordingly. Therefore, using video in classes and seminars could be a great opportunity for both learners and teachers.

The benefit for teachers and students is that videos can be used as a creative and different way to present information. There are many ways and possibilities to integrate them into lectures. For example, watching them to start a discussion in class or using them in the context of a flipped classroom. Also, watching videos on a particular topic might be interesting for a deeper analysis to go beyond the surface and therefore provide deeper learning on a particular field of theory or research. In media education, the analysis of a children's educational programme can be analysed regarding learning theories that fit the targeted age group and give reasons to discuss whether this programme is suitable to learn something or if there are any alterations necessary. Videos could be provided in a Learning Management System (LMS) or on a video platform like YouTube or Vimeo. Students are able to watch videos at home, use them for preparation for a class or they can discuss it on an online platform, i.e. LMS. In this case, videos are easy to use and most of them are available for free.

Another possibility is for students to produce the video themselves. In this case, students can learn how to produce a video and they have to think about how to put special content in a video, how to tell a story and/or how to present particular content. In order to raise students' motivation, competitions could be established or joined, e.g. the European Educational Video Challenge[1] (EDIT). Every year, students are invited producing educational videos in form of a hackathon event with a 72-hour deadline and particular criteria, i.e. a certain topic or the use of particular words or items. In general, teachers can enable students to work collaboratively during video projects and the output created by the students can be graded by the teacher. Students learn how to receive and provide information and how to present information in a different format.

[1] http://www.editvideochallenge.org

3.1.2 Weblog

A blog is an easy-to-handle content management system. It is an informational website published on the World Wide Web, consisting of diary-style text entries, called posts. But it is also possible to publish pictures, audio and video files in blogs. Blogs can be the work of a single individual, a small group or a large number of authors. Usually, they cover a single subject or topic. The authors keep records, write down logs, notes or thoughts. The posts are typically displayed in reverse chronological order, so that the most recent post appears first, at the top of the web page. So, a blog is used for storing notes, providing access to information, thoughts or experiences, furthermore, the commentary function allows a kind of communication between readers and author.

They can be used in different learning scenarios. The three main types of application are information storage, reflection medium or discourse, and publication medium. Depending on the context of the application, blogs can support formal and informal learning situations. In formal learning scenarios, blogs can be used as a learning content management system. Here, students and teachers can collect and summarise the content. It could also be a possibility to support virtual seminars or lessons. In this case, literature or videos could be provided and collected on a blog. In informal learning scenarios, blogs are used as personal journals or public (learning) diaries, as a feedback medium or as a medium for the learning of knowledge in general. Private weblogs can provide access to people, establish communities, and encourage mutual exchange in communities. A blog tool which could be used in courses is *Wordpress*[2].

3.1.3 Online Survey Tools: Kahoot!, Socrative and Mentimeter

Although many online survey tools like *Kahoot!*[3], *Socrative*[4]and *Mentimeter*[5] are becoming increasingly popular in higher education, they are still not utilised as often. Kahoot is generally known for its gamification aspect because it provides a variety of quizzes for use in class. You can also add and create own quizzes. Socrative is a tool that is typically used to conduct polls during lessons. Consisting of one teacher and one student version (app and web version available) small polls can be conducted within a few minutes. Teachers instantly get live results, which are anonymous and can be exported or converted into various types of files while students get instant feedback. Mentimeter is similar to Socrative in many ways but it is specifically tailored towards use in presentations. When you want to present something via Powerpoint Mentimeter will integrate with your presentation and enable participants to take a survey at specific points in your presentation.

3.2 Mobile Collaboration

Within the MINE Project, different online and offline tools in mobile learning were experienced and shared. During an intensive program in Lisboa, a Wiki was constructed and a lecture course, the mobile learning online week, was created to cooperate with teachers and students. All guidance and experiences are resumed in the MINE handbook.

3.2.1 Wiki

MINE-Wiki[6] is an online knowledge network that can be managed and extended by MINE participants. The wiki provides a platform for those who are interested in learning the individual scenarios offered by MINE. On this page, you will also find information about the partners of the project and partner institutions. Above all, you will learn more about the team behind the project on MINE-Wiki. Other subcategories presented on this page are the mobile learning scenarios, under which, for example, the categories video, blog or collaborative learning are linked. Another point is the MINE curriculum: There you will find administrative information about the MINE project. In addition to that, you can find the exact course of the MINE week in Lisbon 2018 to get an impression of a past practical implementation of the project.

[2] https://de.wordpress.com/
[3] https://kahoot.it/
[4] https://www.socrative.com/
[5] https://www.mentimeter.com/
[6] http://wiki.mine-project.eu/Main_Page

3.2.2 Mobile Learning Week

Mobile Learning combines learning in an international group. The content refers to mobile learning in higher education. The participants will be shown, discuss and reflect on various scenarios on how to use mobile tools in higher education. Each evening from 7 pm - 9 pm will be a live online learning session, experts from all over Europe will show the participants interesting tools and solutions. There is the possibility to get in contact with other students and teachers. The users get to know other learning traditions and cultures. This makes them experts in state of the art educational technologies and didactic approaches.

The mobile learning week combines blended learning arrangements with online and offline learning experiences. The learning system links problem-oriented workshops with phases of self-directed learning set up on web-based training and communication via a learning management system in line with requirements (Kuhmann & Sauter 2008, p. 101). In these learning scenarios, analogue and digital learning content merge. The participants can use networking with other participants to arrange self-directed learning networks.

Blended Learning in the online week focuses on the virtual classroom that takes place daily and in which all participants take part. There they learn new learning contents through the tutors and come into direct contact with the experts of the week. After these online events, the participants return to their self-learning phase and work out learning tasks that have been put right for them. During this time they can get in contact with the other learners at any time. The focus of these blended learning scenarios during Mobile Learning Week is the intercultural exchange between learners. They can exchange their learning experiences online and find solutions to problems together. In 2020 the online week will take place from 20th April till the 25th of April.

3.2.3 MINE Handbook

Through the use of new learning methods in university teaching new opportunities and challenges arise. The MINE Handbook is a storybook by teachers and students sharing their experiences about using mobile learning in higher education. The goal of the MINE project was not to develop new applications but to test and evaluate existing solutions in a wide variety of learning scenarios. The M-learning handbook gives an overview of the project, mobile learning scenarios and summarises stories and opinions by teachers, colleagues, and students. It encourages the reader with some success stories to try out new things and thus tread new paths in the area of university teaching. Furthermore, it views different mobile learning scenarios by taking a closer look at benefits for teachers and learners, goals and expected outcomes, possible options for application technical parts and finally pedagogical added values. The pedagogical practice is important if the digital education revolution will be more than rhetoric and will offer students better learning opportunities. Using mobile tools proactively, it can facilitate self-regulated learning and learners are placed in their roles as active actors, the self-controlled their learning process, independently and competently determine the use of the technologies in the centre. The MINE Handbook will be provided online and in a printed version in the first quarter of 2020.

4. STRATEGIC PARTNERSHIP

The three-year MINE project was funded by Erasmus+ and realised within the framework of a strategic partnership between six European universities: University of Education Upper Austria, Linz, Austria; University of Aberdeen, UK; Universidade Aberta, Lisbon, Portugal; Tallinn University, Estonia; Rhodes University, Greece; Johannes Gutenberg University Mainz, Germany.

All relevant documents and results of this project are published under the creative commons license and available to be downloaded from the project website (http://www.mine-project.eu/).

REFERENCES

Cochrane, T., 2012. *Critical success factors for transforming pedagogy with mobile Web 2.0.* British Journal of Educational Technology, [online] https://doi.org/10.1111/j.1467-8535.2012.01384.x [28.10.2019].

Farley, H. et al., 2015. *How Do Students Use Their Mobile Devices to Support Learning?* A Case Study from an Australian Regional University. Journal of Interactive Media in Education. 2015 (1), p. Art. 14. http://doi.org/10.5334/jime.ar [28.10.2019].

Gikas, J. M.M., 2013. *Grant Mobile Computing Devices in Higher Education: Student Perspectives on Learning with Cellphones, Smartphones & Social Media.* [online] http://www.sciencedirect.com/science/article/pii/S10967516130 002 62. [27.02.2017].

Hochschulforum Digitalisierung, 2015. *Diskussionspapier. 20 Thesen zur Digitalisierung der Hochschulbildung*, [online] https://hochschulforumdigitalisierung.de/sites/default/files/dateien/HFD%20AP%20Nr%2014_Diskussionspapier.pdf [27.02.2016].

Kuhmann, M. Annette & Sauter, Werner, 2008. *Innovative Lernsysteme: Kompetenzentwicklung mit Blended Learning und Social Software*, Springer-Verlag Berlin, Heidelberg.

Sung, K. E., Chang, T. C. Liu, 2016. *The effects of integrating mobile devices with teaching and learning on students' learning performance*: A meta-analysis and research synthesis, Computers & Education, 94, 252-275.

Traxler, J. & Crompton, H., 2015. *Mobile Learning In The UK Today: Successes, Failures, Future,* GLOKALde April 2015, Vol. 1, No. 2.

USING MOBILE LEARNING AND RESEARCH BASED LEARNING TO ATTRACT STUDENTS INTO QUANTUM INFORMATION RESEARCH

Francisco Javier Delgado-Cepeda and Marco Benjamín Enríquez-Flores
Tecnologico de Monterrey, Engineering and Science School
Carretera a Lago de Guadalupe km. 3.5, Atizapán, Estado de Mexico, CP. 52926, Mexico

ABSTRACT

Research-Based Learning seeks a new valued perception of scientific research through its inclusion in educative spaces. Mobile Learning promotes the inclusion of different terrains of university education. Research is not an exception. This work presents an initiative to include undergraduate and graduate students in Quantum Information research assisted by a mobile site to learn and collaborate. We analyse the performance in terms of participants, impact factor and scientific collaborations based on analytics included in the site, tracking the participants in their different inclusion spaces.

KEYWORDS

Mobile Learning, Education for Research, Educational Innovation, Quantum Information, Higher Education

1. INTRODUCTION

Nowadays, education has become increasingly oriented to satisfy the immediate human resources necessities in the industry (Kromydas, 2017). Oriented mainly to develop concrete competencies to occupy workplaces in the industry (Corominas, Canals and Villar, 2010). Under this landscape, the former wider vision of university has been overshadowed to be oriented to the masses. On this role, the mobile learning revolution has been mainly exploited to reach different types of education, technical or university inclusive (Wade, 2014), with outstanding examples of deeper education experiences (Hosler, 2014). Nevertheless, it has been expressed also about the absence of educative spaces to develop innovation, original knowledge and research competencies (Healey, 2005), thus boosting initiatives to overcome such deficiencies - STEM education or education oriented to the future- (Prager and Omenn, 1980). Universities have recovered such spaces (West, 2000) modelling the contemporary University behaviour.

The aim of this work is to bring a reflexive assessment of mobile learning as a companion element in education for research, concretely in the Quantum information (QI) trend. We show their evolution becoming a useful and effective resource to attract engineering and science students on this still new technological area. The second section depicts the entire project and it concretes the research objectives. The third section presents the evolution in terms of the attraction of students. The fourth section states the main findings and the discussion. The last section states the conclusions and the future development for the education initiative.

2. RESEARCH-BASED LEARNING AND MOBILE LEARNING

Quantum Information area in the modern era and its education necessities are raising in a traditional educative scenario (EU, 2016). Just in the 21st century they are generating the majority of their non-conventional technological proposals. However, those areas have not been completely settled in the curricula for electronic, mechatronics, nanotechnology, chemistry or computer engineering among others.

The initiative from the Quantum Information Processing Group (QIPG) has been developed to show and to attract students into scientific and technical research (Delgado, 2018a). It includes participation in seminars, a yearly workshop in QI, a formal topic in Quantum computation for undergraduate students, research stays of students in the QIPG and formal work with graduate students (thesis and scientific papers). The entire initiative have been managed as Research-Based Learning (RBL) (Barnett, 1992). Despite the model has been sustained by a few years, it has become a basis for development of research human resources.

Mobile learning has been an important element in the attraction. We prepare the main development to extensively cover different areas of attraction, education and research with students through several levels: Tangle (Delgado, 2018b), including a series of learning modules as MOOC's and MOOR's. They are reconfigurable for several approaches, depth levels and profiles: scientific, engineering and computational. In addition, our university created five years ago, a yearly space of one week for innovation and research, Semana I (from the Spanish of Innovation week), where students enrol in one from lots of activities associated with research, entrepreneurship, design, etc. projects. There, QIPG has created a yearly Quantum Information Workshop for undergraduate students (Delgado, 2018a) with Tangle, showing its usefulness to improve knowledge and performance in the second week, a face-to-face section (Delgado, 2018b).

Is the use of mobile learning technologies useful to improve the impact on the research production in academic spaces oriented to research? We are integrating the whole outcomes with a scope of education based on research within a mobile learning basis, thus the current objectives for this report are:

1) To stratify the attraction of human resources in the entire project with the scientific production generated
2) To evaluate the impact of mobile learning in terms of time, human resources and scientific products

The research is based on outcomes of production and the analytics raised through four years development (Delgado, 2018a, 2018b). Despite, the current report will include entire sets covering not only the yearly workshop: seminars, the research stays (one-year participation in an own project having as a mandatory outcome the publication of a scientific paper) and the graduate thesis and their associated products.

3. FIGURES AND OUTCOMES OF QIPG INITIATIVE

We are interested in the analysis of students' inclusion in the research group covering the first objective. Identification becomes useful to track analysis patterns related to mobile learning and mobile collaboration strategies. We report first the conformation of layers and the relation with students participating in research. The information from other analytics included in Tangle let to understand the whole picture of interactions in a quantitative approach given by the time usage, the number of collaborations and the scientific products.

3.1 Stratification in the Involvement of Participants

Figure 1 depicts the human resources involved and developed with scientific products. Figure 1a shows the layers of the impact of those initiatives. Straight lines depict the inner and deeper involvement.

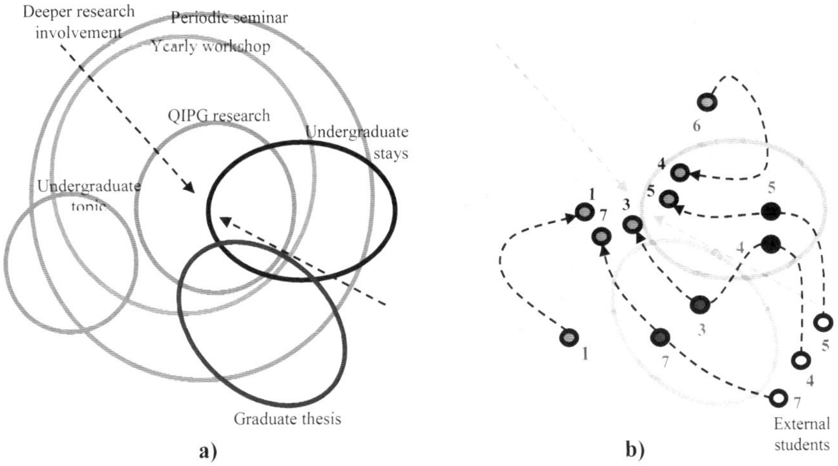

Figure 1. a) Group layers to arrive into the research projects, and b) paths of development into real research from initial students (red), intermediate students through the layers (blue) to finally concreting indexed research papers (black)

Several groups have had a deeper interaction with the researchers in QIPG collaborating in research. From the undergraduate level, the periodic seminar, and the QI workshop are the first contact point before the arrival of the research activities. Some students go through the undergraduate research stays first, others go to graduate studies in nanotech, computer science or engineering whose cloisters QIPG belongs. Some students are totally external ones arriving directly to graduate studies. Figure 1b depicts the paths followed until now together with the final research works being concreted after those relations (blue dots with the numbers in black). Identified tracks are shown with dashed curves going through different groups or activities. All tracks are departing from coloured points (marked with red numbers indicating the number of students) in agreement with their origin group crossing secondary dots through their transiting membership group.

The layers of the students' arrival have been constructed on the time as QIPG strategies generated through the politics and spaces settled and allowed by our institution. Despite, they have been generated good results in terms of students' attraction and scientific production.

3.2 Mobile Learning Impact in Learning and Scientific Production

The use of learning analytics (Greller and Drachsler, 2012) through Tangle tool permitted to follow the advance of learning for the different groups and students (Delgado, 2018b). Particularly, during the yearly workshop, the interaction has been intensively measured inside Tangle. Workshop has become the main attraction boosting deeper collaboration with QIPG. Demographics between 2017 and 2018 are in Table 1.

Table 1. Demographics of the three cohorts in the yearly workshop in Quantum information

GENDER	**Year**	**Female**				**Male**			
	2017	3				22			
	2018	6				22			
	2019	1				26			
PROGRAM	**Year**	**Engineering**		**Computer science**				**Physics**	
	2017	10		11				4	
	2018	10		13				5	
	2019	5		10				12	
SEMESTER	**Year**	**2nd**	**3rd**	**4th**	**5th**	**6th**	**7th**	**8th**	**9th**
	2017	4	7	4	2	2	2	2	2
	2018	4	9	5	0	0	0	5	0
	2019	2	7	7	4	0	1	0	4
ORIGIN	**Year**	**Local (Mexico City)**				**Non-local**			
	2017	14				11			
	2018	14				14			
	2019	14				13			

Despite, in the current analysis, we are not interested particularly in the local impact on the workshop. We analyse the relation of mobile interactions with the final research product years ago. Here, previous research has shown a meaningful impact of the blended learning scheme on the learning effectivity (Delgado, 2018b).

Analytics in Tangle have tracked the entire process by participant through the learning, collaboration and writing processes. We set the maximum number of interactions as 1 in a scale from 0 to 1 where 0 is any register of use. Mapping the whole path followed by each participant during the interaction, gathering each collaboration of any participant with another in each paper published and tracking if it was published in indexed or Conference journals, we set the Figure 2 including such relations and quantitative tracking. Each participant in Figure 1 was mapped in Figure 2 which is a data mining graph including statistical information. Three main points should boost the reading of graph: the three dots reporting the scientific articles published in indexed journals (red for a graduate project and yellow otherwise) or in conference proceedings (pink for undergraduate projects). Each publication is connected with dashed lines to blue dots (final stages of publication of each participant). Nodes of the graph are coloured as in Figure 1 for the several stages of each student. A solid red line implies a collaboration co-authoring certain paper (undergraduates collaborating with graduates). Colour scale reports the level of usage of Tangle in the scale depicted. White, grey and orange nodes are the beginning path of each student. Solid grey lines join the same type of such departing nodes as reference. ES and IS state external and internal students respectively, and US and GS for undergraduate and graduate studies respectively. Thus, eleven master and doctoral degrees thesis have generated scientific papers published in indexed journals and nine conference papers (SCOPUS). Use of Tangle appears in the upper range (0.5-1.0), Figure 2.

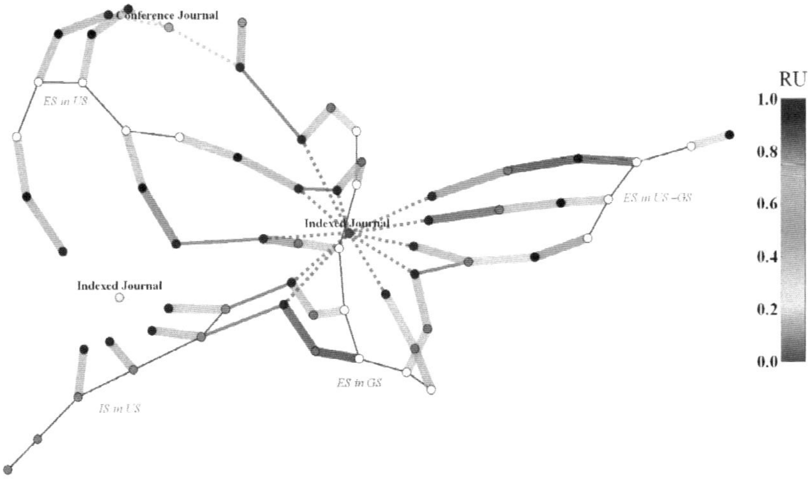

Figure 2. Interaction among students publishing in indexed (red: graduate, yellow: undergraduate) or conference (pink: undergraduate) journals with relative usage of Tangle (bar: 0-no usage, 1-max usage). Solid red lines set collaborations

To verify a possible relationship within groups, we split the group in three as function of the number of periods belonging to QIPG (1, 2, 3), averaging the Tangle level of use. Then, we run a one-factor ANOVA test with $p=0.05$ between groups related with the usage level of the tool. Results are in the Table 2. Test does not give sufficient statistical evidence about meaningful difference among groups ($p=0.062>0.05$) despite averages in Table 2 suggest it. Because populations with collaborations are small, there is no possibility to compare the level of use having or not having collaborations. In the future, this is an important aspect to evaluate as assessment of performance for Tangle as a boosting tool of such scientific collaborations.

Table 2. ANOVA for Tangle usage among students staying a different number of stages in QIPG

Groups	*Sample*	*Sum*	*Average*	*Variance*
1	6	2.110	0.352	0.018
2	12	5.575	0.465	0.008
3	3	1.560	0.520	0.013

Source	*S.S.*	*d.f.*	*M.S.*	F_{calc}	*p-value*	$F_{critical}$
Between	0.073	2	0.037	3.263	0.062	3.555
Within	0.202	18	0.011			
Total	0.275	20				

Finally, we compare the averages of impact factor and time of the development of scientific products. Figure 3 shows the 2017 (Green), 2018 (Cyan) and 2019 (Blue) productions. Size dot shows the average number of collaborations by article, ranging from 1.66 to 1.25. Reduction exhibits growing independence of undergraduates in research. The plot shows an increasing quality and a decreasing time of development.

4. CONCLUSIONS

Research has gained terrain in the aspirations of university students since several years ago (Banner and Bennet, 1999). While, society has been modifying their perception of the value of research as an activity bringing welfare. Quantum Information is still a relatively emerging field of research, but rapidly including a growing number of professionals collaborating to enrich the potential of such research area.

In the report, RBL has become an innovative action to attract students in the field settled in different spaces let by our university. The use of a Mobile strategy to teach, discuss and collaborate the research topics was central. Both initiatives have been harmonically combined showing a real increase in the number of students involved, the number of publications generated, and in the impact factor. Collaborations in quality and number should be evaluated in the next years when more students will be participating in our group. Those outcomes have begun to position QIPG in the world research landscape of Quantum Information.

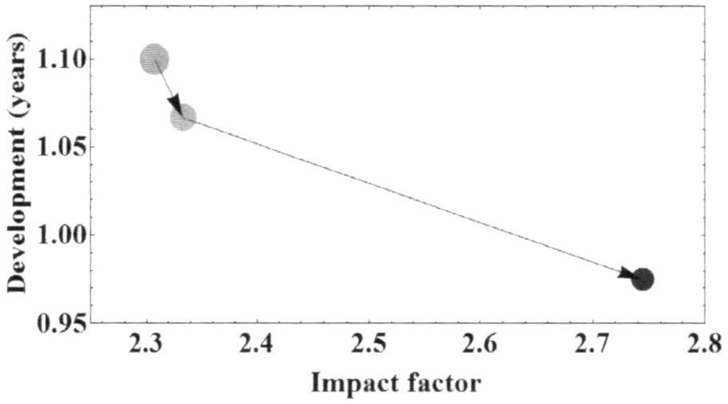

Figure 3. Average time of development versus average impact factor through 2017 (Green), 2018 (Cyan) and 2019 (Blue). Point size reflects the average number of students by scientific product in a range from 1.66 to 1.25

ACKNOWLEDGEMENT

The authors would like to acknowledge the financial and the technical support of Writing Lab, TecLabs, Tecnologico de Monterrey, Mexico, in the production of this work.

REFERENCES

Bauer, K. and Bennet, J. 1999. Alumni Perceptions Used to Assess Undergraduate Research Experience. The University of Delaware. Retrieved form: http://www1.udel.edu/RAIRE/Alumniper.pdf

Barnett, R. 1992. Linking teaching and research: A critical inquiry. *The Journal of Higher Education* Vol. 63, No. 6; ProQuest Education Journals, pp. 619-623.

Corominas, E., Canals, C. and Villar, E. 2010. *The match between university education and graduate labour market outcomes*. AQU: Catalunya, Spain.

Delgado, F. 2018. A learning challenge for a multidisciplinary quantum information and quantum processing workshop during "Semana I". *Proceedings of INTED 2018.*

Delgado, F. 2018. Blended learning in research oriented education: TANGLE, an educative suite for quantum information. *IADIS International Journal on WWW/Internet* Vol. 16, No. 1. ISSN: 1645-7641.

EU. 2016. Quantum Manifesto: A new era of technology. European Union. Retrieved from: http://horizon2020.mon.bg/en?h=downloadFile&fileId=86

Greller, W.; Drachsler, H. 2012. Translating Learning into Numbers: Toward a Generic Framework for Learning Analytics. Educational Technology and Society. 15 (3), pp. 42–57.

Healey, M. 2005. Linking research and teaching to benefit student learning. Journal of Geography in Higher Education, 29(2), pp. 183-201.

Hosler, A. 2014. *Massive Open Online Research: The MOOC Evolves into the MOOR.* Retrieved from: http://www.emergingedtech.com/2014/01/massive-open-online-research-the-mooc-evolves-into-the-moor/EmergingEdTech

Kromydas, T. 2017. Rethinking higher education and its relationship with social inequalities: past knowledge, present state and future potential. *Palgrave Communications* Vol. 3, No. 1, pp. 1-12.

Prager, D. and Omenn, G. 1980. Research, innovation, and university-industry linkages. *Science* Vol. 207, No. 4429, pp. 379-384.

Wade, G. 2014. New model needed to close widening education gap. *University World News* 334. Retrieved from: http://www.universityworldnews.com/article.php?story=20141121091229767

West, J. 2000. Higher education and employment: opportunities and limitations in the formation of skills in a mass higher education system, *Journal of Vocational Education and Training* Vol. 52, No. 4, pp. 573-588.

MODELING A SECURE EXAM MANAGEMENT SYSTEM (SEMS) FOR MOBILE ENVIRONMENT BASED ON FACE RECOGNITION AND GPS TECHNIQUES

Hervé B. Olou[1] and Eugène C. Ezin[1,2]
[1]*Institut de Formation et de Recherche en Informatique, University of Abomey-Calavi, Republic of Benin*
[2]*Institut de Mathématiques et de Sciences Physiques, University of Abomey-Calavi, Republic of Benin*

ABSTRACT

Learning anywhere at any time is the goal of Mobile learning (m-learning). With the proliferation of smartphones, some universities adopt m-learning to facilitate accessibility of documents and online courses for students. Teachers can plan for online assessment and students can join session, answer and see their score directly. During an exam, the challenge is to make sure that students don't cheat. In this paper, we propose a modeling of secure exam management system (SEMS) for m-learning. The system is composed of a mobile app and a server. The mobile app is specially developed for students and will be used during exams. When students start exam, random face recognition and location request will be run automatically to ensure that other students are not in the same place and that it is effectively the learner who is in front of his smartphone.

KEYWORDS

M-learning, Secure Exam System, E-exam, Face Recognition, Geolocation

1. INTRODUCTION

Mobile technology has an important impact in our life. It gives us a new manner to communicate, to access information, to work, to learn and many other facilities. Nowadays, mobile technology offers a new generation of learning tools for everybody, everywhere and at any time. Scholars believe that m-learning is an e-learning regardless location and time (Shukri N. and Razak A., 2011). According to Cavus N. and Uzunboylu H. (2009), m-learning introduces learning opportunities for geographically dispersed persons or students who are not able to go at school or university at a regular basis.

After a certain amount of courses, exams can be organized to validate the knowledge learnt. In m-learning system, the students are evaluated online. Omkar Urunkar et al. proposed a survey on designing a secure exam management system (SEMS) for m-learning environments (2016). They noted that SEMS have many disadvantages like slow services, security issues for exam and not being service oriented. About security issues, we have communication between students through internet, the exchange of mobile devices and the fact that students can be side by side during online exam.

The aim of this paper is to propose a model of system which allow students to take their exam everywhere without cheating. To reach this goal, we have based the system on two main techniques: face recognition and global positioning system (GPS). The contribution of this paper is essentially the integration of these techniques in SEMS for m-learning environments.

This paper is organised into four sections. The first section presents the use of face recognition in the system. In the second section, we talk about the use of geolocation. In the third section, we present the global architecture of the system. The last section resumes our work and presents perspectives for future works.

2. FACE RECOGNITION

Several mobile phones have front-facing camera. This front-facing camera can be used to implement a SEMS for m-learning environments with face recognition. Face recognition is an appropriate mechanism for anti-usurpation. It is a usable, highly secure, and efficient biometric-based authentication mechanism that can be adopted as a second authentication factor (Mustafa K. et al, 2016). Students will be registered on the system with their pictures. Thus, the system can recognize them by using front-facing camera.

During an exam on mobile phone, students can easily cheat by:

- exchanging mobile phone with other students;
- giving their mobile phone to another person who will take exam for them;
- making research on internet or writing to another student to get answer of the questions; etc.

By face recognition, we can limit this cheating. If the system detects that it's not the student who is identified at the front of the mobile device, the session of this student will be automatically terminated. The different steps of the face recognition mechanism in our system are:

- the first step is the student registration. All students must be enrolled in the system with information about email, login, password and pictures;
- the second step is the starting exam session. With the mobile app, the student will be connected thanks to his login and password. Thereafter, he will start the exam session accessing to questions;
- the last step is the face recognition by the mobile app. During exam, face recognition will be done in the background. It will be done automatically at random times. After three failure attempts of face recognition, the session of the student will be automatically terminated.

Face recognition can be affected by the quality of the front-facing camera and the luminosity. Before the online assessment, students will be informed about these and they can make all necessary arrangements for a good face recognition.

Furthermore, the establishment of a powerful facial recognition system must take into account certain parameters like eyes blinking. Indeed, someone can use picture of a student and take exam for another student. So, by detecting eyes blinking in a video sequence, we can ensure the exact identity of the student in the front of the mobile device.

3. USAGE OF GEOLOCATION

During a face-to-face exam, a minimum distance must be set between students to avoid them exchanging information. This rule must also be respected during online exam. Several mobile phones have a Global Positioning System (GPS). Generally, GPS is used for tracking an object, animal or people. In our case, it will be used to track the student's mobile devices during the exam.

By using GPS functionality of mobile devices, the server will get the GPS coordinates of the student mobile phone. Then, it will check if different students have the same coordinates at the same time or the minimum required distance between students is respected. If these conditions are not respected, the server will send a request to the mobile app to close and send the answers of the students. After that, the session of these students are closed and their answers sent to the server for getting marks.

On the system, we use geolocation like this:

- at the beginning and during the exam, the mobile app communicates the GPS coordinates of the mobile devices to the server;
- the server makes the comparison of the GPS coordinates of students mobiles devices. If some wrong thing is detected, the student session will be close;
- on mobile app, students can see the positions of the examination centers and they can choose one of them.

4. GLOBAL ARCHITECTURE

This section shares the global architecture of the system. This architecture is presented in Figure 1. All students are previously enrolled in the system. Before starting exam session, the student chooses the exam.

A teacher can decided to make an exam with a supervisor. On the system, different places like library, primary school, private school or university will be enrolled with their supervisors. Thus, students who are far from the university can decided to take exam on one of the registered centers by using the map frame on the mobile app of the SEMS.

If the exam can be made without a supervisor, the student will start the session. Else, he will see the list of examination centers and chooses one. The supervisor of this center will validate, if the student is there. Thereafter, the student can start exam session. In spite of the supervisor's presence, the system will continue to use the geolocation and face recognition.

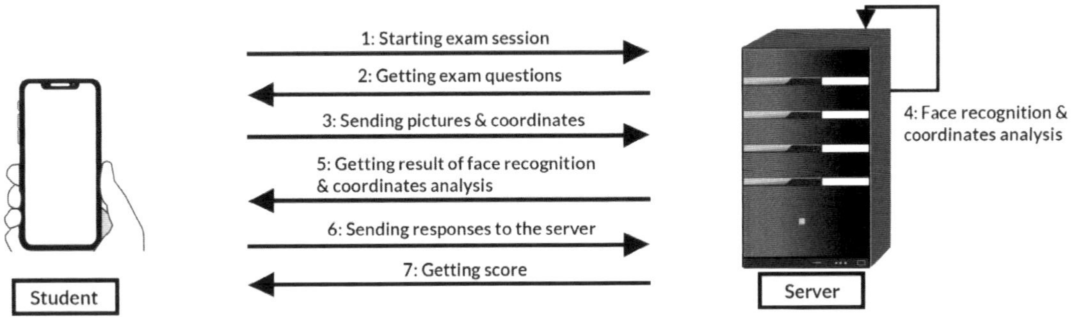

Figure 1. Global architecture

The global architecture has seven steps:

- At the first step, the student starts the exam session after logging into the system and choosing the exam. The mobile app sends a request to the server to get the exam questions.
- Then, at the second step, the server sends the exam questions to the mobile app according to the description of the exam (course, type of exam, duration, etc.).
- Pictures and GPS coordinates of the student are sent to the server at the third step. As soon as the student begins the exam, the mobile app sends automatically these data to the server to prevent cheating during the exam.
- At the fourth step, the data sent previously are analyzed by the server. It's the heart of the system. The main work is done at this step, as described in sections 2 and 3.
- Now, at the fifth step, if some wrong thing is detected, the server will request the closure of the student's session. Else, the session will remain active.
- The assessment of the questions are sent at the sixth step. At this step, the student finished his exam or the server detects some wrong thing at the fifth step. So, his answers are sent to the server.
- Finally, at the last step, the student gets his score. His session will be closed and all restrictions will be canceled.

The mobile app must be able to:

- block incoming calls. During the exam, a call can disturb the student;
- verify if the application is foreground or background. This check is important to detect if the student is using another application (browser, excel, Whatsapp, Facebook message, etc.) during the exam. If he uses another application, his session will be closed and his answer will be sent to the server.
- take pictures, send pictures and GPS coordinates without affecting the student exam. These data will be analysed by the system during the exam.

5. CONCLUDING REMARKS

In this paper, we present the modeling that combines face recognition and GPS technique for SEMS. The aim of this work is to guarantee an effective exam without cheating. By using face recognition, students are constrained to put their phone in front of their face. Thus, during an exam they can't exchange their mobile device with another student. Moreover, no one can take exam for another. The use of geolocation in this system comes to ensure that students are not side by side during the exam. If an exam requires a supervisor, the students will see the closest center to him on the mobile app.

Our system is under development. In future work, we plan to implement the prototype and integrate it into an existing learning management system (LMS). A low energy battery cannot provide power supply for longer period. Hence, improving the energy efficiency in mobile learning framework is also crucial (Asir, D. et al., 2017). The efficiency of this system must be studied too.

REFERENCES

Asir, D. et al., 2017. Mobile Application for m-Learning. *In International Journal of Advanced Research in Computer Science,* Vol. 8, No. 3, pp. 313-316.

Cavus, N. and Uzunboylu, H., 2009. Improving critical thinking skills in mobile learning. *In World Conference on Educational Sciences 2009*, pp. 434-438.

El-Hussein, M. et al., 2010. Defining mobile learning in the higher education landscape. *In Educational Technology & Society*, Vol. 13, No. 3, pp. 12-21.

Kaiiali, M. et al., 2016. Designing a Secure Exam Management System (SEMS) for M-Learning Environments. *In IEEE Transactions on learning technologies*, Vol. 9, No. 3, pp. 258-271.

Moldovan, A. et al., 2014. Energy Aware Mobile Learning: Opportunities and Challenges. *In IEEE Communications Surveys & Tutorials*, Vol. 16, No. 1, pp. 234-265.

Shukri, N. and Razak, A., 2011. Students' Awareness and Requirements of Mobile Learning Services in the Higher Education Environment. *In American Journal of Economics and Business Administration* 3 (1), pp. 95-100.

STUDENT ACCEPTANCE OF LEARNING WITH TABLETS IN A HISTORY MUSEUM

Alan J. Wecker, Merav Yosfan, Billie Eilam and Joel Lanir
University of Haifa
Mount Carmel, Haifa, Israel

ABSTRACT

This paper examines early results of an experiment in students' user experience for in context learning in a museum with a mobile device. We examine 3 conditions. The first is a paper worksheet (approximately 50 pages) vs two types of mobile application (approximately 25 screens). The second set (both mobile applications) compares a constructivist to an informative educational approach. The students preferred the mobile app over the printed worksheet. Students also found the informative approach preferable to the constructivist approach. In the future we will examine which approach had better learning results and delve deeper into examination of the learning process.

KEYWORDS

Mobile Museum Learning

1. INTRODUCTION

One way to enhance student's engagement in humanity-oriented museums is by using electronic mobile devices. Mobile devices, such as smart phones, are ubiquitous today and have become widely available and used. Adults and children alike use mobile phones throughout their daily lives to communicate, organize their daily activities, play, and also learn. Such individual devices may provide customized and personalized learning experiences, building on user's own understanding and making their own choices (Schwartz & Arena, 2013), at their own pace. At the museum, mobile technologies pose both an opportunity and a problem. A multimedia mobile museum guide, e.g., can provide museum visitors with a wide variety of novel and important services. The visitor can receive personalized adaptive information from a vast amount of content sources that can suit his or her personal needs at a particular time. Information can be tailored according to the visitor's learning abilities and preferences (Ardissono et al., 2011). However, a mobile guide as the main interpretive option at the museum can also be problematic. It may focus the visitor's attention on the mobile device rather than on the museum exhibits. Furthermore, for small groups, it might isolate the visitors from their peers, effectively dissocializing the group (Grinter et al., 2002; Lanir et al., 2013).

In order to understand if and how the use of mobile technologies can enhance informal learning at the museum, we first need to characterize the existing mobile applications in such an environment. The integration of mobile devices as tools to support museums has become well established in recent years (Economou & Meintani, 2011). Many mobile museum guides, i.e., classical audio guides or more advanced multimedia guides, are information-based, which means they have been designed to provide context-specific information presented in an information-centered way. Context is often achieved by utilizing location-based services (using QR codes or various sensors), while information is mostly limited to audio, text, images or short video-presentations providing details on nearby exhibits (e.g. Lanir et al., 2013). While these kind of guides may be beneficial for an individual adult visitor, being able to provide relevant and sometimes personalized information and services, they may not be ideal for children or small groups. Children arriving to museums at school trips, or individually with their parents, often require a more engaging form of presentation, especially in humanity type museums such as history museums.

A different approach for the design of mobile learning takes an activity-based approach (as opposed to a guide) that includes interactive inquiry learning and problem solving. In this approach, visitors need to solve some puzzles, find items (e.g., a treasure hunt) or actively produce their own interpretations. This is based on the constructivist epistemology that individuals are active learners and must construct knowledge for themselves (Schunk, 2004). A meaningful learning therefore, involves the granting of meaning to new acquired information by relating it to existing knowledge. Such a learning mode requires individuals' high engagement with meaningful tasks, while actively processing, interpreting and making sense of the information. Retention and deep understanding enables transfer and future use of this newly constructed knowledge in similar situations. In addition, the ability to construct several such connections to different but relevant bodies of existing knowledge or to adaptively re-assemble pieces of knowledge to fit a particular need in a complex context (like a museum) and ill-defined domains (like history), ensure the development of cognitive flexibility and this knowledge being active and used (Spiro & Jehng, 1990). Several works have aimed at designing and implementing such mobile museum guides, for example, by using various games, quizzes and puzzles (see Mortara et al., 2014, for a survey). Other works, used a more direct approach, supporting collaborative enquiry work at the museum using the mobile phone which later can be used at home or in class (Vavoula et al, 2009).

2. BACKGROUND

Museums are one of the primary sites of informal learning (Bamberger & Tal, 2007; Crane, 1994; Wood & Latham, 2011). Museum learning complements formal learning at school by deepening and expanding school knowledge; relating to and presenting authentic objects (Bitgood, 1989); providing concrete ways for the assimilation of complex concepts and their comprehension (Wright, 1980); and applying multimodal presentation modes – visual, auditory and/or haptic, thereby promoting individuals' ability to observe and understand world phenomena (Wood & Latham, 2011). Museum learning is fundamentally different in several aspects from formal learning: the temporal – being for a short time duration; the modularity - requiring no continuity; and the affect - being primarily based on curiosity, intrinsic motivation, selection and self-control (Bamberger & Tal, 2007). Museum learning occurs through interactions involving personal, socio-cultural, and physical contexts, which create the foundation for the learning processes (Falk & Dierking, 2000).

Studies investigating children's' learning in museums were conducted mostly in science museums, aquariums, and zoos and have focused on family visits (e.g., Bamberger & Tal, 2007). Museums presenting information in the varied humanities domains were rarely investigated and knowledge regarding informal learning processes, their processes characteristics, and ways for improving them, are still mostly absent. The inherent importance of childrens' visits to such museums, especially along their school years, can't be underestimated. History museums for example, enable the children direct involvement with "real" objects from the past and raise their awareness of these objects relations to the present (Rosenzweig, 2000); reinforce children's history knowledge and related thinking skills; encourage children to deepen their life-long learning; and support history understanding as a subjective product influenced by economic, social and political factors (Marcus & Levine, 2011).

3. METHODOLOGY

In order to better understand mobile-based learning strategies, we compared three options for informal learning at the museum. Through in-depth observations as well as questionnaires and interviews, we examine and compare students' learning, engagement, and communication patterns, when using the three options.

The study applies the naturalistic paradigm, suitable particularly for examining learning in informal educational environments. This paradigm describes participants' behaviors as they transpire and relates them to the environment in which they are observed. In addition, it allows observation of visitors' behavior without affecting the informal nature of their learning experience. To collect data, we use both quantitative and qualitative methods (microphones, video cameras, screen recordings). The qualitative method focuses on understanding the dynamics of isolated events, in order to achieve a more generalized understanding while the quantitative one enables comparing different conditions and knowledge of specific issues, and allows for inferences and generalization.

The study includes 44 students learning in three 7th grade classrooms. Students' ages (12-13 years old) assures children's sufficient skills to cope with the museums' texts and labels. Moreover, 7th grade children's awareness of the importance of dates is already developed and they can link dates with their own background knowledge regarding the period's events (Brophy & Vansledright, 1997).

The study uses a between-subject design, in which each student is assigned to one of the three experimental conditions. All three conditions relate to the same information and exhibits at the same cognitive level and use an activity based guide (These activity-centered applications support learning while performing various activities based on a question and answer approach in front of the exhibits).

1. ***Constructivist printed worksheet/guide.*** In this condition, Students get printed information with photos and texts (the same information as the audio in the video of the other conditions) and use assignment sheets with a pencil, that supports the interactive activities of the cognitive-activity type in front of particular exhibits/presentations. (approximately 50 pages)
2. ***Informative mobile worksheet.*** The students get short videos presenting them with information about the exhibits. The design of these activities is aimed at enhancing the recall and summation of the information; based on a series of questions and answers activities (with many multiple-choice type questions). (approximately 25 screens).
3. ***Constructivist mobile worksheet.*** The students get the same set of short videos presenting them with information about the exhibits. The design of these activities is aimed at enhancing the integration of information acquired into a coherent body of knowledge, based on the findings that mental engagement with the exhibits promotes learning. These are mainly based on answers to questions that the students must formulate by typing in answers to thought provoking questions. (approximately 25 screens).

4. RESULTS

We present here initial results of the user experience questionnaire of the three conditions (Table 1). The questionnaire used a 7-point Likert scale with the value of 1 meaning agree that it possess trait to an extreme degree and 7 meaning agree that it doesn't possess trait to an extreme degree.

Results show that printed guide was rated as least attractive and least efficient out of the three guides. All three guides were considered easy to use, with the mobile guides considered more interesting and more novel than the printed guide. Also, the mobile guides were considered clearer and more organized than the printed version. Looking at the negatively framed results we see that the informative was considered less annoying, less inefficient and less unfriendly (i.e., the friendliest). The printed guide was considered more boring and uninteresting.

Table 1. User experience questionnaire for the three types of guides used in the museum

	Constructivist			Informative			Printed		
	N	Mean	Std. Dev	N	Mean	Std. Dev	N	Mean	Std. Dev
Attractiveness	14	2.21	1.57	15	1.47	1.18	12	2.75	1.54
Efficiency	14	1.64	1.59	15	1.73	1.16	12	2.92	1.50
Ease of use	14	1.29	1.72	15	1.00	0.92	12	1.83	1.26
Control	14	1.29	1.26	15	1.07	0.96	12	2.75	1.81
Interesting	14	2.57	1.86	15	2.27	1.75	12	3.08	1.31
Novelty	14	1.43	1.82	15	1.87	1.59	12	2.17	1.74
Clear	13	1.92	1.32	15	1.60	0.91	12	3.67	1.87
Organized	13	2.08	1.32	14	2.29	1.77	11	4.64	2.15
Annoying	14	4.86	1.91	15	6.00	1.06	12	4.33	1.69
Inefficient	13	6.23	1.42	15	5.33	2.12	11	5.73	1.00
Not useful	13	5.62	1.60	15	5.53	1.88	11	5.55	1.03
Unfriendly	14	5.43	1.74	14	6.43	0.64	12	5.33	0.77
Unpleasant	11	5.27	1.61	15	6.07	1.53	12	5.25	1.05
Not understandable	13	6.38	1.04	15	6.60	0.63	12	5.75	1.48
Hard to learn	13	6.54	1.12	15	6.53	0.83	11	6.00	0.89
Complicated	13	6.38	1.12	15	6.60	0.63	12	5.58	0.99
Unpredictable	13	5.62	1.12	15	6.60	0.63	12	4.17	1.94
Boring	13	4.69	1.93	15	4.47	2.35	12	3.50	1.93
Uninteresting	13	4.77	2.12	15	4.60	2.47	12	4.00	1.80

5. CONCLUSION AND FUTURE RESEARCH

Summarizing the results, it seems there was an overall preference of the students for the informative guide, while the printed handouts were least preferred. We expected the printouts to be least preferred, mostly because of the novelty effect and since younger students often like technology as a mediator for learning. However, the preference of the informative guide over the constructivist one is surprising for us, and needs further investigation into the observational data in order to explain. A possible explanation is that constructivist methodology called for students to formulate written answers to questions in order to assimilate, while the informative guide allowed for more multiple choice items.

These are early results which show a clear direction for student acceptance preferences. We plan to have another three classes with about 80 students from another school using the three condition. In addition, we have started to analyze student's knowledge questionnaires as well as their recorded audio and video to investigate and compare learning accomplishments and group behavior between the three conditions.

REFERENCES

Ardissono, L., Kuflik, T., & Petrelli, D. (2011). Personalization in cultural heritage: The road travelled and the one ahead. *User Modeling and User-Adapted Interaction*, 22(1), 1-27.

Bamberger, Y., & Tal, T. (2007). Learning in a personal context: level of bechoice in a free choice learning environment in science and natural history museums. *Science Education*, 91(1), 75-95.

Bitgood, S. (1989). School field trips: an overview. Visitor Behavior, 4(2), 3-6.

Brophy, J., & Vansledright, B. (1997). Teaching and learning history in elementary schools. New York: Teachers College Press.

Crane, V. (1994). An introduction to informal science learning and research. In V., Crane, M., Chen, S., Bitgood, B., Serrell, D., Thompson, H., Nicholson, F., Weiss, & P., Campbell, Informal science learning: what the research says about television, science museums and community–based projects (pp.1-14). U.S.: Research Communication Ltd.

Economou, M., & Meintani, E. (2011). Promising Beginning? Evaluating Museum Mobile Phone Apps.

Falk, J. H., & Dierking, L. D. (2000). Learning from museums – visitor experiences and the making of meaning. New York and Oxford: Rowman & Littlefield Publishers, Inc.

Grinter, R. E., Aoki, P. M., Szymanski, M. H., Thornton, J. D., Woodruff, A., & Hurst, A. (2002). Revisiting the visit: Understanding how technology can shape the museum visit. Proceedings of the 2002 ACM Conference on Computer Supported Cooperative Work, 146-155.

Lanir, J., Kuflik, T., Dim, E., Wecker, A. J., & Stock, O. (2013). The influence of a location-aware mobile guide on museum visitors' behavior. Interacting with Computers, 25(6), 443-460.

Marcus, A. S. & Levine, T. H. (2011). Knight at the museum: learning history with museums. The Social Studies, 102(3), 104-109.

Mortara, M., Catalano, C. E., Bellotti, F., Fiucci, G., Houry-Panchetti, M., & Petridis, P. (2014). Learning cultural heritage by serious games. Journal of Cultural Heritage, 15(3), 318-325.

Schunk, D. H. (2004). Learning theories: An educational perspective (4th ed., Chap. 7, pp. 285-328). Upper Saddle River, NJ: Pearson, Merrill Prentice Hall.

Schwartz, D. L., & Arena, D. (2013). Measuring what matters most: Choice-based assessment in the digital age. The John D. and Catherine T. MacArthur Foundation Reports on Digital Media and Learning. Cambridge, MA: MIT Press.

Spiro, R., Jehng, J. (1990). Cognitive flexibility and hypertext: Theory and technology for the nonlinear and multidimensional traversal of complex subject matter. In Nix, D., Spiro, R. (Eds.), Cognition, education and multimedia: Exploring ideas in high technology (pp. 163- 205). Hillsdale, NJ: Lawrence Erlbaum Associates, Inc.

Vavoula G., Sharples M., Rudman P., Meek J. & Lonsdale P. (2009) Myartspace: design and evaluation of support for learning with multimedia phones between classrooms and museums. Computers and Education 53, 286–299.

Wood, E., & Latham, K., F. (2011). The thickness of things – Exploring the curriculum of museums through phenomenological touch. Journal of Curriculum Theorizing (27), 51- 65.

Wright, E. L. (1980). Analysis of the effect of museum experience on the biology achievement of sixth-graders. Journal of Research in Science Teaching, 17(2), 99-104.

SPOC, FUTURE OF MLEARNING AND LANGUAGE LEARNING?

Hamed Asgari and Georges Antoniadis
Laboratory LIDILEM
Université Grenoble Alpes, France

ABSTRACT

Mobile artifacts are objects that surround us increasingly in life. They give us the opportunity to engage in activities outside the traditional context and at our own pace. The objective of this article is the realization of the software on mobile artifacts for computer-assisted language learning (CALL) using the concept of SPOC (Small Private Online Course) for learning FLE (in French Français langue étrangère[1]).

KEYWORDS

SPOC, NLP, MIRTO, Mlearning, SPOC+, FLE

1. INTRODUCTION

Purpose of this study is to provide a complete description of a French language learning system based on SPOC (Small Private Online Course) integrating NLP (Natural Language Processing) tools and the MIRTO project (in French Multi-apprentissages Interactifs par des Recherches sur des Textes et l'Oral[2]) on mobile artifacts with a personalized follow-up procedure for each learner. Currently, a large number of SPOC educational theories and practices have been implemented (Fox and Patterson, 2013), such as the software engineering program at the University of California at Berkeley, the copyright course at Harvard Law School, the Python programming language course at MIT. China has also launched a pilot project of SPOC teaching activities, such as the first SPOC physics courses at Tsinghua University, circuit theory courses at Nanjing University and C language programming courses at the University of Zhejiang. Xuetang Online also created the SPOC platform for English courses. However, these SPOC pedagogical practices are not widely used because they are found only in renowned universities (Li et al., 2019). The emergence of SPOC becomes an innovation of the "internet +" teaching model and constitutes a new form of information-based teaching. At the same time, teachers need to have a good understanding of the learners who choose the course, which can strengthen the management and supervision of learners, making SPOC an effective tool to improve teaching (Chen, 2019). Research on SPOC also shows that SPOC is more attractive than traditional classrooms. It stimulates learners' interest in learning and stimulates their participation (Chen, 2019). In the teaching process of SPOC, depending on the course curriculum, tutor publishes the instructional video and organizes homework assignments. Depending on the length of the course, learners can watch their personalized video, homework and online discussions (Lei, 2019). According to the literature, no scientific work has been done which addressed the use of SPOC in language learning with the integration of NLP tools for mobile artifacts.

2. CONTEXTUALIZATION

Teaching and learning are two words that are born from the birth of the human being. Since the creation of humanity, we are in the phase of either teaching or learning. According to Mike Sharples (Sharples, 2002),

[1] French as a foreign language
[2] Muti-Learning Interactive through Text and Oral Research

the mobile learning movement, also called mlearning, emerged in the 1970s invented by Alan Kay with Dynabook. However, there is no consensus on the definition of mobile learning.

Recently, there are multiple definitions for mlearning; "any sort of learning that happens when the learner is not fixed predetermined location or learning that happens when the learner takes advantage of the learning opportunities offered by mobile technologies" (Vavoula et al., 2004), "learning supported by mobiles device such as cellular (mobile) phones, portable computers, and personal audio player" (Rheingold, 2002) and "learning by means of wireless technological devices that can be pocketed and utilized wherever the learner's device can receive unbroken transmission signals" (Attewell and Savill-Smith, 2005).

The notion of mobility in all definitions is the only one that does not change; the tools used for mobile learning can be different and evolving over time. In this article, we are interested in the notion of mobility for both mobile artifacts, the aspect of distance and the use of telecommunication technologies.

We define smartphone as the new generation of mobile phone, which apart from the current functionalities of mobiles (camera, video, sound recording, GPS connection, ...) which able to communicate from almost anywhere, as long as it picks up the signal that access the internet and by installing third-party applications it can present new functionalities.

2.1 SPOC

With innovation in technology, the educational model is also developing and progressively new modes of teaching are emerging. Currently, traditional software-based education is changing due to poor effects, low efficiency and low quality of teaching. In traditional mode, a single teacher continues to teach in the classroom and learners complete assignments independently, thus due to the low capacity of independent learning. Learners' understanding of the program is not sufficient and learning effect is difficult to assess. Todays, courses need to move away from the traditional model of single-teacher teaching and use modern teaching tools and methods, as well as high-quality teaching and a wide range of learning content in a limited amount of time. Nowadays, with the advent of the information age, the new teaching model is emerging and the traditional offline course and online teaching are constantly being integrated and updated (Lei, 2019).

SPOC, Small Private Online Course, was created by Professor Armando Fox (Fox, 2013) from the American University of California at Berkeley (Chen, 2019) in 2013, also known as the "post-MOOC era"(Chen, 2019) MOOC is the acronym for the Massive Open Online Course.

The meaning of small in SPOC is the scope of the class, where the number of learners is controlled and is limited to a small group comparing to MOOC which hundreds of learners are participated in. The meaning of Private is that the courses are not public on a large scale and accessibility is defined for the courses and scope of the course is limited to specific number of learners. By taking advantage of these restrictions, we look forward to improve learning efficiency and course completion of the learners. SPOC's teaching method is a combination of online and offline courses (Lei, 2019).

SPOC has become a completely new way of teaching, combining the information age with new teaching resources. The "Small Private Online Course" has also revolutionized content and form (Li et al., 2019). SPOC brings different learning experience to learners (Li et al., 2019).

The teaching mode of SPOC is the development of MOOC's mood. This means that SPOC's teaching mode not only compensates for the disadvantages of MOOC in teaching courses; but also places the teaching of offline communication within MOOC's teaching mode. SPOC allows teachers to intervene directly in the whole learning process of the learners (Lei, 2019).

2.2 NLP and MIRTO

Our work falls within the fields of Computer-assisted language learning (CALL), natural language processing (NLP), as part of the MIRTO project (Antoniadis, 2010) invented by Georges Antoniadis and the concept of SPOC, invented in 2013 by Professor Armando Fox (Fox, 2013) teaching at the University of California.

According to the research of Georges Antoniadis, the objective of the MIRTO project is the design of a multilingual system for teaching languages, using:

- The set of NLP software resulting from scientific research and laboratories.
- The diversity and richness of textual and oral corpora.

- A set of NLP functions (NLP function is obtained from NLP software) (Antoniadis et al., 2005)

Our main objective is the definition, the conceptualization of the architecture and the elaboration of a system for the learning of French as a foreign language to the non-French speaker on mobile artifacts with the concept of SPOC that we have just described above. Used MIRTO's previous work to be able to integrate the automatic creation of exercises and their corrections into our solution with a morphological analyzer. MIRTO should be able to implement classic NLP functions within the platform to facilitate the conception, without prior computer skills, of didactic activities (Antoniadis et al., 2005). We will explain this functionality in more detail.

2.3 Learning and Mobile Artifacts

According to (Reynolds and Anderson, 2015) the rapid advances in information and communication technologies in recent years have created new opportunities for education. Now that most people have mobile devices, learning can be extended beyond the traditional classroom (Wu, 2016). Based on the work of Abdous (Abdous et al., 2009) and Wu (Wu, 2014) mobile technologies are reshaping learning and teaching by supporting, developing and enhancing course content, learning activities and student interactions with the instructor, peers, and learning content. The technologies help overcome many limitations and barriers in the traditional classroom, including a lack of opportunities for language use, individualized learning, feedback and interaction (Ahn and Lee, 2016) and can provide a seamless learning experience, i.e., learning anytime, anywhere (Liu and Chen, 2015).

According to Shadiev (Shadiev et al., 2017), in general, students have a positive perception of learning a language with a mobile phone and that the latter has positive effects on language proficiency. They also found that the most used technologies were smartphones and learners were more university students.

Our objective is the evolution of the MIRTO system by integrating mobile learning (mlearning) in order to obtain a system for learning the French language with a complete architecture.

The complete system is composed of different modules: user interface (administrator, teacher, and learner), activity generator, correction module, morphological analyzer, and feedback. This architecture must be possible to follow the evolutions and updates of the tools and mobile interfaces, also should be able to add new functions of NLP modules.

Now we have developed our solution, which is considering all the functional aspects of a complete system. Our solution is composed of a website, a web interface, and a mobile software. (figure1).

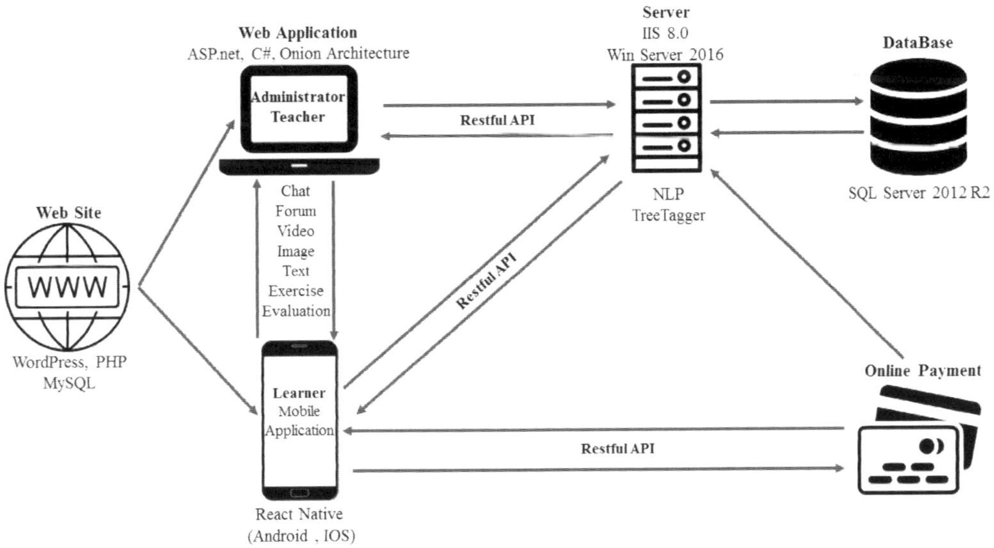

Figure 1. SPOC+ architecture

For doing that, we need a reliable morphological analyzer, which is indispensable for automatically generating activities through our platform. For French processing, two analyzers that are mainly used by the NLP community: TreeTagger, developed by Helmet Schmid (Schmid, 1994) at the University of Stuttgart and Brill (Dejean et al., 2010). Both of them are open source, but only TreeTagger is available for Windows and it has the advantage of being multi-platform. According to the studies of Allauzen and Bonneau-Maynard (Allauzen and Bonneau-Maynard, 2008), the reliability rate of TreeTagger is 95.7% compared to Brill which is 94.6%. With TreeTagger and those 33 labels, we can define and generate automatically MCQ exercises, text with holes, questions, and answers of grammar, conjugation, or spelling.

The website only used for the presentation of the application and our solution. The website made in PHP language with WordPress as the basic CMS. Collecting of colors and the design of our UI (User interface) were carefully considered. We chose blue for its soothing, calmness and relaxation (Singh, 2006) aspect (figure 2).

Figure 2. SPOC+ mobile interface

We have dedicated the web interface only for the administrator and teachers. The administrator plays the role of the traditional administrative service; he is in charge of defining access rights at different levels for teachers and learners. He will also be in charge of checking for the payments of registrations during the course for the learners.

In our system, we chose the project-based pedagogy invented by John Dewey (Dewey, 1986). The learning process organized by the teacher or a group of teachers to reach a predetermined target. According to Stephanie Bell, "Project-Based Learning (PBL) is a student-driven, teacher-facilitated approach to learning" (Bell, 2010).

The teacher will access with his login and password provided by the administrator, he would discover the list of learners with various information about them, including their names, dates of birth, current level, requested course, geographical location and time zones.

With his web interface, teacher will be able to associate the participants to the forums and define the topics to cover in his forums according to his teaching method and based on the needs of learners. Teacher is in charge of adding learners in different forums.

The mobile application is intended only for learners. They will be able to identify themselves using the login and password provided after acceptance of the administrator and pedagogical service. They will be able to participate in different forums that the teacher already gave access them. At any time, he will be able to be in contact with the teacher through the chat tool. The chat tool is the synchronous or asynchronous contact point between the learner and the teacher. In the chat tool and forums, the participants will be able to send any kind of document (text, video, sound, pdf, image, etc...).

We have named our solution SPOC+, its SPOC with a big plus. The choice of the learner's level based on the criteria set out by the CEFRL[3], which our reference point for distinguishing the learner's knowledge. We propose that the learner has acquired the basics of the French language in writing, speaking and

[3] Common European Framework of Reference for Languages

comprehension. This level will allow learners to understand the different parts of the software; and communicate with other learners and teachers; via forum or chat, to answer the questions and to participate in the social life of the class. The audience that is chosen in the concept of our software is an audience that has already acquired the B1 level and would like to start the B2.

Through SPOC+, all four necessary skills proposed for language acquisition including oral comprehension, written comprehension, oral production and written production; are offered to the learner.

Each level consists of several sessions, which are divided into several courses and each course composed of different lessons. The presentation of the content in lessons corresponds to a modular division. Each lesson corresponds to an object of study sufficiently limited to constitute a scientifically and pedagogically autonomous element and is therefore used when it is assembled or detached from the rest of the course. Not all lessons occupy the same volume and do not present the same difficulty. The amount of work time required by the student will not necessarily be the same from one lesson to the next. For each lesson, a set of activities offered to the student. The required time to read, listen, watch, and participate in each session should not exceed 70 minutes; the necessary videos are cut in 15 minutes maximum.

An information sheet is systematically attached to each lesson, giving useful information such as the title, summary, keywords, estimated working hours, date of the last update, objectives, prerequisites, and general advices on learning methods for the learner.

Maximum 25 learners can participate in each class. We have limited the number of learners per class to allow the teacher a personalized follow-up, which is one of the significant differences between the MOOC and the SPOC.

3. CONCLUSION

This article proposes SPOC+, as a new solution for mlearning, which integrated MIRTO and SPOC. Previous research studies have not proposed SPOC in language mobile learning. As we discussed in this article, today, SPOC is one of the solutions for language learning with mobile artifacts. Thus, SPOC+ demonstrates learning anytime, anywhere, sociable, on the mobile device, and with an educator. Our practical contribution tested with three users to analyze the intuitiveness of our solution. The theoretical contribution of this study is that a framework proposed for French language learners and should be tested in other languages.

Our main limitation is testing the solution in the real environment, within 25 learners from a non-French speaking country who have been pre-qualified, evaluating the level of satisfaction of the learners over four weeks of participation. For the future, we propose to extend the research from the basic level of French learners and reach other languages.

REFERENCES

Abdous, M., Camarena, M.M., Facer, B.R., 2009. MALL Technology: Use of Academic Podcasting in the Foreign Language Classroom. ReCALL 21, 76–95. https://doi.org/10.1017/S0958344009000020

Ahn, T. youn, Lee, S.-M., 2016. User experience of a mobile speaking application with automatic speech recognition for EFL learning: Speaking app with ASR. Br J Educ Technol 47, 778–786. https://doi.org/10.1111/bjet.12354

Allauzen, A., Bonneau-Maynard, H., 2008. Training and evaluation of POS taggers on the French MULTITAG corpus 5.

Antoniadis, G., 2010. De l'apport pertinent du TAL pour les systèmes d'ALAO : l'exemple du projet MIRTO, in: 2ème Congrès Mondial de Linguistique Française. Presented at the 2ème Congrès Mondial de Linguistique Française, EDP Sciences, La Nouvelle-Orléans, Etats-Unis, p. 150. https://doi.org/10.1051/cmlf/2010228

Antoniadis, G., Kraif, O., Lebarbé, T., Ponton, C., Echinard, S., 2005. Modélisation de l'intégration de ressources TAL pour l'apprentissage des langues : la plateforme MIRTO. alsic. https://doi.org/10.4000/alsic.376

Attewell, J., Savill-Smith, C., 2005. Mobile learning anytime everywhere: A book of papers from MLEARN 2004. Learning and Skills Development Agency.

Bell, S., 2010. Project-Based Learning for the 21st Century: Skills for the Future. The Clearing House: A Journal of Educational Strategies, Issues and Ideas 83, 39–43. https://doi.org/10.1080/00098650903505415

Chen, J., 2019. Exploration and Application of SPOC-based Belended Teaching Mode in Comprehensive English Course. J. Phys.: Conf. Ser. 1237, 022115. https://doi.org/10.1088/1742-6596/1237/2/022115

Dejean, C., Fortun, M., Massot, C., Pottier, V., Poulard, F., Vernier, M., 2010. Un étiqueteur de rôles grammaticaux libre pour le français intégré à Apache UIMA.

Dewey, J., 1986. Experience and education, in: The Educational Forum. Taylor & Francis, pp. 241–252.

Fox, A., 2013. From MOOCs to SPOCs. Commun. ACM 56, 38–40. https://doi.org/10.1145/2535918

Fox, A., Patterson, D., 2013. Software Engineering Curriculum Technology Transfer: 9.

Lei, M., 2019. Research on Hybrid Teaching Mode of Software Engineering Based on SPOC. J. Phys.: Conf. Ser. 1237, 052009. https://doi.org/10.1088/1742-6596/1237/5/052009

Li, M., Qi, X., Song, M., Li, Y., 2019. The Feasibility Study of Blended English Teaching Based on SPOC 329, 4.

Liu, P.-L., Chen, C.-J., 2015. Learning English through actions: a study of mobile-assisted language learning. Interactive Learning Environments 23, 158–171. https://doi.org/10.1080/10494820.2014.959976

Reynolds, B.L., Anderson, T.A.F., 2015. Extra-Dimensional In-Class Communications: Action Research Exploring Text Chat Support of Face-to-Face Writing. Computers and Composition 35, 52–64. https://doi.org/10.1016/j.compcom.2014.12.002

Rheingold, H., 2002. Smart Mobs: the next social revolution Cambridge. MA: Perseus.

Schmid, H., 1994. Probabilistic Part-of-Speech Tagging Using Decision Trees, Intl, in: Conference on New Methods in Language Processing. Manchester, UK.

Shadiev, R., Hwang, W.-Y., Huang, Y.-M., 2017. Review of research on mobile language learning in authentic environments. Computer Assisted Language Learning 30, 284–303. https://doi.org/10.1080/09588221.2017.1308383

Sharples, M., 2002. Disruptive devices: mobile technology for conversational learning. IJCEELL 12, 504. https://doi.org/10.1504/IJCEELL.2002.002148

Singh, S., 2006. Impact of color on marketing. Management Decision 44, 783–789. https://doi.org/10.1108/00251740610673332

Vavoula, G.N., Lefrere, P., O'Malley, C., Sharples, M., Taylor, J., 2004. Producing guidelines for learning, teaching and tutoring in a mobile environment, in: The 2nd IEEE International Workshop on Wireless and Mobile Technologies in Education, 2004. Proceedings. Presented at the The 2nd IEEE International Workshop on Wireless and Mobile Technologies in Education, 2004. Proceedings., pp. 173–176. https://doi.org/10.1109/WMTE.2004.1281378

Wu, T.-T., 2016. English Reading E-Book System Integrating Grouping and Guided Reading Mechanisms Based on the Analysis of Learning Portfolios. Journal of Internet Technology 17, 231–241.

Wu, T.-T., 2014. The use of a mobile assistant learning system for health education based on project-based learning. Comput Inform Nurs 32, 497–503. https://doi.org/10.1097/CIN.0000000000000089

THE EFFECT OF TEACHING BY (MOBILE LEARNING) IN UNIVERSITY STUDENTS'S ACHIEVEMENT

Omar M. K. Mahasneh
PhD., Department of Basic and Applied Science, Faculty of Shobak University College, AL-Balqa Applied University, Jordan

ABSTRACT

There have been efforts to investigate the effect of teaching by using mobile learning in university student's achievement. However, studies examining effect of teaching by using mobile learning in university students are, thus far, rare. This study adopted a quasi-experimental design with two types of teaching methods. One research group was assigned to the mobile learning teaching Method (n=25) and the other to the conventional teaching Method (n= 25). A multiple-choice test was developed in Unit introduces technology in course of pre-vocational education technology, Within the Bachelor of pre-vocational education program at Shobak university college .The results showed that the mobile learning teaching method was more effect than the conventional teaching method in the achievement of university students.

KEYWORDS

Mobile Learning, University Students, Achievement

1. INTRODUCTION

In 1970, the concept of M-learning (Mobile-learning) appeared by Alan Kay, He developed a portable and hands on personal computer (Dynabook) it was intended to develop children's abilities in dealing with digital technology (Pirttiaho, Holm, Paalanen, & Thorstrom, 2007; Saylor, 2012; Singh, 2010; Pimmer, & Grohbiel, 2008). In 1994, Mitsubishi Electric Corp designed the first smart phone (IBM Simon), since that date telecommunications companies have started developing (smart phones) it was used in education under the name mobile-learning. The educational term (mobile learning) has become a key topic in the educational and social sciences, as mentioned by many researchers (Maxwell, 2006; Masters & Ngambi, 2007; Al Tawarah, Mahasneh and Al-Hawartheh, 2017; Mahasneh and Murad, 2014). After studying the theoretical literature, mobile Learning meaning the use of mobile information technology and mobile devices in the education process (Pimmer and Grohbiel, 2008; Cook and Pachler, 2012). Were explained of mobile learning that makes the learner enjoy in the study successfully. Chan (2011) carried out to mobile learning must be part of school and universities, Therefore, the current study aimed at detection to investigate the effect of teaching by using mobile learning in university students achievement.

1.1 Theoretical Background

Many researchers have confirmed as (Keegan, 2005; Swan, 2005; Moore, 2009; Chan, 2011; Jump& Cochrane, 2013; Crescente & Lee, 2011; Crompton, 2013; Cook & Pachler, 2012) that mobile learning achieves the following advantages (Facilitates access management and exchange of information, Develop student's creativity and motivation, Encourage student learning and enhance their performance, Encourages individual learning, Encourages communication between students, faculty and students with same, Provides a variety of resources used (photos, videos, applications), Allows the application of a wide range of learning strategies, Facilitates student assessment, Make education more fun and Facilitate distance learning. The researcher conducted the procedures (Development of the unit of activities to be implemented using mobile learning, Design a training program that includes sessions, Providing mobile learning for each student in the experimental group, Conducting unit content analysis to make a test specification tablet, Achievement test design, Identification of two groups to be taught in the conventional method and mobile learning).

1.2 The Researches about Effect of the Mobile Learning

The researcher after studied the theoretical literature and previous studies did not find studies on the subject of determining the effect of teaching by using mobile learning in university student's achievement. Studies focused on a set of things related to the subject of the study. Mahdi (2016) carried out a study aimed at investigating the effectiveness of mobile learning service SMS in acquiring and retaining the instructional technology concepts among the College of Education Students at Al-Aqsa university. The study results revealed that there are statistically significant differences at the level of significance ($\alpha = 0.01$) between the average of the grades of the experimental group and the average of the grades of the control group in favor of the experimental group in the technological concepts test. Al-Monim (2017) conducted a study aimed at identifying the effectiveness of smart phones employment in developing of self-learning skills and electronic communication among students of the Faculty of Education at Al-Aqsa University in Palestine. The results showed that there are statistically significant differences reading the marks obtained by the university students in terms of the development of self-learning skills and electronic communication scales on the pre-and post-tests. Mileva (2011) carried out a study aimed at investigating the Effectiveness of Mobile Learning in the Form of Performance Support System in Higher Education. the result showed that confirmed by the students who indicate that the use of a mobile device did not hamper their learning.

All previous studies focused on learning the effect of mobile learning on some variables (self-learning skills, Performance Support System, instructional technology concepts). The present study differs from previous studies in that it is the only studies that researches investigate the effectiveness of the mobile learning in university student's achievement.

2. THE PRESENT STUDY

The aim of this study is to contribute to the knowledge of the effect of teaching by using mobile learning in university student's achievement. The research was conducted on (50) students as experimental group and control. This study is one of the rare studies in this Domain; I distinguished to structure Instrument for achievement test. The study attempted to answer the following questions: Is there a statistically significant $\alpha=0.05$ in differences between the average scores of the students of the experimental group and the students of the control group in the test of achievement?

3. METHOD

3.1 Research Design

The study adopted a quasi-experimental design. The Individuals for this study consisted of (50) students, (25) Experimental and (25) Control. The researcher first made an arrangement to work with the dean of Shoubak University College For agreeing to conduct the study. The researcher then structures the Instruments and verified their Validity and Reliability, and then applied to the Individuals of study.

3.2 Analytical Strategy

In this study, my main focus was on investigating the effect of teaching by using mobile learning in university student's achievement. The theoretical literature and previous studies related to the subject of the research were read to structure the study Instruments achievement. In Appendix, show the example Instruments used as final in the study.

3.3 Instruments

3.3.1 Redevelopment of the Unit from an Introduction to Technology Courses

The researcher redeveloped the unit from an introduction to the technology course to be taught in mobile learning, and the following mobile learning applications were used in teaching (Elearning system (moodel), whatsapp, youtube, facebook, SMS, mail, Bluetooth, web, pdf, Microsoft office, Live chat, twitter). The developed unit was implemented through a training program of 20 sessions and took one month to implement.

3.3.2 Test of Achievement

To determine the effect of teaching by using mobile learning in university students achievement, they have been Measured by the achievement test, the test consists of (25) question, type multi-choice, total score (100).

3.4 Instrument Validity

After the final preparation of the test, the researcher applied the test to a sample (10) Students with the aim of finding the difficulty and discrimination coefficients for test paragraph and the calculation of the validity and reliability of the test as well as the time required for the test to be applied. The validity of internal consistency was verified, by finding correlation coefficients (Pearson) between the score of each paragraph and the total score of the test, using the statistical program (SPSS), that all test paragraph achieved significant correlation with all score of the test at 0.05, demonstrating that the test is internal consistency.

To verify the difficulty and discrimination coefficients for test paragraph, that the degree of difficulty of the test was between (0.45- 0.54), and that the degree of discrimination between the test was between (0.67-0.49), indicating that all test intervals fall within the acceptable level For difficulty and discrimination.

3.5 Instrument Reliability

The researcher used the alpha-cronbach method to measure the reliability of the test as a first method to measure reliability, the coefficient of test reliability was finding using the alpha-cronbach, and the value of the total reliability coefficients is equal to (0.898) which is its value high; this indicates that the test has a high degree of reliability.

3.6 Data Analyses

Using SPSS version 16.0, the researcher used mean, standard deviation and ANCOVA was used to compare the average scores of the students of the experimental group and the students of the control group in the test of achievement.

4. RESULT

To answer the main question: **Is there a statistically significant α=0.05 in differences between the average scores of the students of the experimental group and the students of the control group in the test of achievement?** Mean, Standard Deviations and (ANCOVA) was used to compare the average scores of the students of the experimental group and the students of the control group in the test of achievement, as shown in the tables (1-4). The pre-test was applied to the study subjects to ensure the equivalence of the study groups as shown in Table 1.

Table 1. Mean and standard deviations to ensure the equivalence of the study groups.

Group	Teaching method	N	Mark	pre-test	
				mean	Std.d
Experimental	mobile learning	25	100	10.56	4.14
Control	Traditional	25	100	10.88	4.69

Table 1. shows that there is a equivalence between the study groups, the mean of experimental group (M=10.56), control (M=10.88).

The mean and standard deviations of the students' marks were calculated on the testing of post-achievement according to the variable of the teaching method. Table 2 shows that.

Table 2. Mean and standard deviations of the marks of the students on the test of post- achievement

Group	Teaching method	N	Mark	Post-test	
				mean	Std.d
Experimental	mobile learning	25	100	85.12	6.78
Control	Traditional	25	100	30.56	12.80

Table 2. shows an apparent difference in the mean of student performance Course to test of post-achievement between the experimental group and the control, For the benefit of the experimental group, where the mean of the experimental group (85.12) and the control group (30.56). To illustrate the significance of the differences in the statistical averages of student scores at the level of $\alpha = 0.05$, the analysis of the variance (ANCOVA) of the study individual marks was used to test the skills of post- achievement according to the group variable and the results of Table (3).

Table 3. The results of the analysis of the variance analysis (ANCOVA).

Source	Type III Sum of Squares	df	Mean Square	F	Sig.
Corrected Model	37631.724a	6	6271.954	58.439	.000
Intercept	3215.168	1	3215.168	29.957	.000
Teaching method	36130.479	1	36130.479	336.644	.000
Pre-test	421.804	5	84.361	.786	.565
Error	4614.996	43	107.325		
Total	209520.000	50			
Corrected Total	42246.720	49			

a. R Squared = .891 (Adjusted R Squared = .876)

Table 3. shows statistically significant differences at the level of $\alpha = 0.05$ for the effect of teaching by using mobile learning in university students achievement. The value of (f) calculated (336.644), and the level of significance (0.000), this value is less than the level of significance (0.05), there is a difference of statistical significance between the control group and experimental. The ETA squared of the teaching method is (0.891). It is clear that the effect of the use of the mobile learning on the achievement is very high, indicating the importance of this Compared to the traditional method of teaching.

Table 4. Shows effect size determination for values ($\eta 2$, d)

Tools	Small	Moderate	high	Very high
d	0.2	0.5	0.8	1.10
$\eta 2$	0.01	0.06	0.14	0.20

$$d = \frac{2\sqrt{n2}}{\sqrt{1-n2}}$$ (Abdelhamid, 2011).

Table 4. shows that the values of the square eta ($\eta 2$) field coefficient and the magnitude of the effect are significant, indicating that the magnitude of the effect of teaching by using mobile learning in university students achievement Very High. In summary for research question, the results showed that the mean in the traditional method scores were lower than the mean of the using mobile learning method in university students achievement. The effect size of the treatment was calculated using Cohen's d and found to be d = 1.831. This indicated that the mobile learning treatment had a "very high" effect, using Cohen's terminology, on the common final exam scores of the treatment group (Cohen, 1988).

5. DISCUSSION, LIMITATIONS AND IMPLICATIONS

The aim of this study was to knowledge the effect of teaching by using mobile learning in university students achievement. The results indicated that the mobile learning treatment had a "very high" effect. Indicating that there are differences of statistical significance between the average scores of students in the experimental group and control group in the achievement test, for the benefit of the experimental group. The researcher emphasizes that the method of teaching by mobile learning is a modern method and is rarely used in university teaching. In this study, I strove to explore the effect of teaching by using mobile learning in university student's achievement in course of pre-vocational education technology. Within the Bachelor of pre-vocational education program at shobak university college. I conducted the study under natural conditions in order In order to produce accurate results.

REFERENCES

Al Tawarah, H. Mahasneh, O. Al-Hawartheh, N. (2017). The Effect of Practical Presentations' Strategy on the Achievement of the Ninth Graders Students of the Pre-Vocational Education Subject in Shobak District Schools. *International Education Studies*, v10 n5 p109-114 2017.https://files.eric.ed.gov/fulltext/EJ1142233.pdf.

Al-Monim, R. (2017). the effectiveness of smart phones employment in developing of self-learning skills and electronic communication among students of the Faculty of Education at Al-Aqsa University in Palestine. *Zarqa Journal for Research and Studies in Humanities*. 17(1), PP 97-111.

Chan, S. (2011). Becoming a baker: using mobile phones to compile e-portfolios. In N. Pachler, C. Pimmer & J. Seipold (Eds.), Work-based mobile learning: Concepts and cases (pp. 91–117). Oxford, Bern, Berlin, Bruxelles, Frankfurt am Main, New York, Wien: Peter-Lang.

Cook, J. & Pachler, N. (2012). Online people tagging: Social (mobile) network (ing) services and work based learning. *British Journal of Educational Technology*, 43(5), pp711-725.

Crescente, M. & Lee, D. (2011). Critical issues of m-learning: design models, adoption processes, and future trends. *Journal of the Chinese Institute of Industrial Engineers*. 28 (2): 111–123. doi:10.1080/10170669.2010.548856.

Crompton, H. (2013). A historical overview of mobile learning: Toward learner-centered education. In Z. L. Berge & L. Y. Muilenburg (Eds.), Handbook of mobile learning. Florence, KY: Routledge (pp. 3–14).

Jump, U. & Cochrane, T. (2013). A Summary and Critique of M-Learning Research and Practice. ISBN 9780415503693.

Keegan, D. (2005). The incorporation of mobile learning into mainstream education and traning. IADIS International Conference Mobile Learning, Cagliari, Italy.

Mahasneh, O. & Murad, O. (2014). Suggested Model (Related to the Student Portfolio) Used in Evaluation the Students in University Courses. *Higher Education Studies*; Vol. 4, No. 3. Doi:10.5539/hes.v4n3p72.

Mahasneh, O.Farajat, A.(2015).The Effectiveness of a Training Program Based on Practice of Careers in Vocational Interests Development. *Journal of Education and Practice*, v6 n26 p101-108 2015. https://files.eric.ed.gov/fulltext/EJ1077457.pdf.

Mahdi, H. (2016). The Effectiveness of Mobile Learning (SMS) Service in Acquiring and Retaining the Instructional Technology Concepts among the College of Education Students at Al-Aqsa University. *AL-Najah University Journal for Research (Humanities)*. 30(5), PP 958-988.

Masters, K.; Ngambi, D. (2007). After the broadcast: disrupting health sciences' students' lives with SMS. Proceedings of IADIS International Conference Mobile Learning. Lisbon, Portugal. pp. 171–175. ISBN 978-972-8924-36-2.

Maxwell, J. (2006). Tracing the Dynabook: A Study of Technocultural Transformations. Koblentz, Evan. Abacus to Smartphone: The evolution of mobile and portable computing.

Mileva, N. (2011). The Effectiveness of Mobile Learning in the Form of Performance Support System in Higher Education. *International Journal of Interactive Mobile Technologies (iJIM)*. 5(4):17-21DOI: 10.3991/ijim.v5i4.1692.

Moore, J. (2009). A portable document search engine to support off-line mobile learning. Proceedings of IADIS International Conference Mobile Learning. Barcelona, Spain.

Pimmer, C., & Grohbiel, U. (2008). Mobile Learning in corporate settings. Results from an Expert Survey. Paper presented at the mLearn. The Bridge From Text To Context, Telford.

Pirttiaho, P., Holm, J. Paalanen, H. & Thorstrom, T. (2007). Etaitava - Mobile Tool for On-the-Job Learning Paper presented at the Iadis, International Conference Mobile Learning, Lisbon, Portugal.

Saylor, M. (2012). The Mobile Wave: How Mobile Intelligence Will Change Everything. Perseus Books/Vanguard Press. p. 176. ISBN 978-1593157203.

Singh, M. (2010). M-learning: A New Approach to Learn Better. International Journal of Education and Allied Sciences. 2 (2): 65–72.

Swan, K. (2005). Teaching and Learning with Mobile Computing Devices: Closing the Gap: 25–28. CiteSeerX 10.1.1.508.5837.

APPENDIX

An example of one of question from achievement test.

Who is the scientist proposed programmed education? {ID 11}

- ☐ Skinner
- ☐ John Dewey
- ☐ John Broadus Watson
- ☐ Ivan Pavlov

REFLECTION PAPER

TEACHERS DIALOGUING ABOUT STATISTICAL LITERACY WITH SUPPORT OF MESSENGER APP FOR SMARTPHONES

Sérgia Oliveira[1], Liliane Carvalho[1], Carlos Monteiro[1] and Carolina Carvalho[2]
[1]*The Federal University of Pernambuco – UFPE, Brazil*
[2]*The University of Lisbon, Portugal*

ABSTRACT

Despite the possibilities of interactions and sharing information, only few studies investigated the use of messenger apps as a pedagogical tool. This paper reflects on possible uses of messenger app as a way to share and expand knowledge about the teaching and learning of statistics. The discussion is based on theoretical perspectives on statistics education, critical mathematics education and M-learning. A pilot study was conducted with early years elementary school Brazilian teachers. In this paper we discuss results from participants' responses to an online questionnaire. The results indicated that participants frequently use WhatsApp application and email on daily basis. Regarding the teachers' previous teaching of statistics, their responses suggested that they know about statistical graphs and they already approached pedagogical activities on statistical contents. Further stages of this study will explore in-service teacher education situations in which the use of Whatsapp might assist discussions and elaborations of pedagogical activities in school and extra-school contexts.

KEYWORDS

Statistical Education, Dialogue, M-learning, Messenger App

1. INTRODUCTION

People experience the impacts of mobile technologies in their lives, such as frequent access to a large volume of data, including statistical data (Campos, Wodewotzki and Jacobini, 2011). Cazorla and Santana (2010) emphasize the importance of providing citizens with the possibility of being statistically literate, in order critically interpret statistical data presented by different social medias. Gal (2002) considers that people become statistically literate when developing skills that involve elements of knowledge (e.g., mathematical knowledge, statistical knowledge) and dispositional elements (e.g., critical attitudes). Statistical literacy can enable people to understand and discuss statistical data. The schooling has a crucial contribution to develop statistical literacy, and school teacher have important role to mediate students' learning about statistics, proposing reflective activities that involve dialogical investigative perspectives.

In studies on continuing teacher education to promote possibilities for statistical literacy, the authors Carvalho (2015) and Oliveira, Carvalho, Monteiro e François (2018) argue that dialogic processes permeate all stages of the investigative cycle, from the elaboration of research problem to the communication of results. The teachers participating in these studies argue that face-to-face meetings would have been insufficient to deepen debates and ideas about approached concepts. These results studies motivated us to reflect on technology utilization that could broaden dialogue between teachers beyond presential meetings.

Alro and Skovsmose (2006) define that the action of dialogue is constituted of conversation exercises about research, in which participants want to discover something to construct knowledge and develop new experiences. When we talk, we abandon the convenience of certainties to take risks, expressing opinions and expressing a worldview that can be confronted and challenged. Dialogic interactions promote relationships of equality based on interpersonal communications. The dialogical relationships from interactions presuppose the freedom of each person to exercise their learning processes (Freire, 1972). In addition, such relationships must be situated in collaborative research processes in which individuals reflect on what they know and what they do not yet know. In this sense, dialogic interactions should promote equality, considering the roles of teacher and student, including knowing how to deal with diversity and differences in the classroom.

Considering that vast majority of Brazilians frequently use messenger app for smartphones, such as *WhatsApp*, we would like to explore possibilities in teacher education. In this paper, we present results from a pilot study to diagnose the uses of *WhatsApp* by teachers in school and non-school situations. Our questions related to the possibility of dialogic communication between teachers, in order to develop statistical literacy.

2. WHATSAPP AS A TOOL FOR M-LEARNING

Mobile learning (m-learning) consists of a research field focused on theoretical and methodological discussions on the inclusion of mobile technologies in education. In this paper we base our discussion on the perspective that consider m-learning as a tool that can contribute to a more flexible education, capable of creating new learning contexts through interactive processes between people, technologies and environments (Traxler, 2009). Despite the importance of m-learning in learning, there is a contrast in school with realities which students find outside educational environments (Schofield, 2011). For example, although smartphone are devices which comprise a range of materials that students and teachers take to school and use them, as well as they could contribute to learning processes, they are not usually encouraged to use in teaching situations.

Sharples, Arnedillo-Sanchez, Milrad and Vavoula (2009) states that m-learning is a characteristic of current era that enables mobility of learning. For these authors, it is only possible to conceptualize m-learning by adding to the existence of two components: mobile and learning. The term mobile also refers to movement of people and mobility to access to information, contents and learning contexts. Its use does not impose spatial or temporal constraints, allowing students to learn math with a more focused approach to their needs.

According to Silva (2013), m-learning plays an important role in the development of educational methods, as it deals with a new form of relationship between individuals, learners and learning content. In addition, it allows actions in the educational act to be negotiated and streamlined beyond pre-established contexts. According to Oliveira (2014), one of these possibilities is the use of the WhatsApp application as a m-learning platform, which can be an effective alternative to mediate teaching and learning processes. Using WhatsApp environment allows you to exchange information, share ideas, experiences, resolve questions, gain access to a wide range of resources and materials such as text, images, audios, videos, games, links, news, e-book's and various content. These elements can strengthen interactions between students and teachers beyond the classroom, thus creating possibilities for emerging meaningful dialogues for the educational process.

The use of WhatsApp in the educational context, we can cite as an example the study by Souza and Pereira (2019), which investigated the use of WhatsApp as a facilitating tool in a process of continuing education for teachers in Brazilian rural schools. The choice of WhatsApp was justified for two reasons: first because it was widely used by the research subjects as an agile means of communication and, second, due to the wide range of this software that has an easy, intuitive and free interface. In addition, considering some difficulties, such as long hours, as well as distance and travel time, these authors realized the possibility of including the WhatsApp application as a virtual learning environment, which can be used to minimize adversities and expand the discourses. Through a semi-face-to-face training model, WhatsApp was the tool by which all non-face-to-face interactions between articulating teachers and teachers in training took place. These authors concluded the study by stating that WhatsApp was configured as an important tool to expand dialogues beyond the school environment, promoting instant and reciprocal interaction between subjects, bringing together all participants in this virtual environment. In this space, the articulating teachers were able to propose reflections and activities to the teachers in training, who had the opportunity to interact with each other throughout the activities. Thus, the subjects were able to share knowledge and experiences in order to enhance the training process.

3. METHOD

This paper discusses aspects of a research study in the context of Brazilian mathematics and statistics education fields, in which studies about the use of mobile technologies is still early stages. The ongoing is exploring the use of WhatsApp as a tool to be utilized in teacher education situation about statistics topics. We expect that the development of activities which involve face-to-face and online interactions can contribute to experiences with stages of statistical investigative cycle.

In this article we present empirical data that was collected through a questionnaire available online, which was shared through the WhatsApp application. The aims of this data collection were to identify if and how the WhatsApp app is used by teachers in in-school and out-of-school situations and verify teachers' prior knowledge about teaching statistics from the perspective of statistical literacy.

We used the resources of Google Form and produced a total of 18 items: 4 items were about teachers' professional profile; 6 items asked questions to identify what the teachers knew about statistics topics; and 9 items were related to their use of WhatsApp. Most of items demanded written answers and only 03 items provide alternative responses.

The data collection was developed with teachers from a public school located in the Metropolitan Region of Recife, Brazil. The school pedagogical coordinator explained the study for the teachers and asked them for volunteers. Seven teachers positively responded the invitation and allowed to give their WhatsApp contact to the researcher. The questionnaire was sent on those volunteers by WhatsApp. Six teachers responded the questionnaire. All participants have university degree in Pedagogy, and they teach in early years of elementary education in Brazilian public schools.

Further stages of the research project will have data collection from presential teacher group meetings about statistics education, dialogues from participation in a WhatsApp group. The main statistical topic is going to be investigative cycle from the perspective of statistical literacy. The data analysis is going to focus on characteristics of dialogues with and without WhatsApp use, seeking to verify articulations of cognitive and dispositional dimensions of statistical literacy.

4. RESULTS

The responses pointed out that WhatsApp was the application that the participants use most on their mobile device. Other apps which they often used are related to social networks such as *Facebook*, *Instagram* and *Twitter*. The frequencies of use are lower for apps associated with videos and music, such as *YouTube*, *Deezer* and *Spotify*. Considering the data presented, it is observed that WhatsApp is the application most used by teachers, indicating, therefore, a great potential for use, including for educational purposes. The perspective of academic use of this tool comes from the verification of the previous technical knowledge of this application by the teachers. Therefore, the *WhatsApp* tools are used in everyday situations by teachers. Therefore, it presents a great opportunity that has not yet been properly explored.

Another item asked about how often they use the WhatsApp application in their daily lives, and all participants responded that they use it for different situations in your daily routines. We conjecture that this resource can be valuable in boosting pedagogical interactions between teachers, between the teacher and the educational institution or even in communication with the students' parents. We also asked them if they had already planned any pedagogical activity or carried out any work in the classroom that involved students in discussions about statistics. All teachers reported that throughout their career they have already developed activities with the content of statistics. We also observed a similarity in the teachers' responses, since everyone reported that they managed to approach this curricular content based on statistical research. All teachers also informed that they always choose to highlight and compare students' responses using tables and graphs.

5. CONCLUSIONS

From the analysis of questionnaire, we identified that teachers in the early years of elementary school in Brazilian schools usually carry out pedagogical actions that involve the contents of statistics. We believe that, combining the theoretical knowledge that these teachers already have with their technical skills and experiences with communication through the WhatsApp application, it promotes innovation and dynamism in the pedagogical actions in the classroom. Thus, we believe that projects are needed that approach the current reality of students, contributing to the improvement of the teaching and learning dynamics of Statistics and providing the subjects with greater capacity to understand and criticize the context that surrounds them.

Teachers can take advantage of this resource to exchange ideas and debate about the elaboration of activities, or in the discussion with colleagues about what was worked well or did not go well in their classroom. As for the potential of using this tool to promote the expansion of dialogue between teachers, it could be used in several situations, such as debates and sharing tasks. In addition to the exchange of experiences, it can also favor the emergence of new possibilities for pedagogical innovation that contribute to teaching.

This paper aimed to reflect on the possible uses of WhatsApp in continuing education processes of teachers on teaching and learning statistics. Through the discussions raised, it was possible begin reflections about how this application has been used as a m-learning resource in the context of the formative processes of elementary school teachers. Overall, research, though sparse, provides evidence that WhatsApp can contribute to greater student and teacher engagement in math classes, as well as other areas of knowledge, and that dialogue permeates all interaction actions that m-learning promotes. In addition, the use of technologies can contribute to the development of statistical thinking

ACKNOWLEDGEMENT

This study is financed by the Coordenação de Aperfeiçoamento de Pessoal de Nível Superior - Brasil (CAPES).

REFERENCES

Alro, H. and Skovsmose, O., 2006. *O diálogo e aprendizagem em educação matemática*. Autêntica, São Paulo.

Campos, R. C. et al., 2011. Educação Estatística: teoria e prática em ambientes de modelagem matemática. Belo Horizonte: Autêntica.

Carvalho, L. M. T. L., 2015. Letramento Estatístico: abordagem no âmbito de um curso de formação de professores de EJA. In: Porto, Z. G.; Carvalho, R. T. *Viver o escrever e escrever o viver: lições da prática*. NUPEP, Recife, pp 63-76.

Cazorla, I. and Santana, E., 2010. *Do Tratamento da Informação ao Letramento Estatístico*. Itabuna: Via Litterarum.

Freire, P., 1972. Pedagogy of the oppressed. Nova Iorque: Herder and Herder.

Gal, I., 2002. Adults Statistical Literacy: meanings, components, responsibilities. *International Statistical Review*, The Hague, Vol. 70, n. 1, pp. 1-25.

Oliveira, E. D. S., 2014. Proposta de um modelo de cursos baseado em Mobile Learning: Um experimento com professores e tutores no WhatsApp. - ESUD – XI Congresso Brasileiro de Ensino Superior a Distância. Anais...

Oliveira, S., Carvalho, L., Monteiro, C., François, K., 2018. Collaboration with Ororubá Xukuru teachers: reflecting about statistics education at indigenous schools. *EM TEIA - Revista de Educação Matemática e Tecnológica Iberoamericana*, Vol. 9, pp. 1-15.

Schofield, C. P., 2011. Going Mobile in Executive Education: how mobile technologies are changing the executive learning landscape United Kingdom, Ashridge Business School.

Sharples, M., Arnedillo-Sanchez, I., Milrad, M., and Vavoula, G., 2009. Mobile Learning: small devices, big issues. In: Balacheff, S et al. *Technology-Enhanced Learning: principles and products*, The Netherlands: Springer.

Silva, L. F. Mobile Learning: Aprendizagem com mobilidade. Colloquium Exactarum, v. 06, p. 01, 2013.

SOUZA, V. V., PEREIRA, E. C., 2019. O Software de Mensagens Instantâneas Whatsapp Enquanto Ferramenta Facilitadora na Formação de Professores das Escolas do Campo do Rio Grande/RS. *Revista Latino-americana de Estudos em Cultura e Sociedade*, Vol. 1, n. 8, pp.1-20.

Traxler, J., 2009. Current State of Mobile Learning. In: *Mobile learning: transforming the delivery of education and training*, M. Ally, Canada, AU Press, p. 9-24.

POSTER

ENABLING MLEARNING TECHNOLOGIES INTO INTEGRATING OFF-CAMPUS INTERNSHIP AND CAPSTONE COURSES FOR TECHNOLOGICAL UNIVERSITY IN TAIWAN

Su-Chang Chen[1], Hsi-Chi Hsiao[2], Jen-Chia Chang[3] and Dyi-Cheng Chen[4]

[1]*Professor, Department of Marketing and Logistics Management, National Penghu University of Science and Technology, Taiwan*

[2] *Chair Professor, Department of Business Administration, Cheng Shiu University, Taiwan*

[3]*Professor, Graduate Institute of Technological and Vocational Education, National Taipei University of Technology, Taiwan*

[4]*Professor, Department of Industrial Education and Technology, National Changhua University of Education, Taiwan*

ABSTRACT

The purpose of this study is to develop a concept model of integrating off-campus internships and capstone courses through mLearning technologies. There are five steps of this concept model. The first step is to develop the teaching objectives and digital teaching material for the integration of off-campus internships and capstone course in the technological universities. The second one is to introduce the business mentors to join the teaching plan for integrating of off-campus internships and capstone course. The third one is to design a pretest-posttest control group experimental design. The experiment group uses our course design and based the mlearning technologies to achieve the teaching strategy. Then, the study will compare the result of two groups in pretest and posttest. It will take the pretest scores of employability skills for experiment group as covariates. Finally, it will use ANCOVA analysis to understand whether students can effectively enhance the employability skills through mLearning teaching strategies during off-campus internship and capstone courses.

KEYWORDS

Mlearning Technologies, Off-campus Internship, Capstone, Teaching Strategies

1. INTRODUCTION

Universities across the world are increasingly placing an emphasis on students' gained employability skills within the school curriculum, which should lead them into employment market (Filho, Shiel and Paço, 2016; Hsiao et al., 2019). Therefore, Teichler (2000) deemed that universities should design practical curriculum to shorten the gap between schools and industry. Unfortunately, Taiwan's technological universities rarely considered about developing their curriculum and fail to cultivate talents that reached the needs of industry (Hsiao & Chen, 2001; Hsiao et al.,2012; Hsiao et al., 2019). Walmsley, Thomas and Jameson (2006) said that off-campus internship allowed students to have a deeper understanding of the workplace environment of small- and medium-sized enterprises and to learn valuable work experience. Aggrett and Busby (2011) believed that off-campus internship programs must be highly designed relevant to industry, so that students may learn professional skills and knowledge to satisfy industry's needs. Chen (2018) found that among the 28 technological universities in Taiwan, 24 schools (85.7%) said that there were no teaching materials for their off-campus internship course, indicating that teachers had no established content. It can even be said that most teachers did not conduct actual teaching behavior except for visits.

Capstone is a course aiming to cultivate students' cognitive ability, learning motivation, and self-organization ability (Kostromina & Gnedykh, 2016). All technological universities in Taiwan had set up a capstone course, which was an important component of professional courses in each department

(Wang & Lin, 2001). Chen et al. (2013) argued that the current teaching of capstone course in Taiwan paid too much attention to content in textbooks and ignored the industry's demands for practical technology, innovation, and problem-solving ability. Tang and Huang (2007) considered that universities could promote capstone courses through university-industry cooperation to reduce the gap between learning and application. If students participated in off-campus internship system, they may observe or understand practical business problems. When they returned to school, they could use business problems as their topics for capstone. Under the guidance of school professors and business mentors, they could slove the actual problems of enterprises. In this regard, it is necessary and important to integrate off-campus internship and capstone courses to cultivate students' practical capacity for technological universities in Taiwan. But the students' off-campus internships are scattered all over the place, it is not easy to collect face-to-face discussions. Therefore, it can use the mLearning technologies to discuss between instructor and students. In addition, business mentors who guide students' capstone topic cannot go to school at any time, and it is very important to use elearning technology.

The purpose of this study is to develop a concept model of integrating off-campus internships and capstone courses through mLearning technologies.

2. THE CONCEPT MODEL

There are five steps of our concept model.

The first step of this concept model is to develop the teaching objectives and digital teaching materials for the integration of off-campus internships and capstone course in the technological universities.

The second step is to introduce the business mentors to join teaching plan for integrating of off-campus internships and capstone course.

Thirdly, the study will design a pretest-posttest control group experimental design. The one class will assign as the experiment group. The other class will assign as the control group. The experiment group uses our course design and based the mlearning technologies to achieve the teaching strategy. The control group use traditional manner. All of the subjects will take the pretest and posttest of employability skills.

Fourth, the study will compare the results of two groups in pretest and posttest. It will take the pretest scores of employability skills for experiment group as covariates.

Finally it will use ANCOVA analysis to understand whether students can effectively enhance the employability skills through mlearning teaching strategies during off-campus internship and capstone courses.

3. FUTURE WORK

This is a work in process. The future work of this study is:

1. To accomplish the teaching objectives and digital teaching materials for the integration of off-campus internships and capstone course in the technological universities.
2. To invite the business mentors to join teaching plan for integrating of off-campus internships and capstone course.
3. To ask the experimental students to join this research.
4. To find a suitable employability skills scale.

ACKNOWLEDGEMENT

The authors would like to acknowledge the financial support of the National Science Council, Taiwan for the contract number of MOST 106-2516-S-346-001.

REFERENCES

Aggett, M., and Busby, G. 2011. Opting out of internship: Perceptions of hospitality, tourism and events management undergraduates at a British University. *Journal of Hospitality, Leisure, Sport and Tourism Education, 10*(1), 106-113.

Chen, C. P., Chang, W. H., Hsiao, Y. L., and Yang, J. S. 2013. The construction of the industry-oriented special production capability project and curriculum connotation of the mechanical engineering in higher vocational colleges. *Secondary Education*, 64(1), 85-102.

Chen, S. C. 2018. "*Curriculum planning, materials development and teaching experiment for integrating off-campus internship and capstone courses in department of marketing and logistics for technological universities: Using project-based learning to cultivate students' skill. Grant project research first year mid-report*," Taiwan Ministry of Science and Technology, Grant project number: MOST 106-2511-S-346-001-MY3.

Filho, W. L., Shiel, C., Paço, A. 2016. Implementing and operationalising integrative approaches to sustainability in higher education: the role of project-oriented learning. *Journal of Cleaner Production, 133*, 126-135.

Hsiao H. C., Chen S. C., Chang J. C., Chen D. C., and Chou C. M. 2019. Teaching process guideline of industry-oriented off-campus internship curriculum for technological university. *International Conference on Education and Development 2019.* Portugal: Porto.

Hsiao H. C., Chen S. C., Chang J. C., Chou C. M., Chen C. P., Shen C. H. 2012. Developing and evaluating teaching material for entrepreneurship management course. *2012 Exploring Leadership and Learning Theories in Asia International Conference*. Malaysia: Langkawi.

Hsiao, H. C., and Chen, S. C. 2001. Process of curriculum development for engineering education. *2nd Russian Seminar on Engineering Education*, UICEE: Tambov, Russia.

Kostromina, S., and Gnedykh, D. 2016. Students' psychological characteristics as factor of effective acquisition of visual information in E-learning. *Procedia-Social and Behavioral Sciences*, *217*, 34-41.

Tang, Z. L., and Huang, M. F. 2007. The relationship between the special production courses of colleges and universities and industrial needs: taking the mechanical field as an example," *Educational practice and Research*, 20(2), 157-186.

Teichler, U. 2000. New perspectives of the relationships between higher education and employment, *Tertiary Education and Management*, No.6, 79-92.

Wang, J. H., and Lin, Q. F. 2001. Discussion on the teaching of special topics in technical colleges. *Technical and Vocational Education Bimonthly*, 63, 33-36.

Walmsley, A., Thomas, R., and Jameson, S. 2006. Surprise and sense-making: Undergraduate placement experiences in SMEs. *Education+Training*, *48*, 360-372.

AUTHOR INDEX

Alade, Temitope 39
Antoniadis, Georges 115
Antonova, Albena 31
Araya, Roberto 47
Asgari, Hamed 115
Bastian, Jasmin 97
Bauer, Petra 97
Bontchev, Boyan 31
Botha, Adele 23, 55
Brucker-Kley, Elke 78
Carvalho, Carolina 129
Carvalho, Liliane 129
Casas, Luis Alfaro 87
Chang, Jen-Chia 135
Chen, Dyi-Cheng 135
Chen, Su-Chang 135
Dalkılıç, Tuğberk 71
Delgado-Cepeda, Francisco Javier 102
Dlamini, Sifiso 23
Doğan, Alperen 71
Eilam, Billie 111
Enríquez-Flores, Marco Benjamín 102
Ezin, Eugène C. 107
Herselman, Marlien 23, 55
Hsiao, Hsi-Chi 135
Jahoor, Farshida 55
Karakaş, Buket 71
Keller, Thomas 78
Kolb, Christine 97
Lanir, Joel 111
Machaca, Paula Asto 87
Mahasneh, Omar M. K. 121
Marais, Mario 23
Maremi, Keneilwe 23
Monteiro, Carlos 129
Nichol, Lynn 39
Nunes, Miguel Baptista 11
Oliveira, Sérgia 129
Olou, Hervé B. 107
Räbiger, Stefan 71
Saliba, Chantelle 3
Saygın, Yücel 71
Seychell, Dylan 3
Stymne, Johan 63
Türetken, Berk 71
Wang, Meng 11
Wecker, Alan J. 111
Welch, Ruel 39
Wyder, Christian 78
Yosfan, Merav 111